Dedicated to a group of prayerful women who live in the States, and, of course, to my mum who hears them firsthand every week.

Introduction

Over the past number of years, circumstances have been challenging but I have found the all-time best way to deal with that has been through writing. And so 'snatches' was born. It practises the discipline of taking a difficult situation and finding strength and light within it. My hope is that my putting thoughts on paper/screen will point the way to live with trouble but also see a way out of it. I have found the whole process beneficial to me, and hopefully to anyone who reads it.

I have grouped my posts under the key themes that I/we all have been living with:

Health

I was diagnosed with relapsing remitting multiple sclerosis in 2005. At the beginning this label would be easily ignored or hidden. Sadly as time went on that became harder to do.

Parenting

My two (17 and 15) present different blessings and challenges but always inspiration.

Nature

I only have to look out a window here to see something, a gift, from Nature to talk about.

Encouragement

Every week I am surprisingly given a positive thought to share. I am sure those thoughts are heaven-sent because many times I have no idea what I am going to write about, right up to the day before!

Pandemic

When lockdown took us all by surprise in 2020, it became necessary to find courage and resilience to cope. So, I kept writing and lit a candle to show commitment to everyone most hit by the pandemic.

Faith

Through everything, every struggle, every challenge, faith in a God who is always there and carries us through it all is the lynchpin of my writing. At the beginning I was tentative but as time went on I learnt that my faith was the main thing that carried me through it all and realised that it was foolish to pretend otherwise.

Happy reading!

Lots of love,

Ruth

The first post that started it all…

Writing the bad, reaping the good

Tue, 08 Jun 2010

I have a stone sitting on my kitchen window-sill with my name on it. Most days I don't even to stop to recognise it, and I suppose most days I forget that it tells me who I am - I am more than 'mummy', I am more than a weary housewife or a guilt-ridden family member. Especially, I am more than 'the one who has MS' (said in the obligatory concerned, gossipy whisper). I am Ruth.

Interestingly I got that stone on what was possibly one of the worst days of my life, when my whole identity seemed to be flying away at the rate of knots. That day, I could barely walk. I had to abandon my dignity (and my shoes) at the door of my brother's wedding. And the funny thing was, hardly anybody noticed. I was hiding behind my daughter's push-chair, and behind my son's entertaining ways. And I was glad of that, but heart-broken too. I look at the photos of myself that day, and all I see is someone who doesn't know where she is, or who she is. I am Ruth.

Although, I haven't even been able to be the other things I know I'm meant to be, and live to be. I haven't been able to be 'mummy' either. The mummy who chases her son around the house and never fails to take him a walk every day. The mummy who can carry him up the stairs to bed, or lift him up when he's dizzy or hurt. I have been the invalid who lies down every afternoon and tells him off for bouncing on the bed. Who cries too much and shouts too much. Now I'm getting better, these things must be redeemed. I am mummy.

Sadly too, I haven't been the wife I know my husband hopes I will be. I say no to every spontaneous trip out, and I get in a state if I stay up late, terrified I won't be able to manage the next day. I don't want to be someone that is always tired, and always sick. I don't want to be bound by my lack of energy and my fears about the future. I want to be a good wife, a joyful wife, a loving wife and a wife who is properly alive. I am his Ruth too.

Published: Tue, 08 Jun 2010

http://ruthwrites.online/2010/06/08/writing-the-bad-reaping-the-good/

Contents

Encouragement

Never assume always

Mon, 06 Jan 2020

Update, January 2020 from Ruth...

I remembered this post from November 2013 last night, and thought it was as true today as it had been when I first wrote it seven years ago. So here it is, with a few careful edits...

(First published, Wednesday 13th November 2013)

Every evening, almost without fail, my husband asks me if I want a cup of tea. To this day, after 11 years of asking, I say no every time. I never drink tea at night - it might be all in my head but the one or two times I have, too polite to refuse when I'm out, my mind goes into overdrive. My husband knows this is my reason, thinks it's ridiculous, and so keeps asking, just on the off-chance I'll change.

I can't tell you how freeing it is to have someone believing that who you are is not set in stone. I'm trying to think of people I know that I could show that same openness to, or if I've ever done it in the past. So next time I have to ask a question, I need to throw out my expectations of what their answer will be, and just listen. Someone who's always a bit gloomy, might just need the space to find a glimmer of happiness - a nodding head and eyes looking away do not give them that.

(January 2020 update from here!)

As I face my most recent bout of weak legs and the permanent need to sit down, I've remembered how lonely and limited life can become. All the standing crowds keep their backs to me, not intentionally of course, but when you're below eye level, you might as well be invisible. I have to turn back after twenty steps on the beach and leave my family to enjoy it without me. The crashing waves are silent behind the car window screen. The wind is visible but not felt.

The problem with this is that it can be easy for me, and those around me, to forget I have more to offer. It may take me longer, but I need to do things, achieve something. Just because I'm sitting down doesn't mean I'm not thinking. Or listening. Or writing.

I do say yes to tea in the evenings now. So you see, everyone can change. As you think over the New Year's resolutions you've possibly already broken, believe that you are capable of so much more. And never assume otherwise.

Published: Mon, 06 Jan 2020

http://ruthwrites.online/2020/01/06/never-assume-always/

What's better than an emerald ring?

Sun, 14 Jun 2020

For as long as I can remember, but not really these past twenty years, we've always been told that one day, dad would get my mum an emerald ring. I don't think it was ever a serious request, but the notion hung around many's an after-dinner discussion. Maybe one day, mum had seen an emerald ring and mentioned it to dad. Maybe not, but somehow the thought of it stuck.

This Monday, they will be fifty years married. A good time for that notion to be realised you would think. But here's the thing- mum does not want a ring any more. These days she would give all she had to be in her favourite place, Donegal. And to be well.

It's funny (not really) how life's hard knocks can change what we see as important. How loss forces us to hold on tightly to the things or people we always took for granted before.

It is so hard to accept our new life when we desperately wish for the old one. The way I cope with the sadness I feel about my own illness is to look at the jewels close by me, and be thankful. I saw a photo of me with my children in the sea last summer. We're not splashing around like 'normal' people. If you look closely you'll see my two children each holding one of my hands to stop me from falling. If you could listen, you'd hear them encouraging me to keep walking. That for me was the best chain I could ever wish for.

Tomorrow we'll do a zoom call with my parents and if you ask mum then, I am certain she would tell you that looking at all her children and grandchildren is much more precious than any old emerald ring.

And me? I'm letting go of all my dreams of diamonds now, and revelling in the ones I already have.

Published: Sun, 14 Jun 2020

http://ruthwrites.online/2020/06/14/whats-better-than-an-emerald-ring/

Good changes

Be free

Mon, 21 Aug 2023

Let me tell you a happy story today.

Back in June, after six months of mainly sitting on my sofa looking out at life flying past without me, I was introduced to the idea of trikes, or more specifically, recumbent bicycles.

My physio mentioned a name to me, I got in touch and the next thing I knew, I was going up my street at a reasonable pace, bringing tears to the eyes of the man who had brought it to me and delight to many of my loved ones.

Have you ever had that dream where you need to be somewhere but your legs won't move fast enough? Well that was me. Life in slow motion. I always say it's teaching me patience, but honestly, the predominant feeling I have is frustration. So you can understand how amazing it felt to be speeding down the hill with the wind in my hair.

I had only been out twice when I decided I needed to have one of my own. After a few months, my brother-in-law drove down from Newcastle to Peterborough with his unwell father-in-law to pick the trike up. It was more than a three hour drive both ways. The next week my husband boarded the ferry and crossed stormy seas to get it from Newcastle. Another long drive. Yesterday, finally, it was here!

The man I bought it from conceded that his bad hip and his Parkinson's were making it too difficult for him to continue. That sad news has made me all the more determined to go out as much as I can. He deserves it, the trike deserves it, I deserve it. And thanks to my parents, my aunt and a number of anonymous donors, I have found a way to fly!

So you see, it's a tale of overwhelming kindness, heroism and dedication. Yet again. Today I am not feeling sorry for myself, I'm just feeling thankful.

Does that ring true for you too?

Published: Mon, 21 Aug 2023

`http://ruthwrites.online/2023/08/21/be-free/`

Take one step and then the next

Mon, 25 Mar 2024

If life is getting overwhelming, sometimes it helps to focus on the next step, not whatever lies beyond that. If you're like me and wake up dreading what the day brings, don't look too far ahead. Even getting out of bed is a good start.

Move away from the heap of worries pressing you down, and focus on one thing. If you find lists helpful, don't let them feed your anxiety. Make a list of all the good things you have in your life, and let that lift you up. In my line of vision I see weights I could use to strengthen my arms, or ones I could put round my ankles. Maybe I'll put them on today, or maybe I will start with one set. Step by step is a good approach, because it means you are moving forward. I could sit here for hours fretting about my wasting muscles, or I could lift up one weight and make a start on changing my situation.

Do you feel pushed into the ground by life? Try taking one step and then another. Before you know it, you will be flying. Making a tiny change can lead to better and better things. If you have a dream that your head tells you is impossible, see if you can break it down into small, manageable steps. I have this dream of setting my feet onto a sandy beach. In a few days time I will be in a house right beside one and I'm already trying to figure out how I can get my unsteady self onto it. Maybe a strong man on either side of me.... One foot in front of the other..

If there's a mountain in front of you, turn your attention away from it and see if you can focus on an easier way to walk away. Putting your hand into someone else's can often help. If you can't manage the steps by yourself, is there someone near who can carry you?

I'll leave you with one of my favourite verses. Again, it's a hope for me, and you too.

"but those who trust in the LORD will renew their strength; they will soar on wings like eagles; they will run and not grow weary; they will walk and not faint."

Isaiah 40:31

Published: Mon, 25 Mar 2024

`http://ruthwrites.online/2024/03/25/take-one-step-and-then-the-next/`

The Greatest?

Mon, 28 Jan 2019

Who decides that, when it comes to subjective, unquantifiable things?

In fact, even measurable achievements can be debated. Twenty metres for a person who finds it difficult to walk (like me), could be the equivalent of a thousand metres for somebody else. A bowl of soup could be a feast for a starving person, or a disappointing starter at a banquet.

On Saturday night I watched another episode of The Greatest Dancer and it hugely disappointed me. The week before, a man with Downs Syndrome astounded everyone with his grace and exquisite movement. A deaf performer proved that music could be felt as much as heard. But at the recall stage, both were sent home. The able-bodied, 'normal' contenders were taken through, the tears of the dance captains over the two men completely forgotten.

For me, the greatest dancer would have been the one who danced in the face of adversity, with their disability, not without it. I feel like the show, the powers that be, have, yet again, decided that to be great, you have to fit the same old expectations, achieve the same old things, look the same, be the same. It's like they thought, we'll tick that equal opportunity box and then forget all about it again.

In my world, 'greatest' is far more multi-faceted: the greatest is someone who has given all they've got, despite what they haven't got, to achieve their best. I don't think anyone can decide on that, do you?

Today, you're the greatest mum, dad, friend, human being you can be, within the struggles you face. Don't ever let anyone make you give up on that.

Published: Mon, 28 Jan 2019

http://ruthwrites.online/2019/01/28/the-greatest/

Would you describe yourself as

Mon, 14 Aug 2023

Relaxed? When you sit down and think about it, are your nerves heightened and your worries rising, or are you able to let go and breathe easily?

I am never calm. MS means my reactions are always too quick, so if our dog barks and I'm holding a cup of tea, it will invariably end up all over me. My hands shake most of the time and I catastrophise constantly. The two times I have gone for a massage the masseuse has said they have never come across shoulders so tense!

So when I read yesterday that one word that described Jesus best was 'relaxed', I frowned. Surely, knowing what was ahead of Him meant that He was stressed? Then I remembered He told other people not to worry, He made last minute decisions to go places for tea and He slept through a storm in a boat. It dawned on me then that I let my own stresses colour the way I see everyone else.

My cousin mixed up a foot soak for me the other day that was intended to relax me. She recognised the need and tried to help. Maybe one day soon I'll be able to close my eyes and let the calming aroma do its work.

What about you? If you are like me and no amount of calming techniques work, then think about what does. Where were you when you felt relaxed? What were you doing? Can you re-create it now? I am realising that even if we are far from the sea or bereft of candles, it is still possible to relax. Exercise or music can help. Talking it out with a friend works too. If you pray then pray but maybe leave long pauses and remember most things are not there for you to organise and control. Jesus may have been relaxed but at the end He was 'overwhelmed with sorrow to the point of death'* so don't think He doesn't understand when that is how you feel.

So I'm not going to tell you to relax, because I rarely can. I'll just say seek out the ways that get you as close to it as you can and remember that even the Saviour of the world had to escape to find space sometimes.

*Matthew 26v38

Published: Mon, 14 Aug 2023

http://ruthwrites.online/2023/08/14/would-you-describe-yourself-as/

You wouldn't believe

Sun, 17 Apr 2022

How many present day knights I see.

Maybe this is the one advantage of frequently being in need of help, that people are able to show me their heroic side. You could almost say without any damsels in distress, there would be no knights.

Don't get me wrong, I would love to be the independent, strong Joan of Arc type, but life has had a different path for me. And you know what? Days full of struggle and weakness can also be packed with other people's strength. If you are able to accept it.

Every single day I get to see the heroes that are close by me. My family step up all the time, but outside of that I could tell you about someone who unfailingly stands by the car and gives me his arm into church, the cashier who packed my bag and lifted it in to my trolley without question and the star of the show who valiantly drove his mobility scooter over potholed roads and up steep hills just to see me.

I will never know if these kinds of courage would have happened anyway, but I am almost certain that the way I am, which causes me so much frustration, has created this remarkable world of remarkable people just for me.

Of course, it is possible to rescue someone from a seated position too. The written word has opened that up for me. Can you think of any other ways to save someone? I could tell you of the best Rescuer we could have, the One who holds us fast through every storm, but I'll leave that up to you.

Now that I have shown you my rescuers, I wonder if you can see yours too?

Published: Sun, 17 Apr 2022

http://ruthwrites.online/2022/04/17/you-wouldnt-believe/

Hard times

Blackbird singing

Mon, 17 Jan 2022

In the dead of night.

This past week or more I have been awake in the wee small hours. If I've had sleepless nights before, I've either been upset or relieved that the birds are announcing the night is past. But this blackbird? He's singing at the ungodly hour of half past two! Maybe I've never been awake to hear him before, but in these dark times, I do.

Some might say, 'how annoying', but as the rest of my family isolate, he's actually been my only friend at the darkest of times, when everyone else is asleep. I woke before his time last night and waited for his valiant song to begin. It reminded me to look again for the dawn.

My brother called that Beatles song to mind when I asked which bird sings in the middle of the night. It prompts us to have courage, no matter how broken we might feel...

'Blackbird fly, blackbird flyInto the light of a dark black nightBlackbird singing in the dead of nightTake these broken wings and learn to flyAll your life '

Who will you be a blackbird for this week? Will you listen out for yours?

To be able to bring light into the darkest of situations, in my life or in yours, is a reason to soar, don't you think.

Published: Mon, 17 Jan 2022

http://ruthwrites.online/2022/01/17/blackbird-singing/

Digging in heaven

Sun, 05 May 2013

Twice this week, I have had an extraordinarily happy time doing something very ordinary. During those two times, I have remembered people who aren't here any more, and felt closer to them. What was I doing that created this magic? I was gardening.

Earlier this week, my mum, my daughter and I dug in potatoes. As we did it, mum told me how her father had showed her how to do it, and she passed on his tips to me. I was only 11 when he died, and had very few vivid pictures of him. But as I watched mum digging, I remembered seeing my papa pushing a wheelbarrow round to his vegetable patch in Donegal, and walking with his tall staff round the lane to supervise a bonfire. Somehow, doing what he loved made him alive to me again.

Yesterday, we came home from my husband's granny's with a tray of tiny pansies. They had been sown in pots by his granda, who died last November, and were sitting waiting for someone to plant them out. As I put them in our flower bed today, I felt deeply sad that he wasn't here to do it himself, but so privileged to be able to do it for him. Every time I pushed the soil around a little flower, it felt like such a joyful, right thing to do. And he too, felt closer.

We'll never know, on this earth, how near we are to heaven and to those who are already there, but somehow, this week, in the garden, it came close.

Published: Sun, 05 May 2013

http://ruthwrites.online/2013/05/05/digging-in-heaven/

Don't forget when shadows fall

Tue, 22 Jul 2014

Note to self: when the days get shorter, when the children have gone off to school and you're left alone to find a different purpose, when winter brings unwelcome, much dreaded spells of bad health, or when unexpected troubles come, don't forget that you had a bright summer. That you felt warmth. The kids were often trying, but many, many times you were reminded how much you loved them. The sun shone more than it rained when you were on holiday, and by the end, you could climb a steep hill without a trekking pole. You looked out across the bay, and saw a pod of dolplns leaping out of the water beside a rainbow. That was heaven dancing right before your eyes. Do not forget these things; carry them with you, but don't hanker after them as though brightness has gone for good. Look for it just as you looked for the dolpins that evening, and don't be surprised if you see a rainbow too. Shadows fall...But there's light to their left and to their right*

*Shadows Fall, The Proclaimers

Published: Tue, 22 Jul 2014

http://ruthwrites.online/2014/07/22/dont-forget-when-shadows-fall/

It's the small things

Mon, 27 Jan 2020

Sometimes, for a host of reasons, your world shrinks.

Maybe it's stress over one life-change like moving house or a new job. Maybe your mind is entirely consumed with worry about one person. Maybe that person is yourself. Your world becomes a narrow tunnel, or a cramped cave, as you grapple with this one all-consuming thing.

When I experience this feeling of being simultaneously overwhelmed and pushed into a corner, I reach out and grab at the tiny, inconsequential things that can bring immense reassurance. Like Wilson, the football, in Castaway, Tom Hanks' only comfort. Yesterday, I found myself trying to keep my eyes on a tiny wren in the garden. The huge pigeons, picture-perfect blue tits and noisy starlings kept on trying to win my attention but yesterday, I wanted small. I wanted to be reminded that however unseen we feel, we still matter. Just like the wren. 'Not one of them will fall to the ground outside your Father's care'.*

Recently, as I go through my tunnel, I've been finding it difficult to write. Last week a friend encouraged me to write 'postcard stories' - little stories that could fit onto a postcard. I tried it and found that it worked! When your head is stuffed with worry, try and find a tiny, postage stamp space for yourself. There, you can remember you are more than all your worries, your pain, your pre-occupations. There, you can find a little bit of happiness.

And maybe share it with someone else.

*Matthew 10v29.

Published: Mon, 27 Jan 2020

http://ruthwrites.online/2020/01/27/its-the-small-things/

Looking for the light

Mon, 14 Oct 2024

Our dog is addicted to sunny spots. If left alone, she will invariably be found on the sofa if that's where the sunlight falls. I watched her looking out the window at the sky and then searching the room for the brightest place to be. Do you think it would help if we were a bit like her?

There are, of course, plenty of times when we have to face the shadows, or when they come upon us without warning. It is difficult, even impossible, to see the light in those times. I watched Rag n Bone man struggle on the Graham Norton show to describe the grief he felt over his mum's death. I looked at him and just wished he would see the light of Christ waiting to comfort him. There is no stronger, greater light than that.

If you are struggling in your own darkness, there are sometimes glimmers of light that can help you through. It could be a bright birdsong, somebody else's hand, a child's laugh, a letter from a distant friend, a visit from someone brighter than you feel, a funny pet that makes you laugh. The sun is out today. Can you see it?

So if you are searching in your darkness, look up and see the Son shining for you. That is my prayer, that no darkness would be so great that you can't see the light that is dispelling the night for you.

Published: Mon, 14 Oct 2024

http://ruthwrites.online/2024/10/14/looking-for-the-light/

Over-stretched, tested, wrung out...

Thu, 18 Jul 2019

Do you ever find that, already at your wit's end, something new explodes in and knocks you flat? Before that, you were saying to yourself, this is as much as I can take. Now, the next thing is pressing down on top of everything else.

I come across so many people who have far too many troubles, far too many burdens. Often the only question you can ask is, 'how much more?'

Human capabilities are astounding. I bandy round my 'pushed beyond my limit' phrase but then I meet people who have a parent each in a critical condition in hospital, or the woman I met today who has just found out her cancer's come back.

She's younger than me.

Those things have forced me to look outside of myself and realise other people need help more than I do. After hearing that girl, I felt so ashamed.

Plato said, 'be kind, for everyone you meet is fighting a hard battle'. It is so easy to get lost in our own lives, when people on either side of us are drowning. Sometimes it only takes a minute to get in step with them. Other times, they need your hand for longer.

Maybe you're the person who's overwrought, or maybe you know someone who is.

Why don't we try to share round the burdens for a bit?

Published: Thu, 18 Jul 2019

http://ruthwrites.online/2019/07/18/over-stretched-tested-wrung-out/

Picnics in hard places

Tue, 30 Jul 2019

Last week I was in a slow-moving queue in a sports shop. As I shared an exasperated look with another customer, she turned to her friend and said loudly, 'if I'd known it would take this long, I'd have brought a picnic.' We all laughed, forgetting the heat, expense and stress of our surroundings for a brief moment.

Since then I've been thinking a lot about how we cope when times are hard, when the wait for things to get better is never-ending.

It's not a solution but finding small ways to lift our spirits helps. Things like sitting out in the sun with a cool drink, walking through a rose garden, chatting with a friend, going to the seaside, having a picnic. Even if none of those things are physically possible, we can get there in our imagination.

It takes a bit of a push, but it is possible to find ways to make difficult circumstances a little more bearable. The woman in the shop had a hearing aid and was looking after her disabled friend too. And yet, she was able to lift her thoughts to picnics.

What could you do today to cheer yourself up?

Even in the darkest of woods or the deepest valley, you can still have sandwiches.

Published: Tue, 30 Jul 2019

http://ruthwrites.online/2019/07/30/picnics-in-hard-places/

Pop-up worms

Fri, 18 Sep 2015

Have you ever played that game where little wooden worms pop up, and you have to bash them back down with a hammer? I was just remembering it as I mentally swatted away hordes of worries that flew in as soon as I stopped rushing around and sat down. They appear uninvited, and often unexpectedly, and worst of all, if not halted, they GROW! So, for example, I can't reach a key person regarding our house move, and all of a sudden the sale is never going through. Or, it took longer than I thought to do the shopping, and now I'll never get anything else done today. I am expert at indulging the worries, letting them settle down in my head, and fill it with out-of-proportion, fatalistic concerns.

This is where the hammer comes in. I have found that self-talk is especially helpful, so, if I spot a worry, I tell myself quite deliberately to stop it. Sometimes, I just shake my head and say 'No'. (Not in public, obviously.) I do remember being told that the Christian way was to give it all to God, but I'm afraid I am not great at that. I will do it verbally, but to this day I have never learnt not to take it all upon myself again. On a sleepless night, I actually visualise sweeping all my fears off a table, or pushing them into the far corner of a room. It kind of works, temporarily.

Sometimes it takes someone else to tell you to wise up, because you're so locked in to the swarms you can't see a way out. But that is way down the road. Really, the first step is stamping the thought out, like a pop-up worm. Before it becomes a monster. Writing it down, and forming a plan is the next thing I suppose. Doing something about it as soon as the thought comes to you is a way to gain control.

Sadly, there will never be a time when worry does not rear its ugly head, and once one is sorted out, another will move in. But they don't have to stay there. And the best part is, they can be shared. Hammer, anyone?

Published: Fri, 18 Sep 2015

http://ruthwrites.online/2015/09/18/pop-up-worms/

Raindrops on roses

Mon, 08 Jan 2018

The past couple of months have been tough- for so many people I know and for me too in a smaller measure.

What do you do, think or say when times are this dark? Honestly, I've no idea. Somehow words emblazoned on coffee cups or embroidered on cushions just fly away in the face of this much pain. There is no philosophy that can fix it. Nothing we can do to take it away. But.

I was sitting beside an elderly lady yesterday who had recently lost her husband very suddenly. And what did she say to me? 'We just have to be thankful for what we have. It's the only way to get through this.' Now, because it came from someone who was in the middle of great darkness, I take that advice very seriously.

I am always worrying about bad things happening because sometimes they do. We can't stop that. But how do we keep on going?

We look around, find the good things and treasure them.

(Still struggle to be glad about whiskers on kittens though. I think my dog would back me up on that one.)

Published: Mon, 08 Jan 2018

http://ruthwrites.online/2018/01/08/raindrops-on-roses/

Sorry, moaning Minnie,

Mon, 06 May 2019

The pity party's been cancelled.

I knew early on today that there was going to be a fight. Between self-pity and gratitude. The rest of the family headed off to climb a mountain and I was left to my own devices at home.

Usually one of two things happen at times like this. Either I give in to tears OR I realise this is my chance to do whatever I want, whenever I want. So far, I've caught up on e-mails, hoovered the house and enjoyed a leisurely lunch. I did go out and contemplate my bike and read the back of the packet of garden peas. But so far, that's been all. Until I started this of course.

Having been known as 'the moan' of the family since I was wee, and knowing how easy it is to slip into it again, I'm writing myself back up that dark and slippery slope right now. I have discovered a few antidotes to negativity over the years. One is keeping busy. Another is listening to someone else. But the best one is simply: being thankful.

I'm thankful for the peace of a house usually full of barking dog and grumpy, permanently bored children. I'm thankful for the absence of agenda in my life today. I'm thankful that my family are happy, and that I'm not there to hold them back. And let's be honest: I have never enjoyed mountain climbing, even at the peak of my fitness. If given a choice between sitting on my sofa and hauling myself up a relentless mountain, of course I would do for the former. And they did phone me at the top to show me the view - it's a win-win.

So, I'm pushing out the moany part of me, and looking for someone a lot more perky.

I wonder what version of yourself you will look for today?

Published: Mon, 06 May 2019

http://ruthwrites.online/2019/05/06/sorry-moaning-minnie/

The dark out there

Mon, 25 May 2020

I've always been the type who fears the dark, far-off places, unknown things and future events. When I was wee, an old man asked me why I was afraid of the dark when everything is the same as when it's daylight. I haven't forgotten that, but still the dark figures lurk. The year I went to France, my mum called it my 'giant'. Right now I'm waiting for a letter inviting me to a spinal MRI and wildly hoping it doesn't come...

These were my fears before but now, coming out of my safe lockdown house into the world has become my number one fear.

From when she was little, my daughter has always gone back time and again to her favourite book, Can't you sleep, little bear? We read it again a couple of weeks ago. I think during this scary time of absent friends, cousins, grandparents and school, you have to bring children reassurance and this book was a small way of doing that.

This time it got me thinking. Are we all a bit like little bear right now? A lot of us can't sleep, and when we do, nightmares are common. We can explain it all away and find the little lamps of comfort to get us by, but there is a fear looming that no panacea will get rid of:

It's the fear of leaving our homes and stepping out into a world of two metre distances, unexpected coughs, lockdown breaches, the VIRUS.

In the story, big bear brings little bear a succession of lamps from a tiny one to the biggest one he has, but he is still afraid. The climax of the story is when big bear carries him out of the cave into the night 'and it was DARK.' Little bear finally falls asleep. It's not clear whether he even saw the massive moon or whether it was just the comfort of being in big bear's arms that did it.

If you are feeling afraid, look for the small things that bring hope to you, but also remember there are braver, stronger people (maybe angels in boots?) that can help if you just ask.

You don't have to face this alone.

Published: Mon, 25 May 2020

http://ruthwrites.online/2020/05/25/the-dark-out-there/

The park bench

Tue, 20 Jun 2017

I wonder how many of you ever take time to just sit on a seat in the park. I never used to; always rushing through on a mission, or not wanting to stop when a reluctant toddler was already taking ages to move along the path. When I was on the bike, it was my mission to get through without falling off (more of a possibility for me sadly). Sometimes, in the picturesque walled garden at Lady Dickson park I would see the occasional elderly person sitting down to enjoy the beauty of the place, or young couples wanting to prolong their time together. But mostly, the benches are empty. People are walking dogs. chasing children, jogging past, speed walking with a friend.

Not me. I can't jog, I can't chase and my dog walks are a strict two a day regime, plotted along routes where she can run and I can wait for her to come back. Yesterday the kids took her to the park and I came to be around when they tore about with her. I sat down and told them that was where I would be if they needed me. I reached into my bag and realised I had no phone, no book, nothing to make my sitting look purposeful. And yet, maybe because of that, everyone that passed me spoke to me - two elderly ladies who were illegally driving round the park (there were no signs telling them not to!), a man on a bike with a ball thrower and a Golden Retriever doing what he called 'the lazy dog walk' where he launched the ball as far as he could, the dog retrieved it and he did it again. After those two, a woman came along with two dogs. I thought she would just say hello, but I was a captive audience for her so she talked to me for several minutes. If I had just been walking, jogging, cycling past her, that conversation wouldn't have happened. And maybe it was the only one she had all day, or maybe she thought I needed her more.

So. My challenge to you is this: go to a park, find a bench, don't get out something to do and just wait. You never know who needs you to be present for them.

Of course, you may look a bit odd and no-one might speak to you, but there's always the views. Sitting down can be the complete opposite of wasting time.

Go on, give it a go and you never know who you'll bless.

Published: Tue, 20 Jun 2017

http://ruthwrites.online/2017/06/20/the-park-bench/

Treasure these things

Tue, 20 Feb 2018

Over the past week or so, I've seen people I know plunged into unexpected grief. And I'm wondering, how much does it take before I learn to cherish the people that I have in my own life?

Often we scrabble to retrieve memories after someone dies, and regret we didn't make more when they were still alive. My papa died when I was eleven so the moments I can recall are just a few snapshots- putting my little finger into his massive hand or watching him walking with a tall stick round the lane in Donegal. One of my grannies died when I was a teenager and I have a vague memory of our last conversation when she gave me valuable advice I can't remember now. If only I had treasured it the way that I should.

We can be full of regret at missed conversations, things unsaid. But there is always the present, the people with us now. Last weekend when I was away with my family and my parents I found myself spending time with them deliberately. I saw when my dad looked happy to see me, I hugged mum more than usual and I just kept noticing that we were together. It was one of the most blessed weekends I've ever had.

So I'm just giving you a wee nudge to try living with more awareness of the people in your life. I'll try to do it if you will.

Published: Tue, 20 Feb 2018

http://ruthwrites.online/2018/02/20/treasure-these-things/

Two worlds, two faces,

Mon, 04 Jan 2021

Two sides.

Most days I have to remind myself that everyone has at least two versions to their life- the one that they show and the one they hide.

My mum tells the story of being surprised at how tidy my dad's flat was the first time she saw it. Until she looked behind the sofa!

I wonder what people move out of view when they're on a zoom call, or do they pick an entirely different background to hide it all?

What's behind your metaphorical sofa?

Spending a lot of time on social media can mislead us into thinking that everybody else is living a better, happier, more 'successful' life than we are. Photographs of rosy-cheeked families having joyous (you never see grumpy) nature walks, athletes standing on top of mountains or children in an immaculate kitchen holding a perfect cake, hit us time and time again. On Twitter especially I come across people who have read the best book or had it published.

The harsh year of 2020 either made us into boasters: 'look what I've learned to do', 'here's a list of the three hundred books I read', 'duo lingo has helped me to become fluent in Latin,'

or into shadows.

Often when I spend time reading Twitter I find myself shrinking with a feeling of disappointment and failure; I haven't learnt a new skill, read a library of books or mastered a language. Don't get me wrong, I think announcing our successes is so important, especially this past year. It shows a laudable, fighting spirit that I'll celebrate in another post another time.

I watch as many individuals seem to be doing this whole living thing better than mostly exhausted, defeated little me. But then I remember that everyone has two lives: the one that they show, and the one they hide. Even the most glittery post has a more real, insecure person behind it. They just push that shadowy part of themselves into the dark.

I'm more interested in the parts that people want to hide than the ones they put on display, because those are real and true and in need of our kindness. So this year I'm going to try to approach the presented life with a more discerning eye. I didn't learn a new skill or publish a best seller but now I want to learn to acknowledge the hidden worlds.

And maybe, when we do that, our Twitter, Facebook and Instagram friends will feel brave enough to let us in.

Published: Mon, 04 Jan 2021

http://ruthwrites.online/2021/01/04/two-worlds-two-faces/

Waiting for a rescue

Fri, 13 Jul 2018

This morning I said out loud what most just keep to themselves, 'I wish someone would just tell me to lie back down and they'll take care of everything.'

Of course I got up. Sitting here at the end of most busy things, I'm reminded about something...that full-on take-over rarely happens. But. Through every tough day, more than once, someone or something picks you up. Usually just for a moment. But it matters.

A few hours ago when I was putting a huge amount of groceries in bags, I turned to apologise to the man behind me and he stepped forward to lift the heaviest bag into my trolley. A tiny rescue which was momentous to me.

I'm going through that despondency of publishing and counting on two hands the number of sales I've made. But just then I read a blog by someone further along the road than me that reminded me that it's the writing that counts more than anything. And I'm never going to stop doing that.

I'm sure I'm not alone in my wild hope for a rescue. But I'm learning not to miss the little ones that are offered every day.

I wonder what yours have been today?

Published: Fri, 13 Jul 2018

http://ruthwrites.online/2018/07/13/waiting-for-a-rescue/

While you wait

Sun, 08 May 2022

Looking back over the past couple of years, I have started, but never finished, several posts about waiting. This past week definitely merits that title.

As I'm sure most of you can relate to, being in hospital, especially a&e, is all about sitting, waiting and hoping that something will actually happen. I heard a woman in agony being finally turned away from her bedsores. I saw a man asking for pain-relief and then no-one came near him for a long time. Hospital staff are clearly so overwhelmed with work, it makes it hard for them to see who or what is right in front of them. When the attention is turned towards you, what a happy victory!

So I can't re-vamp the NHS, or step in to give practical help, but there are some things we can all do that cost us very little. When someone is staring frantically around wishing for attention, catch their eye and smile. Send up a prayer for them. If that is all we can give, it is often enough in that moment. A nurse made me the most perfect cup of tea, after hours of sitting without one. A doctor made me laugh with his stories of losing patients off the chairs he was pushing them on. A triage nurse sympathised with my predicament. As I sat staring round the ward I would have given anything for someone to draw alongside and ask me how I was. I hope I would have done the same for them.

Are you in a state of waiting with no sign of a breakthrough, or do you simply want a fellow traveler to get in step with you, even if just for a moment? I would guarantee that almost everyone needs that at some point in their lives. This emergency room world is packed with people waiting, hoping, despairing, looking for even a tiny rescue.

I wonder if you can give that to them?

Published: Sun, 08 May 2022

http://ruthwrites.online/2022/05/08/while-you-wait/

Wonder

Mon, 13 Mar 2023

It has not been a very pleasant week; full of unexpected tragedy that will stay with some for the rest of their lives. I have to acknowledge that first and foremost else my post will seem unsympathetic to everyone who is struggling today.

On the same day I heard that bad news, I was sent an awesome wee clip of my one year old niece seeing the snow. She was on her tiptoes, looking over the windowsill saying 'wow!' over and over. When did we lose that sense of wonder? When did we become so jaded? Have you said 'wow' recently? Has anything happened in front of you that has filled you with joyful surprise?

Think about that for a minute.

A couple of weeks ago I fought outside with my rollator, followed by my delighted dog. It was the purple crocuses that made me do it. I sat on the garden bench and breathed in the fresh air. I was hit by a feeling then.

It was wonder.

It saddens me when the things I used to get excited about just elicits a shrug from my two now. I promised them 20p for every bit of potato peel they cleared up from the floor. They scoffed. I used to get 20p every Saturday for pocket money! Nothing impresses anymore. Me peeling potatoes or managing to put my socks on are massive achievements these days. Is there anything that you have done recently that you're proud of? Even if things seem small to others, it was a wow moment for you. No-one can take that away.

The sea, the mountains, the woods, the flowers, the snow, a running dog, a diving bird, a newborn baby, these can all fill us with happiness. That feeling dear reader, is not only for children. It is for you too. Never be ashamed to show it, because many people are longing to be taken out of their sadness and into something much much better.

Published: Mon, 13 Mar 2023

http://ruthwrites.online/2023/03/13/wonder/

Learning

A glimpse of sunshine

Mon, 09 Sep 2024

Earlier I experienced above and beyond kindness. Do you ever see that one good experience can often open your eyes to more? If I think hard about it, there was at least one thing that happened before I'd even left the house. It is so easy to let negative events cloud your judgement about what kind of day you're having.

Yesterday I announced that it was 'a bad day'. But was it really? If you can, try to find even one little tiny thing that made you smile or feel better.

After 22 years of marriage my long-suffering husband tries every day to make me smile. He is, without a doubt, the light in my life. We never expected the hard vow 'in sickness and in health' to be the heavy burden we have to pick up every day. Without him and our children, my life would be very dark indeed.

If you have someone like that in your world, stop what you're doing and thank them. If they are in heaven now, let your precious memories fill you with thankfulness once again.

Of course, above, beyond and within all that is our ever-present, ever loving Father, who gives us every good thing, even the Sun itself. I walk in the comforting knowledge that even in the darkest of times, His light will always shine for you

Published: Mon, 09 Sep 2024

http://ruthwrites.online/2024/09/09/a-glimpse-of-sunshine/

Albert Einstein said

Mon, 29 Apr 2019

'There are only two ways to live your life. One is as though nothing is a miracle. The other is as though everything is a miracle.'

What way do you live yours? I'm afraid to say, I'm a glass half empty kind of a girl. But I have discovered that expecting the worst, focusing on the bad and not looking for anything good kind of walls a person in.

I'll be honest, there has been a dire lack of the miraculous in my life recently. OR HAS THERE?

I could tell you about the times I've shortened all my walks, the days I've opted to sit in rather than get out, the times of wishing things were as they used to be.

But what I'm going to write about are the days in Donegal when I ventured out to the shore and made it back. Or the beach we visited where the waves were literally a stone's throw away. Or the best window seat ever, where I didn't even need to stand up to enjoy the view. There were other little miracles, like the deep purple tulips that sprang up unexpectedly in our flower bed.

You should try it.

My hope for you is that even in the toughest of times, you can find the miraculous.

Published: Mon, 29 Apr 2019

http://ruthwrites.online/2019/04/29/albert-einstein-said/

Alone doesn't have to mean

Mon, 09 Aug 2021

Lonely.

I was sitting by myself, naturally, when a swan slowly wandered around me. As I watched her it struck me she was perfectly happy being there on her own.

Someone recently said that being alone doesn't necessarily mean you're lonely. Maybe you need peace and quiet, or maybe you need to drop the brave face you keep on all day and just be truly yourself, free from expectations or pressure.

Nearly all the children that passed by shouted 'swan!' Perhaps that was all she needed. To be acknowledged but not pestered. She had the means to fly away and seek out other birds but for now, she was happy being alone

The book 'Five minutes' peace' suggests that time by ourselves can often be hard to come by. Loneliness is an awful state to be in but time alone is lauded as a precious commodity by many. If only the harried mothers could swap with the isolated elderly for an afternoon. Imagine the chaos!

We all want to belong, to be part of a pack, but not all the time. Sometimes we want to potter about doing nothing in our own company.

I dislike the idea of people rarely being seen by anyone else. I love thinking that everyone, at least once every day, hears someone calling their name. We all need be seen, even if we're mostly happy by ourselves.

So next time you pass someone sitting, standing or walking alone, say their name if you know it, or ask them if you don't.

There's no shame in friendliness.

Published: Mon, 09 Aug 2021

http://ruthwrites.online/2021/08/09/alone-doesnt-have-to-mean/

Don't turn back

Mon, 10 Jun 2024

This week has been a life lesson for my son. Every time he tried to do something, he was turned back. This evening I have been thinking about hurdles as well- I'm home alone and it has taken me 35 minutes to get in the position I wanted- lying on my bed! Keeping going can be disheartening. But there's always that mantra- never give up.

Is there something you want or need to do at the moment and you keep hitting a wall? If it is vital, then keep on trying. Get someone beside you if that helps. Today my son succeeded but it took all week. I'm waiting for my family to come back in an hour's time so I can safely get up again!

Having read today about refugees in Rwanda who have been waiting for FOUR years for a change in status I don't have a thing to complain about.

I'm sure people training for actual hurdles have many tips about getting over them. One might be: forget what's behind and just focus on the next one ahead. Anytime I think about my recent past, all the fears I have rise up again. But if I just focus on the next challenge and forget what's gone before, I know it will be easier to overcome. There's a very apt verse for that:

Philippians 3:12-14 MSG[12-14] 'I'm not saying that I have this all together, that I have it made. But I am well on my way, reaching out for Christ, who has so wondrously reached out for me. Friends, don't get me wrong: By no means do I count myself an expert in all of this, but I've got my eye on the goal, where God is beckoning us onward—to Jesus. I'm off and running, and I'm not turning back.'

Published: Mon, 10 Jun 2024

http://ruthwrites.online/2024/06/10/dont-turn-back/

Don't wait

Mon, 08 May 2023

For the world to change. It might, but that doesn't guarantee you will be any happier.

I have noticed that when things go wrong, a kind of paralysis sets in. We just give up. But what if that's the time when we need to learn about making the most of what we have? Like when you're stuck on a beach, build a sandcastle. When life gives you lemons...

The writer Václav Havel once remarked:

Hope … is not the conviction that something will turn out well, but the certainty that something makes sense, regardless of how it turns out.*

There is a tendency to present our situations to other people as works in progress. When asked how we are, we'll say 'getting there' instead of 'terrible', which may well be closer to the truth. But really, is life not better if we can believe things are moving in the right direction? To decide the status quo isn't going to improve is to concede defeat.

If there is something that needs to happen for you, then you have no choice but to wait. But don't let the time you spend waiting be stolen from you. Claim it as your own and put it to use. Like people who read in airport boarding lounges and don't put their book away until the line is beginning to form. I am not that person but I wish I was.

I was told a month ago that my broken hip hadn't healed much recently. They told me someone would be in touch. What am I doing right now? Waiting and wondering what on earth I can do to make myself better. I don't have the answer for that one and no-one has called. At the moment the challenge is to make some lemonade I suppose. To find some sense in this crazy time, as Vaclav would say.

Make a plan if you're stuck in the doldrums. List all the things you can do right now to pass the time. Turn the 'waste' into something useful. Don't stop hoping but never let wishing hold you prisoner. Any time we have is a gift, whether the situation is about to improve or it isn't. I'm sure farmers still make hay whether the sun is shining or not.

So, I think I'll learn how to make lemonade. Who's with me?

*Václav Havel, Disturbing the Peace: A Conversation with Karel Hvížd'ala, trans. Paul Wilson (London: Faber and Faber, 1990). Quoted in Michael Ignatieff, On Consolation: Finding Solace in Dark Times (London: Picador, 2022) p. 230.

Published: Mon, 08 May 2023

http://ruthwrites.online/2023/05/08/dont-wait-2/

Every 'unremarkable' day

Mon, 03 Jun 2024

'today is just like yesterday and tomorrow's going to be just like today.'

Or so says a character in Isabel Allende's The Wind Knows my Name. Do you live a life like that? Is there anyone who doesn't?

I often think my life is a repetition of nothings. But right now I'm saying it's got to stop! You have to believe that you are more than the things you do or can't achieve. As Chris Martin sings 'you're a sky full of stars'. Every smile, every kind word matters. As the frequent recipient of these, I know😊 .

If you ever get stuck watching reels, notice how many supposed 'nothings' get recorded and shared. Somebody thinks they are of value. Of course, you could argue they are a waste of time, but some might be the only way they can do to feel watched or heard.

I love the idea that we are seen and held by the Father who loves us. Maybe you don't believe that, but I do, and it's the only way I can keep walking through this tough life.

See how many stars you can collect today. Even looking up to watch the clouds or listening to the birds can turn a mundane day into a time full of wonder.

If you believe that you are remarkable, you will live your life like that. Try it and see.

Published: Mon, 03 Jun 2024

http://ruthwrites.online/2024/06/03/every-unremarkable-day/

Filling up

Mon, 29 Aug 2022

The emptiness. I know that most would give anything for even 'five minutes peace'. Most can't find a space in their over-packed diaries. Life is hurtling on at break-neck speed and there is no sign of an empty space anywhere.

There is another set of people who find quite the opposite. We have so much quiet, so many empty spaces in our schedules, that we don't struggle to find peace. We have so much of it that it can present an entirely different challenge:

What do you do when you can't do anything?

I was looking out across placid, blue Sheephaven Bay in Donegal last weekend, watching a sail boat not moving across the water. At first I thought it was due to a lack of wind, but then I realised it wasn't moving because it was anchored there. Sometimes just because we are not moving, it doesn't mean that nothing is happening. It doesn't mean that there isn't a purpose to who we are.

Earlier today I was standing by my car with no notion how I was going to get back to the house with just my walking stick. The builder called to me and came down his ladder. At the same time, my neighbour came out of his drive and took my arm. I have lost count of the times I have been still and kindness has arrived. It is humiliating and I wish I could rush away by myself to avoid everyone else. But maybe there is a purpose to all this that I need to learn. Even Jesus sat down, slept and went away to pray. He wouldn't have invited us to do the same if He didn't see the importance of it.

I have lost the knack of superficial conversation because usually I am there for a longer period. But actually I prefer going deeper with someone than running past them. Having an anchor doesn't have to hold us back, it just keeps us where we're meant to be.

For whoever we're meant to help in that moment.

Published: Mon, 29 Aug 2022

`http://ruthwrites.online/2022/08/29/filling-up/`

Hovering

Mon, 01 Jan 2024

On the threshold of the new year I have one resolution: to not let the bad memories fuel fear about the future.

I am finding that it is easier to hold a recollection of badness than to remember the many good times in the past year. Unhappily, the bad things take up a lot of room in your head. They are not welcome anymore! Let's all resolve to cram our heads so full of goodness, that the darkness is squeezed out.

As Henri Nouwen says; 'We must learn to live each day, each hour, yes, each minute as a new beginning, as a unique opportunity to make everything new. Imagine that we could live each moment as a moment pregnant with new life. Imagine that we could live each day as a day full of promises. Imagine that we could walk through the new year always listening to a voice saying to us: "I have a gift for you and can't wait for you to see it!" Imagine!'*

This new year is not an opportunity to look back and expect the future to be as hard as what has gone before. It is a chance to believe that better is waiting for you. It is up to you to see it and take hold of it, never forgetting that our Father God is holding onto you too. As always, these words of mine are for me and for you, so let's hold each other accountable; who will be the first to fulfil one of the promises that you have been blessed with today?

* Advent and Christmas Wisdom from Henri J. Nouwen (Redemptorist Pastoral Publication, Liguori Publications, 2004).

Published: Mon, 01 Jan 2024

http://ruthwrites.online/2024/01/01/hovering/

It isn't finished yet

Fri, 13 Dec 2024

I have been reminded, or have reminded myself, that there is more to come in the future. More beginnings, more chances, more new opportunities.

It is tempting to see our present circumstances as our permanent future, but what if we have got it backwards? Turning away from the fear and dread of things going wrong, can we step into a mindset that expects things to go right?

My dad produces a calendar of photos of beautiful scenes from Donegal every year. Looking through this year's, I felt sadness that I couldn't ever be in those places because of my inability to walk to them. But hold on! 'couldn't ever' is not right. 'Not yet' is better. To believe that circumstances can be worked around or even changed, is to live with hope. I much prefer to believe that goodness is there in my future, than to think unhappiness is all there is.

To live knowing that your story is not finished yet and believe that, even in the midst of struggles, light is still there to guide us through. The line has not been drawn, the book of your life is still open. Don't believe that everything is speeding down hill. Look up and expect at least one mountain top blessing.

If the wise men (or women?) had just shrugged their shoulders and not followed the star to Bethlehem, who knows if Christmas as we know it, would have ever happened. If the shepherds had huddled closer to the fire, angels singing 'Glory to God in the highest' may have never been heard or seen. It is so easy to block out blessings, especially when we don't believe we deserve them. You definitely do!

I'll leave you with one of my favourite verses in the Bible. I am praying them for you,

‘May the God of hope fill you with all joy and peace as you trust in him, so that you may overflow with hope by the power of the Holy Spirit.’ (Romans 15v13)

Published: Fri, 13 Dec 2024

http://ruthwrites.online/2024/12/13/it-isnt-finished-yet/

Let them be more

Mon, 28 Sep 2020

Than you've decided they are.

On Saturday my husband was looking for shoes online. When he showed me a picture of the ones he was 'drawn to' I was lost for words. They were bright and very sporty looking. 'Not him at all' I thought, and thankfully managed not to say. I suggested getting the type he always wore but this time, he wanted a change. What was this? Unexpected, that's for sure.

Thinking about it soon afterwards, I realised what I have done: categorised someone because I think I know who they are. When we say with surprise, 'but that's not you at all' we are banging the final nail in the coffin of someone who wants to try something new. For a change. A few years ago I wrote Never assume always, and today I'm back thinking about giving people the chance to be different.

It applies to my children too. When my timid son tells me he loved the high waves breaking into his sailboat, I need to hide surprise. When I hear my daughter acing her scales during her piano lesson, I have to remember she is always learning and will continue to get better at everything.

Sometimes, people need space to be more than we give them credit for. Sometimes we will be pleasantly surprised. Forget the words 'that's not you' and be something else. When someone asks you 'what do you do?' remember that you are so much more than the one word answer they're expecting to hear.

When was the last time you did something out of character? My challenge to you is to find that unpredictable thing and go for it. Don't let that phrase 'be yourself' be limited by what other people have decided you are.

The crazy shoes aren't here yet, but when they arrive I promise I'll hold my tongue. Twenty-three years of being with someone does not mean they will never surprise you.

Published: Mon, 28 Sep 2020

http://ruthwrites.online/2020/09/28/let-them-be-more/

Living, not just

Mon, 30 Aug 2021

Surviving.

Do you ever feel like you're counting down the days until something is over, hoping for a positive change or gritting your teeth until the bad spell passes?

I've caught myself being exactly like that. And I can't remember when it started. Just days strung together by relief I got through them. By a 'things have to get better soon' mentality. The problem with having something that is supposed to be relapsing/remitting is that you become a survivor hoping for things to pass. 'They' have decided to stop calling it that now because in fact, over time, you don't see a clear recovery after a bad patch. It's just all quite bad or very bad.

If you find yourself wishing for your life circumstances to change and never truly see that happen then you're just surviving like me. I remember seeing other babies cutting teeth, walking or potty training before my baby and wishing that would hurry up and happen for them too. But then, when they're managing everything by themselves you long for the days when they needed you more.

This past week I have decided to walk badly in public, lean against everything and just keep going. Because I want to make the most of my current situation. Someone with MS herself once asked me, 'do you let it stop you?' Yes, sadly I do.

I watched a rather stoical woman making her way round the shop where she worked as if limping was a fact of life, not an impediment. Covering ground doesn't have to look easy or graceful. I wonder if I stopped trying to look like everyone else all the time I would achieve more. Looking normal is exhausting. Ask any paralympian if they got their medal by hiding.

There are many ways to pass through life: hoping, wishing, hankering or reminiscing. None of those help with the now. Life is full of ongoing goodness, whatever we're enduring, however we feel. Faith can keep us. Family can hold us. Good friends can stick by us. Nature can surprise us every day.

I watched a little ladybird do circuits around a saucer on the window sill yesterday and it made me smile How about you find something today, even a tiny thing, to remind you that you are not just counting down the days. You are living them.

Published: Mon, 30 Aug 2021

http://ruthwrites.online/2021/08/30/living-not-just/

Look how far we've walked!

Tue, 13 Aug 2019

As I was walking up a hill towards our house in Donegal two days ago, I had a memory of my cousin and me deciding to walk in our bare feet the whole way from the beach on that road. Every ten metres we would stop and cry out, 'look how far we walked!' That feeling of achievement carried us the whole way home. This time, however, it was hard for a different reason. This time, I didn't look back. I pushed on, sights set on a chair to rest in, a cup of tea to drink.

We always have the choice. Looking back can give us the resolve to keep going. But sometimes, that can be too painful and we just need to push on. My family often ask, 'did you see-?' Every time, I remind them that all I ever look at is the next five metres on the path ahead.

'Do what you can' is what my Pilates instructor says every week. I love that. It makes everything so much less daunting, so much more achievable.

So, look back on all you have done and congratulate yourself.

But then look ahead and know that you can do the same, and more, again.

Published: Tue, 13 Aug 2019

http://ruthwrites.online/2019/08/13/look-how-far-weve-walked/

Looking for the instead

Mon, 05 Jul 2021

Recently I heard two people on different occasions redeem the idea of doing something the wrong way. A piano teacher called straying from the set music playing a 'jazz note'. Artist Bob Ross said, 'we don't make mistakes. We just have happy accidents.'

We all punish ourselves with the idea that there is one, perfect way of doing things and if we don't manage that then something has gone wrong. I have painful memories of trying to do something I should have realised was beyond me. Equally, I try to cover up the trips and unsteadiness by avoiding walking in public, or opting out of ever showing my 'mistakes' at all.

But what if the things that people think are wrong could be seen as our jazz notes? What if we look for other ways of getting through? What if the 'instead' is as good?

When I'm sitting on a park bench I often think everyone that passes me; the parents with their buggies, the couples walking slowly by, the old women out for fresh air, the joggers, the dog walkers, are living a better life than me. A life free from mistakes. A life I wish I had.

But how can I be so certain? Maybe the parents wish they could have time to sit and rest, maybe the couples, the old women, the dog walkers and the joggers long for a time when they could stop striving and just sit down.

If you feel pushed into a corner of doing the things you think you're expected to do, if you're stuck with all your unfulfilled dreams and shoulds, I suggest you consider the insteads. Maybe things that you think are not going right are in fact going a better way. Maybe you should look out for them and see the jazz notes. Not wrong, just different.

That's where the unexpected brightness lies.

Published: Mon, 05 Jul 2021

http://ruthwrites.online/2021/07/05/looking-for-the-instead/

Nothing is

Mon, 07 Nov 2022

One dimensional.

The way you see things or experience them is not the same as anyone else. Recently I have been learning that. Have you ever heard one event being related by two people with entirely opposite versions of what they thought had happened? Yesterday I realised, to my shame, that I have been so wrapped up in my poor health that I forgot everyone around me is involved too. Nothing in life impacts just one person.

On another note, it is easy to pigeon hole children into the path you assume they will go. My son used to talk about engineering but when asked directly in the summer he said he was interested in medicine! Never say, 'but I thought you liked'... Always let people step outside of the person you have pegged them as.

The question, 'what do you do?' is a very restricted question too. No-one deserves to be pushed into one word. You might be self-employed, part-time, retired, unemployed or too unwell to work at all. But what are you besides that? So much more.

We sang a kids' song yesterday, 'you are a promise, you are a possibility... You are a great big bundle of potentiality'. It's slightly silly but actually, true. Never think that you are all out of chances. Don't let anyone push you into one dimension. If someone asks you that constraining question I would follow it up with 'and what else?' Life is a multi-faceted, surprising mix of experiences.

You are not one-dimensional.

And no-one else is either.

Published: Mon, 07 Nov 2022

`http://ruthwrites.online/2022/11/07/nothing-is/`

Out of your hands

Mon, 31 Oct 2022

There is always something going on in our lives that we cannot control. I was talking about that today with someone and they said if the queue of traffic was too slow-moving, they would just get out and walk. To do that was to re-take control. (I didn't ask about the other poor person left to mind the car!)

I found the photo above earlier and realised that when I feel powerless, I often clasp my hands together. Like at the dentist, or the doctor. Allowing another more qualified person to take over can still be a challenge. Especially if we don't have confidence in them. My son would probably tell you that's how he feels every time I drive.

None of us can predict the future. Life may seem like it is on a certain path but sadly bumps and barriers can arise. Like when you watch a program like Grand Designs the predicted finish time always disappears as complications occur. Never say to Kevin McCloud that you'll be in by Christmas.

Never put a deadline on expectations. Hope, yes, but don't be surprised if things don't fall beautifully into place. I had a timeline for our extension but as it disappears into a cloud of plaster dust, I am trying, very hard, to concede defeat.

Someone else said recently, 'hope for the best but be prepared for the worst'. I'm not sure I would like to live by that. To always be thinking of the worst, we might forget that sometimes life can pleasantly surprise us. I hate feeling out of control, but I would rather think that things will work out ok than live expecting that nothing will. I would definitely rather trust in the Father who holds me fast, than step out onto a tightrope of uncertainty and fear.

If you are feeling out of control, if your circumstances are shaking you, then clasp your hands together and trust that someone else has got this for you. That's a challenge in itself.

Published: Mon, 31 Oct 2022

http://ruthwrites.online/2022/10/31/out-of-your-hands/

Re-imagining the future

Mon, 14 Jan 2019

There's a photo of me standing on our front door step when I was four, dressed up as a nurse. Work experience twelve years later confirmed that actually, I would be terrible at it.

I never lost that desire to help people though. Glandular fever stopped me from building schools in South America and then, sadly, my MS diagnosis kept me firmly, permanently, close to home.

It's taken a long time for me to move away from those laudable intentions to care for others. There are times, most days, when I have those 'what if' moments. You have them too, I suspect.

Here is my tentative solution to all that: so I can't change societies or rescue the poor. I can't trek through the Andes or walk the Camino. I can't stand and serve in soup kitchens or run children's clubs. I can't run full stop.

But, I can write. I can take you away from your dark places and create a better world for you to be in, even just for a short time.

(I still can't understand why authors would want to plunge me into punishing, dark places when they could create an escape plan from all that.)

So, my readers, you are my patients whether you like it or not. The best thing about having me as your nurse: my medicine is always served with a spoonful (or three) of sugar.

Published: Mon, 14 Jan 2019

http://ruthwrites.online/2019/01/14/re-imagining-the-future/

Say what you mean,

Mon, 13 Mar 2017

and mean what you say. I've no idea who first coined that phrase but it is one that rings around my mind a lot.

Not that I do it, as my bad haircut will testify. I've spent the last two weeks trying to convince myself that I meant it when I said the words I always say, "that's lovely, thankyou." But it wasn't really true. And the thing is, nobody will ever tell me that it is not 'lovely', because they play the same game as me. Only once in my adult memory do I recall someone asking me, "what happened?" after I had a crazy pregnant moment and got my hair highlighted. Like a tiger. The person commenting was genuinely concerned for me and my state of mind. I'm laughing now, but was silently offended then.

That's the problem - it's all very well speaking your mind, but if it is at the cost of someone else's feelings, should you do it? Sometimes (read most of the time) I say what I think the person with me wants to hear, and afterwards my true opinions fester inside of me. It often comes from a place of kindness, but other times, it is out of fear of a hurtful confrontation. Simmering, repressed feelings do nobody any good.

Nevertheless, I will always contend that considering other people's feelings trumps (can we bear to use that wretched verb these days!) speaking our mind. Sure, speak into the hidden tension, but tread softly.

It happens all the time in the workplace as well. Back in my days of working in an office, I encountered people who always threw their weight around, regardless of the damage they were causing. But I rarely stood up to them and so the balance of power never shifted. Of course, I would come home and say the things I should have said or done, but then and there, I suffered in silence. On the other hand, if a colleague shows you a poorly thought out idea, or a terrible attempt at solving a problem, then the only way to save them is to tell them. But make sure you're armed with a better suggestion. Criticism only works if it points in a positive direction.

Maybe next time, I'll tell the hairdresser to change their work. Or maybe, I'll choose the kinder way. Say what you mean and mean what you say. But don't ever be mean.

Take it from the hedgehog.

Published: Mon, 13 Mar 2017

`http://ruthwrites.online/2017/03/13/say-what-you-mean/`

Searching for self

Wed, 21 Mar 2018

Hearing of how Cambridge Analytica used a personality type questionnaire via Facebook to access personal records got me thinking. Why do so many of us do these quizzes and what makes them so appealing? The answer lies in that universal question - who am I?

I can remember the times when someone told me who I was. I was sitting in the backseat of the car about 30 years ago and my dad said "You are Irish." That statement started a feeling of pride in me that has never gone away. More recently a fellow writer told me "you are an author now" after I'd sent away my book to get it published.

Both of those declarations about who I am are difficult to say - one for political reasons and the other because of self-doubt. There is something very powerful about statements of identity, especially in this era of uncertainty. That's why people do those surveys - to read the words, 'You are...'. We need to know we are something, that we mean something, that we matter. When you don't have a career, or the job title, or the recognition you feel you deserve, then it is difficult to say who you are as a person.

For me, the solution is simultaneously easy, and hard to accept. My faith tells me I am a child of God. It tells me that the eternal Father has a plan for my life.

Just like that, the craving for self-definition is blown away by a rock-solid truth. So next time a 'what Star Wars character are you' or 'what's your personality type' quiz appears on Facebook, why not ignore it? Why not take all those question-marks over who you are to the Bible. The answers are all there.

And that, my friend, will blow your mind.

Published: Wed, 21 Mar 2018

http://ruthwrites.online/2018/03/21/searching-for-self/

Sometimes the cake

Mon, 01 Mar 2021

Turns out just fine.

I don't know about you, but I set out every day expecting things to go wrong. And then I can say 'I knew that would happen' or 'of course' or, worst of all, 'I told you so.'

How Eeyore of me.

There are always remembered failures, accidents and disappointments that can fuel up our expectation of disaster. One time, I went alone to get a diagnosis. One time, the cake didn't turn out right. One time, or a few more for this one, I tripped and fell. Because of those remembered bad times, I worry every time I go into hospital by myself, put a cake in the oven or step outside my front door. Living with that amount of negative anticipation does not make for an easy life.

What if we expected things to go well? What's there to lose? If you're wrong, you'll have to deal with the same consequences. But at least you were happy until then. Expecting bad things just gives them power over you before they've even happened. There are definitely more pleasantly surprised moments in my life than disappointments. And yet, I persist in expecting the worst. 2020 did not help with that mindset, let me tell you!

Starting a habit of thinking things are going to be ok, looking back over the darkest of situations and being able to see a chink of light in them, carrying a happy anticipation of something working out: these are the way to a happier life.

When you look ahead, can you see a risen cake, a kind person when you're facing something alone, an outdoor experience that brought you more joy than pain? If you can, why not join me today in expecting good things, even when bad odds seem to be stacked against you.

Even if it's just eating the perfect cake someone else has baked for you.

Published: Mon, 01 Mar 2021

http://ruthwrites.online/2021/03/01/sometimes-the-cake/

Staying power: a phenomenon under threat

Mon, 10 Oct 2016

I fear that my generation have lost the ability, or the desire, to stick with things, even when the going gets tough. Tired of re-painting your house? Move. Sick of the sight of your partner? Leave them. Finding your friends too needy? Get new ones. Stuck in the same job for five years? That's too long - go get out the JobFinder.

Looking at the generations before this one, I see people who stayed with the company that first employed them right up to retirement, marriages that lasted a life-time, houses that remained home for many years. For some reason, this kind of same-ness is no longer seen as a laudable achievement, but as a depressing failure to change. But was it really?

I know that life is different now, and the pressures have changed. It is all about life-long learning, re-training, finding something more suitable. Or someone. But a lot of the time I wonder is it just that we have no staying power, and a short attention span?

I see it in myself - looking at my 'same-old, same-old' existence and feeling dissatisfied when actually, what I have is good. Enviable even. This searching for something else, something more rarely ends well. Yes, for a year or two people might say, 'it's the best thing I ever did', but how long before the change grows stale as it turns into normal, and nostalgia for the old ways kicks in?

One of the worst aspects of this societal malaise is what it does to friendships. There is a recommendation that you keep people round you who make you feel good, and cut out the rest. Here's a topsy-turvy idea: maybe the friendships that are the most challenging, are the ones that make you a better person. (That's not a hard and fast theory though.) Looking back now, I wonder at the choices I made about the people I wanted to spend time with, and feel sad about the ones I moved away from.

So what to do? It's not clearcut - change can be good and empowering, but sometimes, we need to appreciate what we've got. The best transformations happen internally anyway. Change your heart and your mind, and then look at your world.

Now that's a subtle revolution right there. And it lasts.

Published: Mon, 10 Oct 2016

http://ruthwrites.online/2016/10/10/staying-power-a-phenomenon-under-threat/

The danger of snapshots

Wed, 23 Apr 2014

I was out in a beautiful forest park with the family on Easter Monday. It was fairly busy, so as we walked through the trees, we met a good few people - couples jogging, families with crying toddlers, people who didn't fit into any neat category. And that's when I got to thinking about how, with one glance, we can decide who somebody is, and whether they're worth considering, or should just be overlooked.

I'd brought my purple walking stick, but found myself hiding it as much as I could. Sitting down on a wooden bench, waiting for our picnic, I actually put it behind my leg when people walked past. At one point, my daughter took it out and started pretending to be a sentry. She wasn't ashamed of this part of me. I was.

Taking a short-cut up the hill on the way back, I found myself walking alone in front of groups of people sitting close to the car park. Either they would look over at me and quickly look away, or they would smile as if they felt they should. 'That poor girl, so young to have to use a stick.' Of course now I'm as much at fault as my observers - seeing one thing, and assuming many.

A presumptive snapshot of young parents dressed for the town in a forest park does not speak of their laudable decision to take their kids to the countryside for a change. Maybe they go all the time. It doesn't tell the story of two men in their thirties, walking closely, talking happily together. And it doesn't tell mine. I hope that this lesson will change how I look at people. Not to stare, but not to glance away either.

Published: Wed, 23 Apr 2014

http://ruthwrites.online/2014/04/23/the-danger-of-snapshots/

The golden moments

Mon, 12 Aug 2024

Are not always when you're winning. I have been watching some of the Olympics, but the moments that have stuck with me have been when someone has not achieved the time they expected or things have gone wrong for them. I found myself empathising with the tears cried by a runner who expected to win and did not, or a cyclist whose legs gave up before he finished his race. I related to the dashed hopes and ruined expectations.

Thinking about those who are not riding home in victory. I wonder how they are living with the disappointment now. Have you got hurt from the past that you can't shake off? Every day I notice the points when my legs shake and I get afraid of falling all over again. I'm sure every time the athletes set out to run another race, they have a similar battle.

There's a great verse for that in Philippians 3: 'But one thing I do: Forgetting what is behind and straining toward what is ahead,14 I press on toward the goal to win the prize for which God has called me heavenward in Christ Jesus.'

So, the challenge for us is to look away from the past and look forward to the better things that lie ahead. The surprising idea is that there might be something good for us in the future. I know that is very hard to believe, but can you dare to expect good things in your future?

It is so easy to let bad things fuel your doubts about your future but let's try. I hope the Olympians who came home with empty hands will find a different way to win. Coping with disappointment may build up strength to withstand the past memory of losing and go on to be a winner in the tomorrows ahead of you.

So today I will step out and be a winner in the small, unseen battles I face. Who's with me?

Published: Mon, 12 Aug 2024

http://ruthwrites.online/2024/08/12/the-golden-moments/

There is no 'just'

Mon, 30 Nov 2020

I watched a very funny video clip on Friday about 'just' changing a light bulb...

A man arrives home, flicks on the light switch but the bulb has blown. He goes into the cupboard in search of another one. The shelf is collapsing. He pulls out another drawer to get a screw driver to fix the shelf. The drawer is stuck. When he gets the can of oil for it, the can's empty. He hurries to his car to go to the shop to get more but it won't start. His wife comes home and finds him under his car in the garage. She says, 'the light in the kitchen needs fixed'. He calls from under the car, 'what do you think I'm doing?!'

Most things in life are like that aren't they; you start off doing something that should be straightforward and a hundred obstacles rise up. These pandemic days, everything has got more complicated. 'Popping to the shops' now involves picking the least busy slot, figuring in queuing times and remembering to wear your mask and sanitise your hands.

The words 'I just want to hug my mum' have become a painfully impossible dream this year. 'It's just for a wee while' can become unintentionally lethal.

No, there's no such thing as 'just' this year. I used to get exasperated when people said 'it's just round the corner' when they were giving me directions. When you can't walk very far, even getting round the corner can be overly ambitious.

I wish all the 'just's would sweep back into our lives again. I wish one simple thing could be that: simple. But maybe I'm looking in the wrong place. Maybe they do still exist, but they've changed into other things. My hope is that as we get used to the new routines this pandemic has forced us into, we'll begin to look beyond them and see they're making a way for us to get to the place we want to be. When I use my stick, 'just round the corner' becomes just that. When we use our words and smiles 'just a hug' can be replaced with other expressions of love.

Just can be a cruel understatement, but it can also be a gentle encouragement. So today, why don't you see how many simple things you can still do? My blog used to be called 'snatches' because with two children under the age of three that was all I could manage. Why don't you see how many precious moments you can snatch today?

They're just wee things after all.

Published: Mon, 30 Nov 2020

`http://ruthwrites.online/2020/11/30/there-is-no-just/`

There is another way

Mon, 17 Oct 2022

You need to remember that, even when you think you're all out of chances.

It is always so disheartening when you hear of a child who didn't get in to their school of choice, when you see someone's hopes being crushed on a talent show, or a friend doesn't get the job they interviewed for. Or, worse still, someone gets a devastating health diagnosis. It can seem as if there is no way out.

In Grand Designs this week, the client was embarking on a building project by herself, shortly after being told she had breast cancer. She would say that was the reason she was determined to succeed with her new house. It made me realise again that when the odds are stacked against us, we often muster the strength to defy them. Or as Dylan Thomas says, 'Rage against the dying of the light'.

I do find that the resolve to not let circumstances win can help us keep going. It can be tiring and often too much but other times, there is enough frustration or annoyance in us to fuel a fight to make things better. It sometimes bothers my family when I step out to do something that they could do much more easily than me, but when I say 'no! I am doing it!' they know to stand down.

If we can let go of the things that are lost to us now, and accept that there are other ways, it can help us to keep on going. If certain things are impossible, look for what is possible. If we are fed up with wanting, look more closely at what is already within our reach.

Maybe you haven't arrived at the place you always planned to be. Maybe that makes you sad. Just remember this: there is another path for you, and good things are waiting on it, if you have the faith, or the friends, to help you find them.

Published: Mon, 17 Oct 2022

`http://ruthwrites.online/2022/10/17/there-is/`

There will always be

Mon, 28 Mar 2022

Another chapter.

This week I have been struggling with the feeling that things are stuck and will never change. Then I started thinking about my inability to write a sequel to any of my stories and I realised: I need to make room for things to turn a page and start a new story.

Do you feel trapped in your circumstances? Can you not see them changing? I know that feeling, but in those times when a new chapter feels impossible, start to write one anyway. It could be the smallest thing, like deciding to go sit in your garden instead of your sofa, or having a coffee with a friend, or pulling out a jumper from the bottom of the pile that you haven't worn in ages.

Of course, big changes are possible for you too. If you're not happy with the status quo, there are often ways to alter it, like getting a new job, cutting your hours down to part-time, starting an evening class, finding a new hobby or a group of people that share your interests or life experiences. I don't do any of those things anymore and am realising that I have let my disability stop me. If the objections are building up in your mind, don't let them have the final say. There are always ways around things.

If that is too daunting, or if even the smallest of new steps feels too hard, then look out your window and think about how every day is different and the seasons will always change, no matter how much of a rut you find yourself in.

Meeting new people at the shops or in the park can give you a lift too. To share a hello or a smile can make your day. Even when you think that nothing is different, let the changing people, scenery and weather carry you through.

To have a life that is hard to add new chapters to doesn't mean that your days are meaningless. In fact, they are wide open to exciting, new things. Look out for tiny chances and grab onto them with both hands.

There is a blank page in front of you, just waiting for you to write on it.

Published: Mon, 28 Mar 2022

http://ruthwrites.online/2022/03/28/there-will-always-be/

Trying to

Mon, 27 Feb 2023

Find a sense of achievement.

When you're at school, tests track your progress. When you're at work, often one-to-ones with your manager record how you are getting on. When you are an athlete or do some form of sport there are personal bests or step counts to measure your activities. However, when none of those feature in your daily life, different challenges need to be found.

I don't know whether any of you are struggling with a lack of purpose, or an inability to physically do much. Every time I see groups of runners I feel a wee bit envious of them. (A nice cup of coffee and a chocolate biscuit on my sofa soon sort that one out!)

In these days of minimal activity, I still make lists in my head. They're shorter than before but still help me through the day. It might be writing for a couple of hours or doing an extra round of my physio exercises but still it's something.

I'm sure if you feel stuck in a job you hate, you could make a list of tiny tasks that you can sneakily do or look forward to doing when you get home. Again, it might involve a chocolate biscuit or two!

We live in a world where obvious things mark success: awards, promotions, pay rises, A's in school exams, firsts at university, publishing deals and lots more. There are cards for most things these days. But what about the times you overcame your fear, the first occasion when you felt well enough to go out, the time when you got through a whole day by yourself or succeeded in making your own dinner. For some, these are huge challenges that deserve to be called an achievement too.

So if you have made yourself proud in an unseen way, congratulate yourself. Not all battles are acknowledged or even seen but they are won nonetheless and I salute you for that!

Published: Mon, 27 Feb 2023

`http://ruthwrites.online/2023/02/27/trying-to/`

You have your own story to tell

Mon, 23 Oct 2023

Have you ever realised that every single person you encounter is a walking story? Beyond the hellos and the blank faces there is a whole life, a wealth of experience- some to be forgotten but others to be learned from.

As a writer, I let my characters direct the story. But no created person can ever hold the complexities, idiosyncrasies and contradictions that a real one does. As I was cycling past an elderly couple earlier, the gentleman told me to slow down. I just smiled and said I couldn't. But now I'm thinking that is exactly what we need to do.

When someone tells you the story they always tell don't inwardly roll your eyes. Slow down and listen. It is obviously significant to them. Each remembered experience makes up part of their story. As it does for you.

I'm thinking especially about older people. I worry that so many of their stories will go with them; either because no-one has the time to listen, because they can't remember them any more, or because they don't think anything is worth holding onto. Only a week ago I heard a story that I have never been told before about my granny. And the sad thing is, she did so much in her life that most will fade away. Every person we meet is remarkable, if we slow down enough to listen.

Do you believe that you hold a story worth telling? I speak to my mum every night and I try to find something notable to tell her. It's not easy, when life becomes a thing to get through, not to really live. So here's a challenge for you- either collect a story from someone you know, or make your own.

Believing you are a story worth telling may well change how you live.

Published: Mon, 23 Oct 2023

http://ruthwrites.online/2023/10/23/you-have-your-own-story-to-tell/

Positive thinking

A day like today

Mon, 26 Oct 2020

Do you ever have a moment, a short time, even a day, when you think, maybe life is not so bad after all?

I hope you do. Yesterday, my walking felt stronger, my family was happy and my mum was feeling better. I'm writing to mark it down as a good day.

For most of this year, I've dwelt upon my up and down health, the state of the world and the struggles people close to me are going through. It is very difficult to push through that to notice when good things happen.

Thankfully, if you allow it, there are always happy moments to be celebrated and cherished. In fact, when life is particularly dark, the chinks of light sometimes shine even brighter.

I've noticed a surprising feeling of gratitude rising up at times that I would have taken for granted before. A couple of days ago, I stood on my aunt's doorstep and talked with her for a short while. Both of us marked the time shared as special. And said so.

That's key. If you notice you're enjoying someone's company, even for two minutes, two metres apart, tell them. So much of our day is spent listening to bad news, fearing bad things and talking about them. Now, more than ever before, we need to spot and remark upon the good. I suppose that's why clapping for the NHS became so important during the darkest days.

When life is bad, we have to search for and remark upon the good. Even if it's just a short, cold doorstep conversation, a tasty takeaway or a long-awaited haircut. These things are good! Let's push out the wearing conversations about covid and talk about them instead.

Published: Mon, 26 Oct 2020

`http://ruthwrites.online/2020/10/26/a-day-like-today/`

Always believe

Sat, 13 Apr 2024

That you can win. I was reading an article on BBC news about Ukraine, and one general from here was saying that 2024 was likely to be the year when Ukraine has to concede defeat. 'The reason, he says, is "because Ukraine may come to feel it can't win".That made my heart sink. The moment you start thinking you can't win is the moment defeat begins.

I am no expert in global affairs, but on an individual level I can relate to the idea of losing self-confidence. Up until last year, medical professionals would tell me my legs were strong. This week I got a letter saying my bones were weaker. That was all it took for me to lose faith in my ability to improve. Once that awful thought takes root, it is hard to step beyond it. But, for all our sakes, that is the time when we need to gather up our courage and believe that things will get better.

Maybe you feel like you are fighting a losing battle, maybe you have been told 'it's impossible' too many times. But remember the things that gave you hope, remember your tiny victories, hold your head high and keep going. Even if the odds seem to be stacked against you, do your best to move beyond that feeling of defeat and take steps to keep up your courage. For me, I am going to work hard to increase my strength and not let the dreaded word 'weakness' blight my future.

I am well aware that sometimes it is beyond our power to change impossible situations. That is the hardest thing. But even in the darkest time, light can shine. I have to believe that, and I truly hope you can too. To live looking for light is to live as a winner.

Published: Sat, 13 Apr 2024

http://ruthwrites.online/2024/04/13/always-believe/

Better things

Mon, 04 Nov 2024

Are waiting for you. So I'm out the other side of our trip to Rome. Sadly, the reality I thought I was prepared for was worse than I expected. The cobbled streets were almost impossible to get across on my wheelchair, and some sights were out of reach this time I was so thankful that I had been there before as the FOMO was not as great. St Peter's was definitely one I was sorry to miss. But, you know what? I saw things and people that I might have missed if I hadn't been down lower than most.

Have you ever found a new community you would never have seen if circumstances were different? I exchanged smiles with people in wheelchairs that seemed to be more meaningful than usual. Mutual understanding is a precious thing.

However, I found Michael Angelo's self-portrait in the Cistine Chapel, deep beside the other ones in the Last Judgement, and I thought, well I am not as low as that! I want to rise up, shake off the pessimism that weighs me down and reach for something better.

Don't ever consign yourself to a hopeless state. Look up and see the light that is waiting for you. Aptly I was staying in a building that once was a place where old furniture was restored. I would love some of that for myself! We all wish for an improvement of some kind. Never consign yourself with the hopeless. Believe that the clouds will part and the sun will shine again. Especially in these grey November days.

Published: Mon, 04 Nov 2024

http://ruthwrites.online/2024/11/04/better-things/

Courage

Fri, 22 Jan 2016

It's actually often hard to recognise it when it's right in front of you. I have always thought of my dad when the word comes up, because he did so many things when I was growing up that were incredibly brave. Then, at the start of this week I watched a Panorama progamme about a possible cure for MS, that followed a few individuals who were taking part in the medical trial. None of them faltered, or complained as they went through intense chemotherapy, 18 days of isolation and the humiliation that is physiotherapy. They were all SO courageous. Watching it, I was petrified. Some people have enthused about this wonderful programme, and the encouraging discoveries that have been made. I agree of course, but the whole thing terrifies me, as I wonder if I have the capacity to be as courageous as those amazing individuals.

A couple of days ago the sun was out and prompted by my daughter, we walked to school. I had no idea whether I would make the walk home, as the last time I'd tried it it was a nightmarish lamp-post to lamp-post struggle. I sat on the bench waiting for my son to get out and felt as far from courage as you can get. But, I stood up again, asked the kids to go slow, and I did it. It wasn't courage that brought me home, it was sheer determination.

Maybe everyone starts from there.

Published: Fri, 22 Jan 2016

http://ruthwrites.online/2016/01/22/courage/

Don't let the memories

Mon, 17 Apr 2023

Of 'better times' stop you from making more right now.

It's amazing how recollections can turn into good ones and the bad things that happened that very day are wiped out by a smiling photo. I found the picture above painful because it recorded a time when I could walk as far as I pleased and the notion of needing a stick or any form of support was far from my mind. That was a 'good day' at a good time in my life.

Or was it? Less than an hour later, I was butted to the ground by a ram. I had to go back, drink some water and wait for my baby to kick again, showing me he was ok. That was an anxious time, not as good as the photo records.

You see? Memories can mislead us. So I think, even if present circumstances are hard, there is still space for a bit of happiness too. On Saturday I was at Florence Court with my family. Because I was on a scooter I was able to be right beside them and see what they saw, in a similar but different way to what I was before. When we put the 'once's and 'back then's out of the picture, look past the walking aids and see the smiles, every day becomes so much better.

Do you find yourself looking back and hankering after times that your mind tells you were better than the present? Look again and see the wonder of what you have right now. Contraptions or difficulties can't take that away. It just takes a bit more strength of mind, but hopefully then you will see the goodness that is right in front of you.

There will always be 'ram' days ahead. Hold tight to what you have and you will be able to get through. As the song goes, 'Keep your eyes on the prize. Don't be dismayed, cos everything's gonna be alright some day.' *

*taken from the movie Green Card.

Published: Mon, 17 Apr 2023

http://ruthwrites.online/2023/04/17/dont-let-the-memories/

Don't wallow, don't dread,

Mon, 19 Oct 2020

Just take each moment as it comes.

Examining my attitudes a few days ago, I recognised two opposite forces at play. Either, I'm looking at my past self and feeling sad at its disappearance, or, I'm looking ahead, filled with dread about the things coming up that I know my future self can no longer do.

Backwards and forwards are both hard for me to think about.

When I saw a photo of me carrying my then toddler in his baby carrier I wondered how on earth I had managed it. These days most photos of me are either seated or with trekking poles. Standing strong with a baby on my shoulders is an image that prompts a deal of wallowing.

Equally, because of all those times when I've failed, I don't feel excited about future events any more, just worried it will be yet another memory of me hiding in the car while the others stride on without me.

Boo hoo. That's enough gloom! What do we do when we're caught up in the pull of wallow and dread?

We set up camp in the blessed present and ban all those black feelings from getting in. Rather than looking back and mourning the past, look at that memory and see how happy you were. Rather than expecting the next outing to go wrong, plan it carefully so that it is bound to be a success.

I'm fed up squandering precious energy hankering after the past or worrying about the future. So your past self is gone, but have you ever considered that who you are now is better? The girl carrying the baby was most likely complaining about how heavy he was. That baby is now a tall thirteen year old who could probably carry me!

The past has turned into a present that is full of good things. I forgot that. Even yesterday, the baby from the photo marched out, took over hoovering the car and sent me in to sit down. Would he have shown kindness if I was always able to do everything myself? Would my quiet daughter have the space to tell me about her day if I wasn't sitting on the sofa waiting for her to talk?

I would encourage you to turn away from the golden days that were and the dark ones you fear will come. Just take a seat and count on your fingers all the things that are good about this present time. I know that's a big challenge right now, but it's still possible, I promise!

Are you ready? Let's start...

Published: Mon, 19 Oct 2020

http://ruthwrites.online/2020/10/19/dont-wallow-dont-dread/

Favourite things

Mon, 13 Jun 2022

What do you think about when you're feeling a little beaten?

I'm not going to talk about my own difficult circumstances again, you'll be glad to hear. This time, I want to think about people, places and objects that make me so very thankful for my life.

Every weekday morning I stand and wave my two off to their school bus. Even better, I watch them coming home with more of a spring in their step. They are my two shining lights. Thankfully they have never asked the crazy woman with messy hair in a dressing gown to stop waving out the window at them. Yet!

I can't even begin to speak of the countless times my parents, siblings, friends and other half have helped me without question or pause. They are the strong arms beneath me when I'm falling, the supports on either side when I can't find anything to grab on to. I can only hope I am ready to do the same for them.

Last week I was looking across the blue of the Back Strand in Donegal, remembering not to wreck the beauty by wishing I was closer to it. There's a pool I'm dreaming of swimming in. One day!

Right now I'm sitting with my feet up under that favourite blanket and there is nothing I have to get up and do. The cleaner has been, the groceries were delivered, the dog is sleeping and I am content.

Sometimes it is possible to stop the bad thoughts racing in and just focus on the good. I say sometimes, because it is a battle to keep that up. Do you have someone or something or somewhere that can help you do that? I really hope so. For me, faith in a heavenly Father who is always there steadies me. But I know how easy it is to feel stuck in the darkness. If you can, try and think about some of your favourite things.

And then, as Julie Andrews sings, you won't feel so bad.

Published: Mon, 13 Jun 2022

`http://ruthwrites.online/2022/06/13/favourite-things/`

Feeling like yourself

Mon, 11 Nov 2019

"'I don't feel very much like Pooh today,' said Pooh.

'There, there,' said Piglet. 'I'll bring you tea and honey until you do.'" —Winnie-the-Pooh

Do you ever have times where you've lost any sense of who you are, or what you're supposed to do?

I felt like that last week. As you already know, I write these blogs to find the positive in an otherwise challenging situation, to celebrate what I can do and turn away from what I can't. On the good days of course.

Last week I had to attend an assessment for eligibility for PIP (personal independence payment). As I spent an hour talking about the things I found physically challenging, I felt as though so much of what I stand (ha!) for was being stripped away. My husband told the assessor about what I used to be able to do. I couldn't bring myself to talk about that. I felt the assessor's eyes on me as I walked out of the office, and the pressure to show her my weakness. It was a truly disheartening, humiliating experience.

This, right here, is more who I am than the person I had to portray in that horrible interview. This is my tea and honey. You all are my Piglet. I don't want to focus on what I can't do. The negativity of that robs me of any thing to live for.

Don't let someone or something take away your sense of the wonderful person you are.

Watching Seven Worlds, One planet last week, I saw an albatross chick struggle to climb back into its nest because if he's not in there, his parent will not recognise him. As he struggled to climb back in, I recognised the battle we all face: to convince people of who we are, to fight to be recognised. I did not recognise myself in that cold interview. I'm finding myself again now.

So, thank-you.

Published: Mon, 11 Nov 2019

`http://ruthwrites.online/2019/11/11/feeling-like-yourself/`

'It's time to sing,

Mon, 04 Apr 2016

time to sing, sing a powerful song.' So The Saw Doctors reminded me last week. It has been a month stuffed full of tragedy, horror, bad news and heart-break. It's seemed as though not a day can go past without something horrible happening. You think you've heard the worst, and more comes to kick you when you're already down.

In all honesty, there have been times when I have not wanted to click into BBC news, or go anywhere where someone might tell me something bad. The initial response to everything - to the tragedy in Buncrana, the terror attacks in Brussels, the floods in Pakistan, the refugees in Syria, Greece and Turkey, the devastating news closer to home - is to scurry into a hole and never come out again. Then there's the anger about it all - directed towards God, the people nearby, life in general. I spent a good deal of time there too. The tears are held back, knowing that many are closer to the tragedy than I am.

But, that song shook me out of this self-indulgent state, and gave me the response that I needed. The notions of 'rallying', or 'bucking up' or even 'brushing yourself down to fight another day' make a lot of sense, I think. I have found in the past that a determination not to be beaten, and a chin-up attitude carry you further than anything else. Not to show a lack of compassion or empathy, but to be strong when others can't be, to offer help to the helpless and hope to the hopeless. This is humanity. This is why God keeps us here.

So, shake off your despair, stand up tall and sing the powerful song, even with tears still in your eyes and pain in your heart. It's time.

Published: Mon, 04 Apr 2016

http://ruthwrites.online/2016/04/04/its-time-to-sing/

Push against the darkness

Mon, 09 Nov 2020

Every year I have an opinion about imperfect Christmas trees, premature decorations, too early celebrations. This year, unpredictably, tragically, everything has changed...

It has gone dark. Hospitals are running out of beds, cities are digging more graves, nursing homes are locked in, people are terrified, defiant, frustrated and desperately sad. When I heard Fairy Tale in New York playing on the radio, I didn't feel outraged at the timing. In fact, I nearly cried.

Now, more than ever before, we've got to search for joy. And hope. I heard a lot of that last week when the American elections found their president and the whole of New York was exploding with celebration. I saw it when I noticed our overeager neighbours have put up their tree in the first week of November. Other years I would have objected, but not this time. We can't have our extended families in for Christmas dinner but we can shine our lights for the whole street to see. We can't meet for Christmas concerts, but we can open our windows and sing for the world to hear to ones online.

Christmas brought joy to the world thousands of years ago. We have the chance, with our gaudy decorations and overplayed Christmas tunes, to bring it again. To remember again that God saw our darkness and sent His light.

So go on, buy too many chocolate Santas, eat all the turkey, kiss the people you can, put all the tinsel you have on your tree, leave a gift on your neighbours' doorstep and do your bit in pushing back against the darkness.

This year, it's never too early to begin. (And I promise I won't complain about it in next year's post!)

Published: Mon, 09 Nov 2020

http://ruthwrites.online/2020/11/09/push-against-the-darkness/

Reject the absolutes

Mon, 06 Nov 2023

Perhaps you remember a time when someone said something about you that made you feel hopeless but has never left your mind. It is funny (and yet not funny) how a few spoken words can stick, and direct many of your future choices.

Last week I used a wheelchair to get through an airport on our way to Paris. The special assistance staff were excellent but sadly one of them said three words that have weighed me down ever since: 'elle marche pas'. She doesn't walk. That statement was true at the time, but I cannot accept it as a forever truth.

I suppose there are two reactions to absolute statements. We can either let them discourage us or we can try to prove them wrong. I am attempting to drive out those words by going out on the trike and trying to get an appointment with a physiotherapist. The determination to prove people wrong is a great motivator.

Are there any words that were spoken to you that you are struggling to move past? Don't let them become an indisputable truth for you. You and you alone have the power to change the statements weighing you down. They are not absolutes.

Sometimes it is difficult, even impossible, to step out of the things people have decided you are. Sometimes, sadly, they are true. But how you live with them is key. Whatever the decree, you can be weighed down by it, or you can dance within it.

So remember how those spoken words made you feel every time you talk about someone else. Especially children. A statement can change the course of their life, for better or worse. Think carefully before you speak today. Maybe something you say will lift the hearer and make them believe in themselves again.

Here are my words for you: you are capable, you are strong and God loves you more than you can ever comprehend.

Published: Mon, 06 Nov 2023

http://ruthwrites.online/2023/11/06/reject-the-absolutes/

Rise and shine

Mon, 20 Mar 2023

So, I searched for photos of people jumping with energy and joy and the only one I could relate to was this one! I think I used to be a morning person but now when my husband calls 'rise and shine' I pull the quilt back over my head. To get up at the minute means facing reality and I'd rather not.

Does your immediate future look bleak or are you loving life? Do you jump out of bed looking forward to what the day might bring? Or does the snooze button on your alarm not work as many times as you wish it would?

I have hoped many times that things would be cancelled. Sadly the pandemic made that a frustrating, unsurprising fact of our lockdown life. Then I broke my hip and was literally forced to stay in. That has not been fun. Well, to my shame, I have quite enjoyed aspects of it. But the rare times I have been out, I have felt so much better. When I get up and out, I remember that we were made to live, not hide away.

That children's song I mentioned in the title has another line that goes 'get those children out of the muddy muddy'. Do you feel pulled down by the muck of life? Is there anything that will help you out? Apart from my amazing family and friends, I find that there is always something to help me rise again. Today it was the yellow snatches of budding daffodils. Tomorrow? Who knows!

So, if you are struggling, remember this: better things are coming your way.

Luke 1:78-79. "A new day will dawn on us from above because our God is loving and merciful. He will give light to those who live in the dark and in death's shadow. He will guide us into the way of peace.”

I really hope that rings true for you one day soon.

Published: Mon, 20 Mar 2023

http://ruthwrites.online/2023/03/20/rise-and-shine/

Start your day with laughter

Mon, 11 Nov 2024

I read a joke this morning that had me chuckling all day. It wasn't that funny so I'll not re-tell it but the principle is true: laughing at the start of the day is much better than crying

When I look back on potentially hard times, I can remember the funny gems that glimmer in there too. Like the time the head flew off the hammer when the consultant was testing my reflexes, or the fellow patient who made us all close our eyes as she rolled past in a wheelchair just covered in a towel.

My mum says 'you'll either laugh or cry' when life gets harder. I often cry at the end of a tiring day, but I am so thankful for the people that bring happiness in too . As it says in Ecclesiastes, there is a time for everything, so hold tight to the chance for laughter and get close to people who can bring it to you.

Make it a resolution to smile at least once a day. Life is stuffed full of hidden joys for you to uncover. I watched a clip of a sausage dog jumping across the snow in her garden, and another one where a litter of golden retrievers raced to greet their nurse. When a bird sings outside my window, it brings me so much happiness. Our rescue dog sleeping with relaxed abandon is another one. What forgotten gifts can you find today?

Published: Mon, 11 Nov 2024

http://ruthwrites.online/2024/11/11/start-your-day-with-laughter/

Swans and icebergs

Mon, 14 Sep 2020

Do you ever realise when you walk past other people, or sit near them on the bus, that they are all hiding something?

Yesterday I got a positive letter. It told me that I had 'no active inflammations' on my brain or spinal cord. As I shared the news I felt anxiety; what if people think that's all my problems over? What if they don't understand when I talk about my current struggles with walking? I mean, if there's no evidence now, what's the problem?

As I pondered this I started thinking about those who have lost someone or something precious a long while ago. Do people still ask them how they are, or do they think the scars from that must have been healed by now?

I would venture to suggest that at least 90% of us are either serene swans paddling furiously, with everything going on beneath the surface, or icebergs, where most of what we are is not even visible.

We need to remember that every single day. Someone is smiling brightly but inside they're aching. Someone else is answering 'never better' but sighing as they walk away. Don't get me wrong, it is always good to expect happy responses from our friends and family but we've got to allow them to have struggles too.

Ask the question but really, truly consider the answer. If we're all the walking wounded, then we need gentle understanding.

So, next time you shake your head about a gruff cashier or a snappy text, you have to remember that. Think about the swan and the iceberg. What is going on beneath the surface? The scars may not be new, the lesions may not be 'active' but sadly, they are still there.

Published: Mon, 14 Sep 2020

`http://ruthwrites.online/2020/09/14/swans-and-icebergs/`

That dratted Pollyanna

Wed, 11 Mar 2015

It's amazing how things you read when you're wee stay with you. A lot of the books I raced through when I was ten had a very optimistic outlook. Just as well, inheriting my mother's bias towards happy endings, I wouldn't have tolerated anything else - even Matthew Cuthbert and Beth March dying was pushing it a bit, in my opinion. But then, there was Pollyanna. At the time, I didn't think the book had any impact on me. Certainly the film was more irritating than anything, with the squeaky voiced Hayley Mills pirouetting around telling everyone to be happy.

But I find myself remembering it now. And the power of positive thinking it encourages. Life certainly wasn't a breeze for Pollyanna, and yet she had this 'glad game', trying to see something good in every seemingly terrible situation, something to be glad about. (Of course I know that's biblical too.)

I'm not good at looking on the bright side. If Pollyanna were a real person, and she came to see me, she'd have a case on her hands. There are no rainbow-making chandeliers in my house either. I am spectacularly good at being miserable. But, knowing that tendency, I find myself trying to be thankful in every circumstance, playing the glad game you could say.

Someone commented on facebook yesterday, 'Lovely day, great God'. A very true statement, but all day today, I've been fighting the urge to respond with 'Terrible day, still a great God.' I won't do it, of course. I'm just telling you. When the sun was shining yesterday, I was going down the stairs on my backside because my legs were weak. It was not a lovely day for me, and I was not being glad about anything.

But wait: there's an overly high-pitched voice in my ear: the sun was still shining, the sky was still blue, the kids' dad was able to walk them home from school. And I could go on too.

I have so, so many things to be thankful for, so bring it on Pollyanna, I'm ready to play!

Published: Wed, 11 Mar 2015

http://ruthwrites.online/2015/03/11/that-dratted-pollyanna/

The padlock

Mon, 18 Feb 2019

Two Fridays ago, I was walking the dog in an unusually quiet park. I only saw one other dogwalker and they were heading out as I went in. The sun was beginning to set, but there was still more light than shadow.

When the park keeper's van drove round the outer lane I thought nothing of it. There was still a jogger in high vis lapping the pitches. When the van drove past a second time I just thought, oh he's forgotten something. BUT THEN I walked back to the gate and it was, you'll never guess (of course, anyone with a whit of sense would) padlocked. I'd be lying if I said I wasn't panicking. My legs were running out of strength, my dog was confused and I was already imagining a night on the park bench. The jogger knew a squeeze-through-a-hedge way out but I wasn't convinced.

Anyway, I phoned a rescuer and it all ended up ok- the farthest gate is always open. Since then, I've been seeing that padlocked gate in my mind's eye, and philosophising.

When your way is barred, or your life is turned on its head what do you do? In the park I was very glad I had my dog with me. I also sought help from someone in there and from someone outside. When you're stuck, it can be reassuring to know both those kinds of people- one who has been there, but also one who knows the way out.

When I saw that padlock, I forgot about the peaceful park, the silver light behind me. All I could see was a blocked way out.

I've been thinking about all the children who got their transfer results the day after that incident. Some of them will now have their dream of a favourite school padlocked. It will seem that their life is over. But it's not. There is another path, and it might even be better.

I'm sure you have felt like that, or are standing still with your way blocked at the moment.

Just don't forget there are joggers.

Published: Mon, 18 Feb 2019

http://ruthwrites.online/2019/02/18/the-padlock/

The power of two

Mon, 05 Feb 2024

It is amazing how things that feel so overwhelming can be overcome when you share them with somebody else. There was a huge wave of human connection last week when Sesame Street's Elmo tweeted the words 'how are you' and got millions of responses. People just want to talk to someone about how they are, if that someone is brave enough to hear the truth. Of course, sometimes it is good news!

I'm as guilty as anyone when I don't truly follow up that throw -away question to pursue the reality behind the first safe answer. If you are in a rush, then don't go beyond 'hello', but if you have the time, then ask it twice, waiting for the real reply. The worst thing to do is to answer for the other person. 'You seem great' shuts down the conversation before it has even started.

The power of two could also mean the power of two eyes noticing struggle, or two ears actively listening to the response. I remember being sorely tempted to bang my finger on the table and tell my doctor to look me in the eye when he asked me how I was and turned to his screen when I replied. I didn't of course, but maybe I should have.

So the next time you are in contact with another person, try and remember that you might be the only one to see them that day, the only one to hear them, the only one to follow up your enquiry about how they truly are . This is the gift you can give, if they want it. And I hope that somebody else does it for you too.

So how are you right now? Truthfully?

Published: Mon, 05 Feb 2024

http://ruthwrites.online/2024/02/05/the-power-of-two/

'The rat, on the other hand..

Mon, 10 Sep 2018

was running round the room busily, with his arms full of weapons...saying excitedly under his breath as he ran, 'Here's-a-sword-for-the-Rat, here's-a-sword-for-the-Mole, here's-a-sword-for-the-Toad, here's-a-sword-for-the-Badger! Here's-a-pistol-for-the-Rat, here's-a-pistol-for-the-Mole-here's-a-pistol-for-the-Badger!' And so on, in a regular, rhythmical way, while the four little heaps gradually grew and grew.'

Reading this to my daughter last night, I was reminded of myself, and mothers in general, as we rush around with invisible check-lists each morning before school. I have lost count of the times I've said, 'I wish you could hold some of this in your head like I do.' Chance would be a fine thing.

Now that our eldest is in secondary school, you'd think that those things would be smoothly transferred on to him. But still, every morning, I'm checking he hasn't forgotten anything. Of course, when I wasn't there, he left his school shoes in school.

When I'm not there, things get burnt to the bottom of saucepans, washing sits in a damp heap in the machine, notes aren't retrieved from school-bags, lunch-boxes lie unfilled on the counter. Well, in my head that's what would always happen.

But what if it didn't? What if I said nothing, did nothing, prompted nothing. Would everything still come together or would it all go wrong? (Of course, I'm only ever going to wonder about that and never put it to the test, controlling person as I am.)

My son is in fact quite organised, and if left to fend for himself, he just might pull it off. What has happened is that all my 'four little heaps' of over-preparation have taken the wherewithal away from everybody else. I might feel ready, but they're not. Because I never give them the chance.

In the story, Badger points out to the flapping Rat that all they really need is a stick each. And he was right. As they all brandished their simple weapons, the weasels flee, shrieking.

Badger tells Toad,

'Don't pretend to be stupider than you are.'

Put a different way, don't assume your children need you to do everything for them, because most times they will prove to be more capable than you might think.

Published: Mon, 10 Sep 2018

http://ruthwrites.online/2018/09/10/the-rat-on-the-other-hand/

The surprising benefits of predictability

Tue, 28 Mar 2017

What's this? I'm posting my blog on a Tuesday, not my usual Monday. Crikey.

In fact, it's a deliberate break from the same-old, same-old nature of my life. Yesterday, as I was summing up my morning to someone, I stopped and looked at the text. It was the same as nearly all the others. I tried to think of one single, tiny thing I had done which was different.

Nothing was different.

If you were to call me at any point in the morning, I could tell you what I would be doing. 8.40: dropping the kids to school. 8.55: cycling. 9.20: housework - a questionably pleasing variety of cleaning the bathroom one day, hoovering the next, tidying every day, dusting (rarely). 10: preparing the dinner. 10.30: making a cup of tea and settling down to write. And so it goes on - hardly ever changing.

The funny thing is, I don't mind my days being the same. It's reassuring, stabilising, even satisfying. It's only when my routine is reported that I feel ashamed. In private, I am fairly content. And why on earth not? Mostly, life is a consistent road of identical stepping stones, and when the route or the path changes, we find it unsettling - sometimes in a good way, sometimes not.

Of course, you never hear the word "typical" said without it sounding negative. Anytime a rebellious child, or adult, transgresses, they are accused of being predictable, and not in a good way. The French saying 'metro, boulot, dodo' that I've referred to before paints the act of doing the same thing every day in a bleak light. But then, usually after their death, people are praised for faithfully going to the same place every day and consistently doing the same thing.

So here's a suggestion for you: predictable living is too often called 'boring'. Why not try 'faithful' this week instead?

Published: Tue, 28 Mar 2017

http://ruthwrites.online/2017/03/28/the-surprising-benefits-of-predictability/

The way is

Mon, 16 Sep 2019

Blocked. You had a destination, a carefully devised plan, everything was in place. But. Just when you're half way or even nearly the full way there, something unexpected happens. You face the locked door, the raised hand, the 'road closed' sign and see no way round.

This happened to me over the summer in a literal way. I was driving back from Donegal with the kids and all of a sudden the road ahead was closed. I don't know Omagh very well, so panic ensued. I stopped at the local garage and the girl assured me I could ignore the signs and just drive through. A man coming in the opposite direction shook his head and said there was no way I could keep going. But I did drive on until the next traffic cones and stopped again. This time, a surprisingly helpful, rough-looking man put out his smoke and lifted the cones to make a path for me. We got home ok in the end, by the usual route. Today my drive has been blocked for Virgin to dig up the road, and again I found myself smiling at another grubby man to get into my house.

There have been unwelcome barriers in my life over the years and often the way round, out, or over is hidden. It has taken a long time for me to accept the 'road closed' signs, and even longer for me to find the diversion. Acceptance is a fitful thing - sometimes I catch it for a while, other times it eludes me. But I know that when we accept what we cannot change, it can set us free to see a different way. That takes a lot of courage and imagination.

Now I know that I would never have found my love of writing, experienced immeasurable kindness, even moved to this amazing street, if the road hadn't been blocked against my original plans. And this is a good way!

I'm sure you have road blocks in your life too. Look out for the grubby road-workers or smoking strangers. I bet you they'll say, "Just give sit tight, love, and I'll show you the way."

You'll get there in the end.

Published: Mon, 16 Sep 2019

http://ruthwrites.online/2019/09/16/the-way-is/

Too many burdens

Wed, 29 May 2019

I don't know why, call it the Baader-Meinhof phenomenon if you will, but I keep on seeing quotes about worry these days.

It's quite apt really, as several things have happened which merit a good deal of anxiety. I would describe myself as a worrier even at the best of times, but it's when the unexpected badness happens that the negativity really kicks in. I hate that type, you know it - an accident, an unexpected illness, an out-of-the-blue redundancy...Fill in yours.

When things like that happen, I have to fight the urge to think, 'this time yesterday things were fine'. We are so good at either hankering after yesterday or fretting about tomorrow. What about the todays? Right now, I'm warm, well-fed, surrounded by good music and safe from the bad weather and yet...And yet, I'm not free from worry. Do you think that one day we'll learn how to stop worrying and just relax? Doubtful.

I remember telling myself 'my skin will be free from spots in my twenties' and 'I'll have more confidence when I hit thirty.' Neither has turned out to be true. I'm at the end of my thirties now, and nothing has got any easier.

It is so hard to live in the moment, when the present you're enduring is taking place on a chair in the a&e of a chemical filled hospital where the number you have is 300 places higher than everyone else's, or when you are stuck in a traffic-jam you can't see the end of, or when you are experiencing pain that no pills seem to be able to take away. At those times, maybe it's ok to live for tomorrow. Maybe telling yourself 'it'll be over soon' is ok. Maybe thoughts of the future can help with the impossible present.

When I think about it, I draw either from the past or the future to help me cope with the present. Memories of happier times and hope for things to get better are my ways to deal with the here and now. Although a good friend and a bit of faith are the best help when times are tough.

I have to apologise for not having an easy fix or neat conclusion for this one. As it turns out, some things in life are far too messy for that.

Published: Wed, 29 May 2019

`http://ruthwrites.online/2019/05/29/too-many-burdens/`

Treasure kindness

Mon, 01 Jul 2024

And use it to push back negative thoughts. I discovered again how you can train yourself to think positively and drown out the bad.

A few nights ago, thoughts about my health, ongoing tensions and fears about what lay ahead started to take over, but then I blocked them all by fixating on a picture of the silk flowers I was sent by a dear group of American women last week. The thoughts were trying to fly in, but I was able to block them with those beautiful flowers

Do you ever feel overcome with darkness or anxiety, helpless to move beyond it? This doesn't always work, but try and focus on one good thing that has been done for you. Or maybe do something for someone else who is struggling at the moment. A few days ago I came to a stop on my trike in the park. I looked round for help. An unlikely, slightly rough-looking person was closest to me so I asked for a push. He didn't need to think twice about it. If I had let the negative thoughts in, I would still be sitting there.

Don't let the darkness win. You are worth a million kind deeds. Sometimes you don't even have to ask. Expect kindness and more often than not, it will find you.

So next time the cruel thoughts start to build, beat them down with kindness. I know that sometimes it is too hard to do, but remember you are stronger than you think

'When Jesus spoke again to the people, he said, "I am the light of the world. Whoever follows me will never walk in darkness, but will have the light of life."' John 8:12

Published: Mon, 01 Jul 2024

http://ruthwrites.online/2024/07/01/treasure-kindness/

Try and make today

Mon, 06 Feb 2023

A good day,

So often we can find ourselves in a hard place and cannot see a way out. But what if we can hold onto the little snatches of possibility and see them for the good chances that they are? Chances to feel better in yourself. An opportunity to find something good when everything seems to be wrong.

When my children come home with their heads down after a hard day in school, I sometimes try to ask them to tell me about one good thing that happened to them that day. It is a practise that I think can help us to see things from a different perspective. At the end of a holiday I ask about the best bit, their favourite thing. Taking stock of the good can work to cancel out the bad, usually.

This way of living is not an exercise in grasping at straws or denying when things are tough, but it can be a lesson in survival, especially when you feel that life is getting on top of you. My granny used to say, 'this was the best day' after a trip out. No-one dared to point out the events that could have spoiled it. If the declaration of a good day has been made then a good day it will be.

You should try it sometime.

The sun may rise but not be seen. The whispered compliment may not be heard. But if you have decided to have a good day, you won't miss them. Notice the best things about today and don't let them go.

I'll do it if you do.

Published: Mon, 06 Feb 2023

http://ruthwrites.online/2023/02/06/try-and-make-today/

Was it all just a waste of time?

Thu, 08 Feb 2018

How many times has that question punched you in the chest over the years? It can be the little daily things like watching your dog, muck to the eyeballs, jumping over a freshly mopped floor, or driving through a massive puddle in your newly washed car, or giving your kids lollipops straight after a trip to the dentist's. Those really grate on me. Every task, however small, can feel like a huge feat when you're tired already. Especially if it means you need to start all over again.

Speaking of do-overs, I've been having a crisis over my latest attempt at novel number five. The plan was, write it in 2016/17, edit it 2017/18, publish in the summer. I'd finished my second edit, and had a few days of feeling like it was done.

Fool.

Last week, a more experienced writer than me talked about choosing where to start your story. The beginning does not necessarily mean the beginning. It might all start in the middle, or even the end. What?! My story starts at the start, and follows a neat, linear pattern until the end. And I can't bring myself to upend it. It's like dog muck on a clean floor. I tried this morning, and failed. My next thing to do is to go through all the novels I admire, and justify my choice. If I find even one that starts not at the beginning, so help me.

If you have done something and later question why, affirm yourself with what you learnt through it, who is all the better for you having done it and why it was actually worthwhile, even if the outcomes were unsatisfactory.

It's the process that matters, more than the end result. I got a lot of joy out of writing this story, and re-lived some of the pain too. I had to go through the process, step by step, holding on to the beginning through the middle and right to the end. Like a chain for your wrist where you pick up both edges to fasten it.

Interestingly, that's where the story really begins and ends in my book. With a gold bracelet. So sorry if I am not adhering to a more clever way of storytelling. I'm just too fond of the way things were before. Including clean cars and floors...

Published: Thu, 08 Feb 2018

`http://ruthwrites.online/2018/02/08/was-it-all-just-a-waste-of-time/`

When there is nothing

Mon, 19 Feb 2024

I was given an amaryillis at Christmas time and still all that is there are four green leaves and no flower. For the past few weeks I have been faithfully phoning to get a date for my next, now long overdue, infusion. When I think outside of all this minimal frustration, I am aware of the dear people I know who are living with a horrible health diagnosis, or terrible, heartbreaking loss, recently or every day for many years. So all in all, living with nothing is a common struggle for most of us, at one point or another. I am writing this conscious of the words of Henri Nouwen who said, 'The great illusion of leadership is to think that man can be led out of the desert by someone who has never been there."* I don't see myself as someone who has been through the darkness you have, so all I write is a gentle pondering.

I could never lay down some foolproof instruction for living without. I don't think that even exists anyway, thankfully. All I can do is tell you to hold on to one another and eventually find a little bit of hope to keep you going. It says in 1 Corinthians 13, 'now three things remain: faith, hope and love, and the greatest of these is love.' So the amaryllis might never bloom, your health problems might never go away, you can never replace the person you have lost, but love will always remain. Right now that might feel like an empty consolation, but, in time, I pray that you will see that love will always endure and will always show up when you need it most.

Yesterday afternoon I was cycling in the park and had to slow down because a little girl by the name of Hope was happily trudging along behind her mother and big sister. She is still very young but in that moment she was the beautiful, timely reminder to me to always keep hope in our sights and let it lead us forwards.

My heart aches for anyone who is living with loss, but I truly believe that there is one, true, never-ending thing that will catch you when you fall, comfort you when you mourn and be with you when you can't see or feel anything else. That is the love our Father God has for you. And it never fails.🩶

*Henri Nouwen, The Wounded Healer (London: Darton, Longman and Todd Ltd, 1994), p. 72.

Published: Mon, 19 Feb 2024

http://ruthwrites.online/2024/02/19/when-there-is-nothing/

When there seems to be

Mon, 30 Jan 2023

No way. Do you feel like you're out of options? Have you given up all hope of getting out of the situation you're in?

On Friday our long awaited sofa for the extension upstairs arrived. Well, sort of. They couldn't fit it through the door of the new room. So downstairs it came again. The delivery men left me staring at that wretched piece of furniture sitting in the wrong room. What on earth were we going to do now?

Well, we contacted family and friends and yesterday afternoon, our sofa was lifted through the upstairs window by a group of kind people. Moral of the story? Don't despair. Help is there if you ask.

Most days I face a stuck sofa situation and most days I try to struggle through, usually unsatisfactorily. Do you ever do that? I know it's easier if you can get things sorted by yourself but sometimes that is just not possible. It is annoying, especially if you're an introvert like me, to bring others into your life, but it is almost always a helpful experience. I made myself a coffee earlier and realised how much better it would have been if someone else had made it for me. When I was sitting on my new sofa today I could have said it again: getting help is worth it

There's a song I remember from my teenage years that says 'God will make a way when there seems to be no way'. Often that happens through the people around you, so keep asking and see how impossible situations can be turned around.

I am very aware that some things do not work out the way you think they should. At painful times like that, we need friends more than ever to stay by us and remind us that in the darkness, we are not alone. I pray that you know that too, when all hope seems to have gone and all ways are closed for you.

All I can say in those impossible times is what I do: look to our Father and ask friends to help you find a way through. As it says in Isaiah, 'See, I am doing a new thing! Now it springs up; do you not perceive it? I am making a way in the wilderness and streams in the wasteland.' God knows all about stuck sofas and He knows how to get them/us out too.

Published: Mon, 30 Jan 2023

http://ruthwrites.online/2023/01/30/when-there-seems-to-be/

When you look at the sky, do you see..

Mon, 02 May 2022

The blue or the black?

Most of the time, it's fairly easy to see the good side of things. My blog posts kind of keep me in that discipline. The majority of people answer the question about how they are with a cheerful 'fine' or 'not bad'. My mum always insists blue sky is on its way. Only yesterday she told me that her friend in Donegal said she could see a tiny sliver of blue after a day of persistent rain. My granny used to say she was 'tip top'. People always like it when you are positive.

But some days the sun doesn't shine. Some days granny was very lonely. Some days you can't even pretend to be fine. The dark clouds gather and that is all you can see. It can happen for many reasons, or for no reason at all.

So what can we do, when we find ourselves in a dark place? It's hard to rally, or find anything to keep us going then. I struggled onto a wooden bench in the garden last week. After I had looked away from the weeds I couldn't clear, I saw a tiny, violet and yellow pansy, pushing up in between the concrete slabs. That flower made me smile. It wasn't in the wrong place. It was just where it needed to be at that moment.

If you are stuck, overwhelmed with black clouds, think about the unexpected miracles that can keep you going when life is too hard to bear. Maybe you can't even see a mouse's waistcoat of blue sky, but it's there, waiting for you.

Come on, we'll find it together.

Published: Mon, 02 May 2022

http://ruthwrites.online/2022/05/02/when-you-look-at-the-sky-do-you-see/

Why not?

Mon, 18 Sep 2017

I've been bouncing from one mood to another about my writing these past couple of days. Yesterday I heard someone say 'what a waste of hours' about an unpublished writer and the dark feeling came over me - have I just frittered away the best part of a year on something that nobody wants to look at, never mind read? I looked over my first draft again, willing myself to see it the way I did when I was writing it. Nothing.

Earlier today I heard a pro-Brexit (hmm) politician extolling the virtues of our great country and something he said made me stop. He described Britain as being full of creative people. And then I remembered - if you are a true writer, you don't write for critical acclaim; you write because you love it. If you're an artist, a composer, a musician, a cook, you do it because you can't imagine life without it. Whatever you are good at, do it. No matter what the skeptics say. They only criticise because they have nothing better to do.

This morning I tried to imagine a life where I didn't write every day and it terrified me. We have the freedom in this country to express ourselves, to make new worlds, to inspire and delight. Why let the gag of self-criticism ruin that?

I'll post this blog, even though my nasty head is telling me it's terrible. And I will keep writing, for better or for worse.

(I do still think we should stay in the EU. I'm not Boris Johnson for goodness' sake!)

Published: Mon, 18 Sep 2017

http://ruthwrites.online/2017/09/18/why-not/

Work in progress

Mon, 15 May 2023

It's easy to forget, when life is tough or just very busy, that change is possible. I have heard many times the words 'I'm done' or 'I have nothing else to give'. I think most of us can't imagine that something new or different could ever be within our reach

Last week I saw an excellent physio who gave me the exercises I needed and I spoke to someone who can get me outside again on an adult trike. All of a sudden, I was able to see that there was life beyond what I have right now. I had forgotten I was not stuck forever. I had stopped believing that progress was possible.

Do you feel that your life is always going to be the same? Does the idea of something better seem too good to be true? Perhaps you don't have the energy to make something happen, or you don't know where to begin. Speak to someone you know who has drive, and let them help you.

I've come across a number of people and situations recently where it is taking longer than initially expected for things to improve. There is a point, many points, when it would be easy to lose heart. Believing that you are a work in progress means you know that you are not done. So don't give up. You are better than that beat up car!

The good thing about 'work in progress' is that it can take a bit of the pressure off. Like leaving the vacuum cleaner out when visitors come so it looks like cleaning is about to happen, or giving that as the answer when asked how a project is coming along. That car looks like it is ready for the dump, but put a few red markers on it and hey presto, it's being fixed!

When you look at your future, believe that there are always opportunities to get better. I know that is hard to do, and some days it seems impossible, but we can do it, one tiny step at a time. If you take a tiny step every day, then where will you be after 365 of them?

Published: Mon, 15 May 2023

http://ruthwrites.online/2023/05/15/work-in-progress/

You are of use

Mon, 01 May 2023

It is easy to think that in a world of visible achievement, you are looking on with no idea of what on earth you can contribute.

Every day I think that, as I sit on my blue sofa and look out the window. Every day I struggle to think of what I have done for anyone else. My amazing neighbour made a spectacular cake yesterday, refusing payment saying 'one day you will repay me.' How? I wished I could see a way.

Earlier on today I read a remarkable sentence 'you might be the answer to the prayer you have prayed'. How about that?! Even if you are unable to do much, you are there.

Every message you send, every smile you give, every prayer you pray, you are doing something. There is no-one exactly like you, which makes your contribution so valuable. We will never know how we made someone's day or turned it around in some way. Remember that when you smile at someone today or tomorrow.

So I will keep on sitting, or writing, or praying, because we all need somebody to lean on.

Never forget: you have more use or purpose than you will ever know.

Published: Mon, 01 May 2023

http://ruthwrites.online/2023/05/01/you-are-of-use/

Your root self

Fri, 19 Mar 2021

I'm reading Matt Haig's The Midnight Library at the minute and there's one phrase that has stuck with me: the main character always holds onto or returns to her 'root self'.

Over the past ten years as my body weakens, I've felt like I'm losing big parts of myself. Every day when I drive past a particular footpath I remember I used to be able to cycle up it. I watch my family walking our dog to the park and I think, that used to be my job. I look out at the untidy flower beds and hate that I can't bend down and fix them, the way I used to.

The problem with looking back is we start to believe that the things we think we don't have or can't do anymore means that we are less now. There are days when I feel someone has turned a turbine on me and left a shred of the person I once was.

I'm learning, very slowly, that my root or Ruth self is still there and that it is definitely worth holding onto.

Have you lost something you feel was what made you you? Maybe a loved one, a pet, a gift or, like me, your good health? How do you think you can find your root self again?

I was remembering a funny story this morning... When I was a wee girl I fell out of our family car when it was driving round a twisty street. My oblivious dad asked, 'is everyone all right in the back?'. My pragmatic brother replied, 'Ruth's not here'. Car brakes and everyone turns round to see a tiny figure lying on the road. I was ok and now everyone laughs about it.

Maybe you're looking back at a distant figure of yourself and worrying that it's never coming back. I'm here to tell you that you are still here. Your root self remains. Through the mists and disappearing, weakening times something strong is holding on. Some-one strong. And it's you!

As a Christian I have a particular hope that when the storms rise, I will never be left behind. I always loved standing in the water as the wave breaks, runs towards me and then retreats again, pulling away the sand around my feet but leaving two small lumps for me to stand on. I stand on my faith and know that my root self will always be there because the One who formed it is holding on to it more tightly than I am.

Published: Fri, 19 Mar 2021

`http://ruthwrites.online/2021/03/19/your-root-self/`

Faith

Angels with boots on

Mon, 18 May 2020

Even if you don't believe in the supernatural, the human sort of angel is pretty common.

Throughout my childhood and even now, my mum would spot angels everywhere, in many situations. Because of her, I'm getting pretty good at it too. I'm not talking about the flimsy, feathery kind. I'm talking about the rough man with a smoke in his mouth who moved traffic cones out of my way, the nurse with the prominent chin and a strange name whose calmness helped my nerves, the boatman with a thick Kerry accent who helped me onto a rib in the summer, and even today, the people who have sent messages of kindness about my mum on Facebook.

I find it's when I'm in my darkest place, at my lowest ebb, that angels appear. All of the situations I listed in the last paragraph were times like that. Sadly, there are times when it is impossible to recognise any good beside us, and any thoughts of angels fly away. But, sit tight and look sharp because they will come back. Sometimes, it's only when we look at something retrospectively that we see a tiny flash of light.

Thinking about these dark covid times, can you see any angels? I can- the Tesco man who carries food to my front door every Thursday, the neighbours I see clapping in their porches, the postman, the bin men, the chatty person stopping at a safe distance to speak to me in the park and many, many more. There are angels (not all the time of course!) in my house- my children unexpectedly holding my hand, doing the jobs I struggle with and my husband, always picking up when I've reached my limit.

There is a snag about spotting angels though. Over time, the kindness you have experienced starts to work on you, and, without realising it, you become an angel too.

Published: Mon, 18 May 2020

http://ruthwrites.online/2020/05/18/angels-with-boots-on/

Be amazed every day

Mon, 30 Dec 2024

'Our goal should be to live life in radical amazement,' writes Rabbi Abraham Heschel because 'everything is phenomenal; everything is incredible; never treat life casually. To be spiritual is to be amazed.'

As this new year stands full of potential for you to enjoy and explore, it is as much for you as for anybody else. This blog post does not revolve around my experience; it celebrates everyone, the whole wide world. There is a wonderful lightness to be felt when we look up and around ourselves. Every time I write I look up at the sky and remember that everything is bigger and better than the world I struggle in, and definitely more expansive than the one I create. I was reminded that the stars are more numerous than grains of sand. And yet, how much greater is the love our God has for you🩶 .

Published: Mon, 30 Dec 2024

http://ruthwrites.online/2024/12/30/be-amazed-every-day/

Beautiful Coincidences

Mon, 13 May 2019

Saturday was a very sad day, as we said goodbye to our uncle John. He was the kindest man I have ever known, noticing and wanting to fix the things that other people wouldn't.

I've had very direct encounters with that side of him over the past few years. Another instance of being more obviously in need of help than most I suppose.

My auntie's cottage sits at the top of a nearly impossible (for me at least) to scale hill. Any time I managed it, John greeted me at the top and ushered me to the rocking chair beside a roaring fire. Always, he wanted everyone else to be happy, well-fed and cared for. He never ever failed to do those things for me and I will never ever forget that. It was a beautiful coincidence when he and my auntie came out of the house to meet us. I know that the next time I consider climbing up will break my heart.

My son couldn't be with us on Saturday as he had already made plans to go sailing with his friend. I passed on his apology at the time but it was only later I discovered that he had been sailing at Whitehead, the very place where John was from, the very sea that he had boated on when he was a boy. I felt that, without us knowing, my boy had said goodbye to John in the most perfect way. I don't know how heaven works, but I like to think that John was watching him too.

Have there ever been beautiful coincidences in your life?

Can you see how you could make that happen for someone else?

It has really comforted and helped me to think over mine.

Almost like feeling the wind in my sails again.

Published: Mon, 13 May 2019

`http://ruthwrites.online/2019/05/13/beautiful-coincidences/`

Beyond the full stop

Mon, 30 Sep 2024

I'm beginning to hate absolutes when we all deserve a chance to tell another story about ourselves. For example 'she has MS' only defines one part of a multi-faceted, diverse histories person. Maybe we should think about expecting more from someone and not getting out a one covers everything stamp.

Last week I discovered yet again my tendency to share more information than is necessary. I started to speak but my husband put his fingers on my arm to stop me. All the receptionist wanted was my name, not my whole life story.

I do it all the time, saying more than I need to. Thinking about it, I just want people to see beyond my wheelchair or trike. I want people to see me

But am I seeing beyond my own assumptions to let the person in front of me be more? If they reduce me, what am I doing to them? So allow yourself to be surprised, even proven wrong. The world is made up of a kaleidoscope of people. It can't be divided into black and white. If that's all you can see then you are missing out.

I often turn on the app Merlin to identify the birds I can hear in the park. But a list of names doesn't do justice to the clarity and beauty of their songs. Who are you and what joys are you withholding? The Bible tells us we are 'fearfully and wonderfully made' (Psalm 139:14) . Do you believe that about yourself, and those you rub shoulders with every day? I wonder what the world would look like if we started to give people room to be more than we have decided they are. As ever, expect to be pleasantly surprised, even contradicted. The world is a storehouse of colourful people. It's up to us to see them, and enjoy being seen like that ourselves.

Published: Mon, 30 Sep 2024

http://ruthwrites.online/2024/09/30/beyond-the-full-stop/

Buckets and bicycles

Mon, 26 Jun 2023

One of my favourite verses in the Bible is Isaiah 40v31. It says 'but those who hope in the Lord will renew their strength. They will soar on wings like eagles; they will run and not grow weary, they will walk and not be faint.' Yesterday I started to notice things and people around me that are constrained or held back in some way.

I am frankly fed up using my own experience as an example but sadly, it is very easy to come across others going through similar things. The most painful one yesterday was seeing a teenage girl in a wheelchair stopped from going down to the beach as the steps made it impossible for her to get there. She seemed fine as her phone was her main focus, but her parents were clearly frustrated. Later on, I looked down my street at the cars half-way across the kerb and thought how annoying and perilous they had unwittingly made it for anyone in a wheelchair or pushing a pram.

I watch people doing things all the time that are nothing for them, but could be a huge struggle for someone else. It is a hard observation, but if you find things easy to do, maybe do them for the person beside you who finds them hard. When I have my rollator in front of me, usually people realise they need to give me space. But what if the need is more difficult to see? The second feature on Jeremy Vine this lunch time was about people needing and often failing to get a seat on the train. Most people nowadays are primarily caught up in themselves and don't notice that someone else may be struggling. A woman in her 80s stood the whole way from York to London as no-one thought to give up their seat!

Can you think of a way to help people fly when they are stuck or weighed down? It could be as simple as parking by the pavement not on it, or pulling your chair in to let people walk past.

The latest freeing thing that happened to me was I was introduced to a recumbent bicycle. Suddenly my existence was transformed from stationary to flying. I felt the wind in my hair as I whizzed downhill in the park. That discovery was the unexpected fulfillment of that verse in Isaiah. Before, I was grudgingly thinking that life for me would always consist of sitting watching life race past without me, but now I see that there are other options, alternative ways to live. All I did was look around and ask, and this miracle was within my reach!

Can you think of anyone you know who can make things easier for you? Or is there anything you could do for someone else? I remember last summer when I couldn't make it down to the shore, my cousin said she was tempted to bring a bucket of sea water up for me to put my feet in😍 .

I wish I had been able to find a way for that young girl to be on the sand but even her parents couldn't do that. What can I do? Maybe I'll become that person who writes regular letters of complaint to people who do have the power to effect change.

Buckets and bicycles may seem like nothing, but they meant everything to me. What seemingly insignificant thing can you do to help someone else fly?

Published: Mon, 26 Jun 2023

`http://ruthwrites.online/2023/06/26/buckets-and-bicycles/`

Clinging on

Mon, 02 Dec 2024

I noticed the final leaf hanging on for dear life on a birch tree in our garden. Do you ever feel like that? Someone once described themselves as ' hanging on by my fingertips'. Not great then.

So what do we do when we're barely managing? The temptation is to give up, hide away and let the storm rage past. I was reading that Bible story this week where Jesus falls asleep in the boat when the waves are overwhelming the fishermen disciples. Do you ever wish that someone could do something to make your crumbling life better? What I realised when I was reading that story was that everything was made good in the end. Jesus calmed the storm he obviously was always in control of.

These days, there are storm calmers everywhere, if you're able to spot them. Every night I sit down with my family for dinner and feel joy. Crucial people come round to remind me I am not alone in this. And that leaf shows me that everything has an ounce of strength in this world.

So if you are struggling, look round and ask for help. Remember that there will be a rescue. Jesus was asleep but He's awake for you right now, telling you not to be afraid. You are not alone.

Published: Mon, 02 Dec 2024

http://ruthwrites.online/2024/12/02/clinging-on/

Don't be a shadow

Wed, 04 Jan 2017

Gloomily reflecting on my narrow existence last night (blame the pressure of a new year), I realised something. When physically you are limited, when that monster fatigue is always the one making all the decisions, when you feel you have lost most of yourself, it's time to choose how you will carry on. Look at the things that sap your energy and reinforce your feelings of inadequacy, and then turn away, towards the people and the activities that you love, that make you feel a bigger person again.

There is one silly problem that I have with that though - I'm told to stop cleaning the house, and start enjoying my family. In all honesty, there are times when peacefully mopping the floor is preferable. That's the difficulty - cleaning is one thing that I can control, one purpose that nobody else will ever take up (to my satisfaction:/), one commitment that can always be fulfilled.

But when I struggle with the last stretch walking home with my daughter, I know I need to look at what really matters. For her sake.

Outside of poor old me, I recognise that sort of diminishing self in many people: the cruel tragedy of dementia clawing a person away from all they love, the fragility of old age where every day throws a different, disabling body punch knocking them further away from their former selves, the pain of being betrayed, bereaved or abused, the loss of a much-loved career or business. We define ourselves so often by what we have, or what we do, and when those things are threatened, or completely taken away, we become shaky versions of ourselves, with no point of reference to who we are.

But wait! I'm going to tell you who you are now. You are a child of God and you are loved with a love that never leaves and always endures. Through everything. Don't define yourself using something that will one day fade away. Make it God. Anchor who you are in Him. Why?

Because He will never be a shadow.

Published: Wed, 04 Jan 2017

`http://ruthwrites.online/2017/01/04/dont-be-a-shadow/`

Even in the valley

Mon, 10 Apr 2023

I'm sitting here with what would be an amazing view if it weren't for the rain. Except that I know what's really there in front of me*.

It's Easter Saturday today. There could be no better day to think about being in a state of emptiness or waiting for something to happen. This morning I was reminded of so many who are stuck waiting; people on a never-ending list for surgery or transplant, foster children longing for a family, the unemployed wondering when a suitable job will come up, expectant mothers already a week overdue...the list goes on. A lot of the time it may seem like things will never happen. But we have to remember this is not a forever valley. And even there, the sun can shine.

If you are familiar with the song, Sovereign over us by Michael W Smith you will know the line 'even in the valley You are faithful'. That keeps me going; the knowledge that God does not ever leave our side, no matter how deep the darkness we are in.

As well as that, there are always moments of goodness or brightness to keep us hoping for better. Of course there are days when nothing seems to go right. Relentless, punishing times. As I looked at that dark hill the other week it was a long time before it changed. In fact, at one point I couldn't see it at all. But then the rain stopped, the clouds lifted and the sun broke through to show a green, verdant landscape..

I pray that you can believe that the light will shine again in your valley, whatever it may be. I'll try and hope for that if you do.

*written when on holiday last weekend in Donegal.

Published: Mon, 10 Apr 2023

`http://ruthwrites.online/2023/04/10/even-in-the-valley/`

Even so

Mon, 29 Jul 2024

No matter how deep the valley or dark the night, hold on tight. I've been looking out my window today and watching the birds landing and sitting still as the dark clouds gather and threaten rain. I was wondering- what do you do in times of crisis?

One of the exercises the physio used to do with me was to get me kneeling down and gently shove me to teach me how to keep myself steady. I would definitely fall over if I was subjected to that now!

When life shakes you, how do you stand strong? Do you run away and hide? Or do you dig your feet in and withstand it? I have discovered that anytime I try to avoid things, they don't disappear. The birds are all flying every direction now but I can guarantee I'll see them lining up on the rooftops again.

The storms will come to all of us, but it is how we endure that is key. I feel frightened writing this because I know all this blithe advice may come to nothing. My only certainty is in the even so. Whatever happens, God can be our strength. Test it and see. I really hope you discover I'm right. Even so.

Published: Mon, 29 Jul 2024

http://ruthwrites.online/2024/07/29/even-so/

Fight for the light

Mon, 06 Jan 2025

In these dark, freezing January days, light and warmth become a top priority. The short days and long stretches of darkness make it difficult to feel happy about anything. Looking back over this first week of 2025, I have found a lot of aspects of life a real struggle and I know I'm not alone. So what to do?

As the faint sunlight glimmers through the grey clouds, I am reminded that we are not alone, that God is light and in Him there is no darkness (Psalm 139). It might feel right now that darkness has won, but that is not the end of your story. You can't rally or artificially make your life better all by yourself. Little steps are the way to go. I put my hands round a warm cup of coffee this morning and the sun became so bright I was blinded. Two little things that lifted me. Do you have anything like that? Go make yourself a warm drink, sit on your favourite seat and let the warmth do its work.

I am greatly reassured by the knowledge that there is nothing, no darkness too great, to phase our Prince of Light. You can run to Him and hide in that Truth. There are people strong enough to not flinch at what you are struggling with. If faith is an ask too great for you yet, if all you can say is 'help' then start there and watch the light grow stronger as you wait.

It is cold today, and, asking permission, my cleaner lifted a blanket and tucked it round my legs. Kindness can bring light and warmth too. Is there something you can do for someone else today? I'm thinking as well.

Published: Mon, 06 Jan 2025

`http://ruthwrites.online/2025/01/06/fight-for-the-light/`

Fill your heart

Mon, 12 Jul 2021

With thankfulness.

Not that long ago, I was having a 'not ok' day. All the things I physically struggle with were right in my face. I was feeling very sorry for myself. But after I had a cry, I thought, it's time to turn away from all this and think about the good things that are also all around me.

This is a tough discipline when life is hard, and I know sometimes it's impossible. But if you can, listing what you're thankful for can really hoist you out of the doldrums. You know, Pollyanna and her 'glad game' have their advantages...

That day I had to dry my eyes, come down the stairs and look at my family. I smelt the dinner being cooked for us, listened to my dog rustling round her bed and lifted my phone to see how my friends were surviving this thin, covid time. And that's only a few out of the many that can pull me out of misery into thankfulness.

We can't force ourselves to be happy. We can't manufacture contentment. But we can find things to be thankful for, no matter what we're dealing with.

Maybe our hearts are broken, grieving, lost, lonely, despairing. My hope and prayer is that you will be able to fill them with thankfulness.

I'll have a go, if you do too?

Published: Mon, 12 Jul 2021

http://ruthwrites.online/2021/07/12/fill-your-heart/

Flying without wings

Sun, 28 Apr 2024

I heard this week that the centuries old Moulin Rouge windmill in Paris has lost its sails. For no explicable reason. When I read that, I couldn't help but relate. But for some reason that cheesy song, You're flying without wings by Take That (edit: oops, Westlife) came to mind. Scrabbling away from dangerous self-pity I thought, now there's my challenge. So what if you've lost your sails or your wings, you just have to find a different way to fly.

One of the most crucial ways to help you take off is to help someone else. An outstretched hand or a shared smile can give the person going past the lift they need. Every time I cycle past someone in the park I see that happening.

Another way to fly is to let yourself be loved or helped. Every day my family show that uplifting love to me. Every time I ask for help, I see friends running to give me a hand. It is humbling but we should never feel humiliated. You don't know how much kindness bounces back to people who give it.

If you feel stuck in a situation, look round and you might see there is somebody or something that can help. Is there someone you know who needs to be picked up? Is there anything you can do? Even sitting with them can help. Praying with them can add wings to your concern too.

Another gift is nature. I can't run but I love watching my dog tear along the beach. I can't paddle but my heart lifts when I watch waves crashing against the sand. I laughed a lot today, just watching crows bouncing onto the smoke coming out of a chimney to clean themselves. Once they'd nearly burnt themselves they flew off.

There are many ways to fly, even if you are weighed down by your own troubles. Writing these posts every week is one of mine. So, thank-you! 🩶

Published: Sun, 28 Apr 2024

http://ruthwrites.online/2024/04/28/flying-without-wings/

From a distance

Thu, 22 Jan 2015

When I was growing up, every Sunday evening while we were eating barnbrack, mum put on 'Sounds Sacred' with Noel Batteye on Radio Ulster. I'm afraid to say that me and my three siblings always groaned at this - we were certainly not the target audience, as Noel oozed through dedications to 90 year old Elizabeth, or from 90 year old Elizabeth to her 60 year old and older children. Mum groaned too, when The Old Rugged Cross or Onward Christian Soldiers came on. She had a problem with loving a method of torture, and with marching as to war. But, there was one song that really got my goat, and that was From a Distance, sung by Bette Midler. The singing was pretty good, the tune fairly catchy, but the words, well, they were something else. Even as a young Christian I didn't understand why God would be at a distance, or why everything would appear air-brushed to Him. Lines like

From a distance we all have enough,

and no one is in need.

And there are no guns, no bombs, and no disease,

no hungry mouths to feed.

were baffling. But there are people in need, there are guns and bombs, there is disease. Why would someone write a song telling us that God is oblvious to suffering? I didn't get any oblique meaning to that song then, and I still don't now. 'Sounds Sacred'? More like 'Sounds wrong'. It's not poor old Noel's fault, but when you tear down the pleasant background to that song, what you hear is abandonment, and a picture of an apathetic God.

God is NOT watching from a distance. He has already got His hands so dirty it killed Him. He is the ever-present Father, the Friend who mourns, rejoices, lives right beside us. That is the hard Truth, standing when everything else falls. Put on a song about that, Batteye, and maybe I'll tune in again.

Published: Thu, 22 Jan 2015

http://ruthwrites.online/2015/01/22/from-a-distance/

Harassed and helpless

Mon, 23 Jan 2017

I read that description of the crowds following Jesus in the gospel of Matthew last night and realised that it was also an apt observation of the people milling around the edges of my observation too.

Last week was a killer blow in the States, with the bad-haired, orange faced, misogynist, racist, egotist Trump pushing his stubborn, blinkered way into the White House. When I scrolled through the news pictures I saw more people with their heads in their hands, a grimace on their face, despairing tears in their eyes, than ones who had their fists in the air like their Stalin-esque new leader. There was nothing they could do- the deed was done. The power was out of their hands.

But wait! Did you see the global protests, or hear any of the bold speeches inviting generosity and compassion the day after? That volume of support for goodness, equality, tolerance, freedom of speech was truly astounding. I can only hope that it is this voice of many that somehow wins through in the end. They are taking their feelings of helplessness, and standing strong against it.

In the less remarkable venue of the Bow Street Mall in Lisburn a few days ago, I saw so many people who were beyond harassed. They had obviously given up. Everyone I saw was alone. No-one had a smile or brightness to their face. They were not looking up or around themselves, they were just following their feet to the place they needed to go. I walked into a card shop, looked for the funny cards section and saw it was completely cleared out. How apt. I spoke to a sales assistant in another place, and she glumly told me what was on the shelves was all that was left. There was nothing else.

One friendly person was all I wanted, one answering smile, but there were none. I tore home, and got on my bike to grab some fresh air and cycle off the gloom. All of those people I had seen needed a friend. They needed to be set free from all the things that were weighing them down. They needed to watch those protests and see that there was another way, another response.

Don't ever be beaten, or if it's just too hard to see a way out, stretch out your hand, lift your face, and look for a friend. Or even just a smile.

Published: Mon, 23 Jan 2017

`http://ruthwrites.online/2017/01/23/harassed-and-helpless/`

Held

Mon, 26 Dec 2022

I was thinking back over this hard year, and further to the other difficult times in my life a few days ago, and it struck me; through it all, in many different guises, I have encountered something good. My memory gets so swamped with darkness I lose sight of the light. So I thought back and made myself notice how much goodness I have seen. Even right in the middle of the bad.

It was no accident that our builder was there to put ramps down to help the trolley get to the ambulance. It so happened that there was a trainee paramedic on duty who gave his all to deal with my pain. Mistakenly dialling the number for a friend instead of the MS helpline meant I heard concern instead of an answering machine. I was put on a ward with someone who was missing a relative who had recently died called Agnes, the very name that the nurse introduced me as when I arrived. That brought unexpected comfort both to the patient and to me.

So when I remember, I'm able to feel warmth. I've been told many times that I'm being held in prayer, but now I see I was never let go. By the One I walk with, but also by the many acts of kind people along the way. When I am tempted to say, '2022 was a nightmare', I have to see how tightly I was surrounded by the care of others- by family and friends but also by people I have never met before. The kind eyes above surgical masks, the gentle hands washing me, the sympathetic words from an overworked staff, the empathetic sighs from fellow sufferers, the cheers when I manage to take a few steps and so much more.

So when you reminisce about a hard time, see if you can find a feeling you hadn't noticed at the time. See if you can recognise you were never alone.

Always, you were held.

Published: Mon, 26 Dec 2022

http://ruthwrites.online/2022/12/26/held/

Hope

Mon, 12 Apr 2021

When I say the word 'hope' to you, what image comes to mind? Light at the end of a dark tunnel? Green shoots pushing through dark soil? An outstretched hand?

A week ago, Hope was toddling down our street, away from her home and towards another that she had seen her older siblings going to before. She was by herself and was going as fast as her little legs would take her.

Never looking back.

For over a year there's been a picture of a rainbow beside our front door, like many others. Children painted hope on stones, rainbow cakes were made, rainbow t-shirts worn.

At the beginning, when we didn't know how long the pandemic would last, hope was easier to muster. As the months passed, the deaths increased and the restrictions were lifted then imposed then lifted then imposed again, hope faded.

Now that the vaccines have been rolled out and spring has come, our flickering hope can flare up again. Are you finding that harder now? So much has happened, it's difficult to think things are going to get better. I'm certainly not ready to take that poster down.

But then, why should I? Life often pushes us down into many dark situations where hope is hard to find. For some of you, grief and sickness are holding you down and light is a fading memory...

I'm here to tell you hope is still there; bird lovers are looking to the skies for the swallows' return, farmers are ploughing fields, thick coats are being changed for lighter ones, garden furniture is being hauled out, tentative plans are being made.

Bright things are on the horizon. Set your gaze on them and keep moving forwards, just like little Hope. And you know the best thing? As I was watching Hope tear along, her big sister came running after her to make sure she was ok, to pick her up if she fell and show her the way home.

Even if hope is hard to find, someone else can do the searching for you and bring it to you.

Look up and see that hope is on its way; it comes with every sunrise, every birdsong, every kind word, every new bud, every rainbow. My question for you is- which sign of hope are you going to find today?

Published: Mon, 12 Apr 2021

http://ruthwrites.online/2021/04/12/hope/

Hoping for the best

Tue, 24 Apr 2018

So many bad, painful, shocking things have happened recently - to the world, to people I know. What's a body to do - retreat into the dark and never come out? Cry until there are no tears left? Never dare, never change, never try anything new?

Never hope?

This week started for me with stomach-punching bad news about someone I know. Later that day, I saw two rainbows. Looking out at them, I remembered about hope. Life is often terrifying and cruel. You think you've had your quota of trouble, and another thing happens. I would never presume to speak into someone else's pain as if I understood so I won't, I'll just say it to myself.

It strikes me that, after however much time is needed, there is an eventual choice of response when life gets ugly. That's where hope comes in. I have to wake up in the morning with it, walk through my day with it, and lie down to sleep, still hoping. For what? For something good to happen, for things to get better, for the ability to survive the day, for friends to come. Only a few examples, but I could list a hundred more.

If we lose hope, all that's left is fear. And I don't want to live like that. Do you?

I wonder though, if a person in our lives is in despair, can we be the one to bring a little hope in? Sure, we can't conjure up rainbows or say anything that would remotely help, but sometimes just being there can make a difference. I know that. I've experienced it many times - a random text, a bunch of flowers, a home-cooked meal on the doorstep. And every time, I've started to believe that things would get better. I've started to hope.

Published: Tue, 24 Apr 2018

`http://ruthwrites.online/2018/04/24/hoping-for-the-best/`

How I got over

Mon, 28 Feb 2022

About two years ago I watched the documentary 'Amazing Grace' featuring Aretha Franklin. There was one song that I noted down back then called 'How I got over'. For two years I have wondered if I can write anything about that.

When I was putting away my daughter's notes from a youth meeting yesterday, I saw that she had defined hope as 'waiting for good things to happen'.That made me sad because I remembered the many times when I tried to wait for things to get better. Even now, I often attempt to survive on that. But the fact is, we can't get over on a desperate wish. For me, it has got to be by pinning everything I hope for and everything I am going through on God; the Father who sent His Son to die for us. Every day I try to remember that a stronger, eternal presence is holding me.

This isn't just a crutch. This is everything that I live for. So when I talk about light or birdsong or kindness, they all find their source in my faith. I don't like to alienate people who don't share that with me, but today as my heart feels as shaky as I am, all I can do is to hold on to the steadiest thing I know.

How I got over is by reaching my hands up to my Father, helped by the people around me. That is the only, the best, answer I have.

The darkness of Ukraine is weighing us all down right now. But as the old hymn says, 'My hope is built on nothing less than Jesus' blood and righteousness. I dare not trust the sweetest frame, but wholly trust in Jesus' name... When darkness seems to hide His face, I rest on His unchanging grace.' I pray that for the people in Ukraine today, but I'm also praying it for you, my lovely readers.

Published: Mon, 28 Feb 2022

http://ruthwrites.online/2022/02/28/how-i-got-over/

If the door is closed,

Mon, 14 Feb 2022

Look for a window. (A direction that has been adapted from Malachi in the Old Testament but still makes sense today.)

Sometimes in life, things that we used to do become impossible. It could be that a baby has ruled out the option of heading out spontaneously. Or the death of a loved one makes us feel that we just can't go to those places where we remember them the most. Or, as all of us can relate to, the not so new restricting rules of lockdown, self-isolation and social distancing mean that so many of our past freedoms have been unexpectedly blocked over.

These past two weeks I have experienced the limbo of watching as someone else cleans my house. The old structures of 'bathroom on Tuesdays, vacuuming on Thursdays, kitchen on Fridays' have been lifted away as they are all done for me. What bliss you may say. And it is. But it has also left me adrift. Before there was work. Then there were babies. Recently there was housework and exercise class. Now? Well that is up to me.

It is hard to re-create our purpose when the former scaffolding of our days is taken away. When our usual way is inaccessible, what direction do we turn to? The question, 'what is it that you do' becomes more and more difficult to answer. Harder still is 'who are you?' Sadly, in this world, those two questions are inextricably linked together.

Do you find them as hard to respond to as I do? It struck me that in fact, we don't have to answer them neatly. If the first is just about getting through the day and the second is unknown right now, that is ok. It is ok to be lost. You just need to look for the markers to get your bearings. Markers like family, friends and faith. For me, the answer lies in the hands of God. He is the most qualified to see me and to find my purpose.

What we do and who we are do not have to depend on eachother. One does not lead to, or equal, the other. The essence of you is not what you have achieved or how much you get paid to do it.

As I stand at this fork on the road I'm looking round for the next step. There is another way. A window. I'm just waiting to find it. How about you?

Published: Mon, 14 Feb 2022

http://ruthwrites.online/2022/02/14/if-the-door-is-closed/

Immanuel

Mon, 16 Dec 2019

Sitting here, I can see a card with one word, one name on it: 'Immanuel'. Every weekend I let thoughts and ideas circle round my head, trying to find something to blog about. Something that will give you a wee bit of courage to carry on. Thinking back over this last year, I see many pieces of writing that encourage mindfulness, gratitude, positive thinking and the push to look beyond our selves, if we can. These are all laudable, and I have no doubt there will be many more posts like that in the days to come.

Over this past week, I have encountered people who are 'holding on by their finger tips'. No amount of clever words or rousing speeches are going to help them. Even for me, there are many moments when I can't stop the blackness taking over. You can try to hold it back with friends, self-talk, small beautiful joys in the world around us, but sometimes...

I have hinted at my faith before, but never want to come on too strong. So let me just tell you about the One person who gives me the strength, hope, light and love to cope in the darkest, most hopeless, most desperate times. When I am in the dirt, He's there.

When the tears rise, He's there. When I've managed something I thought was beyond me, He's there. I can't see Him, hear Him or physically touch Him, but I believe in Him. He is my Immanuel. He's yours too, if you want.

He came in weakness, poverty and vulnerability. He became like us. He was a real, tangible baby, and He became the only One who can hold back that darkness.

I'll leave that thought with you to take or leave. I can only pray that this Christmas, you consider Him.

Nothing else will do.

Published: Mon, 16 Dec 2019

`http://ruthwrites.online/2019/12/16/immanuel/`

Life as a journey

Mon, 06 Mar 2023

I don't know why but the word 'pilgrimage' keeps coming into my mind. My cousin sang about her week-long experience walking part of the Camino de Santiago, bringing me alongside with her rhythmic strumming. Someone else compared giving things up for Lent as joining with Jesus when He journeyed to Jerusalem and His death on the cross. Then I was reading Christy Lefteri's The Beekeeper of Aleppo and read these words: 'I can walk to the other side of the world and there will still be darkness... This darkness is inside me and has nothing to do with the outside world.' That line struck me as the heart of the matter. It doesn't matter how far we can walk or how beautiful the scenery, if we are struggling with the hardships of life, it is impossible to be impacted by the wonders close by.

At the minute I am largely housebound. But now I am beginning to understand that sitting in the same place everyday does not mean my experiences have stopped. We are all on a journey, however stuck we think we are. This is but one chapter in the book of your life. The pages will keep turning, you will keep growing. At times you will be in the 'slough of despond' like John Bunyan's Christian, but hopefully there will be glorious mountain top experiences too.

It comforts me to think of life as always moving. Because that means difficult times pass and good ones arrive. The question is, can you believe that? Is there a sunny world of hope in you that will take you through the darkness? I hope and pray that we can look up and see that the dark clouds are always moving past, the bulbs are getting ready to burst into the light, better times are coming.

Can you join me on that path? Please do, as somehow that walk is easier when there's someone beside you.

Published: Mon, 06 Mar 2023

http://ruthwrites.online/2023/03/06/life-as-a-journey/

Lift your head

Mon, 13 Nov 2023

When we're going through something tough, it becomes so difficult to look beyond it to other things and people. Everything becomes related to our situation and consequently blocked out. This is not good. And so I am feeling the need to look beyond myself and allow others to have the full understanding and compassion they rightly deserve.

I've just finished reading A Tale of Two Cities, one of my favourite books of all time. As I read it, I noticed again that the thing that makes Madame Defarge so monstrous is that she is entirely shut into her own suffering and shows no mercy to anyone outside of it. Do you ever catch yourself being like that too?

I don't deny that most, if not all, of us are bent down with hardship. But I wonder if you can find the strength to look above it and see something, someone else who deserves your attention. In Dickens's book, the unlikely hero, Sydney Carton, pulls himself out of his drunken behaviour to give up his very life for someone else. After his decision is made, he changes for the better, helping the person nearest him, the little seamstress, right up until the end. In a thankfully smaller way, you can see how helping someone else can lift you up too.

So, I will try and do that for someone today if you try too. When we look up or around ourselves we begin to focus less on our own difficulties and more on things and people around us.

A few days ago I was surprised by a flock of tiny birds I didn't recognise when I looked out my window. Apparently another person in a different place going through a horrible time saw them too. Maybe they were recognisable to a more trained eye, but I like to think they were little reminders that when we look up, small wonders may bless us.

My son discovered a word recently, 'sonder'. It means 'The profound feeling of realizing that everyone, including strangers passing in the street, has a life as complex as one's own.' Remember that, next time you feel alone in your trouble. More importantly, remember the Son of God has been there too, and is still with You now.

Published: Mon, 13 Nov 2023

`http://ruthwrites.online/2023/11/13/lift-your-head/`

Like little pieces of the sky

Mon, 15 Feb 2021

I was listening to Rich Mullins at the weekend for the first time in years.

One of his lyrics registered with me, 'So may peace rain down from HeavenLike little pieces of the skyLittle keepers of the promiseFalling on these souls, the drought has dried'.

That's what we need right now isn't it? A little hope, a little connection with something greater than us. So many of us are dried out. It is hard to open our minds to grasp the idea of things being better, let alone consider the notion of heaven when life is so hellish right now.

I'm on a mission to find something good to tell my mum when I phone her every night. These days, that's tough to do. Then this song reminded me that every day, there are moments that can hold blessing, if we let them. Having to look for little pieces of heaven every day helps me to remember that all is not dark, that there is always light somewhere.

After several wet days, the sun came out this morning. The spring bulbs are pushing up. The snowdrops have been out for weeks now. Thousands of people have had their vaccine. Good things are easier to spot these days. But, when they're hard to find, when it's dark and dry, what do we do?

We always have a friend who is able to be a piece of heaven for us. Would you ever consider that you are one too? So many have been lauded as heroes this past year. I think there's a need for little pieces of the sky as well.

For me, the only way to really tap into that 'sky' is to look up to its Creator, the One who came down for us. I've heard and also asked myself the question, 'where is God in all of this?'

He's where He has always been: right here, next to you. Your little pieces of sky are just there to remind you of that.

Don't lose heart. Look for the reminders of God's relentless love for you. Look for the little keepers of the promise that everything is going to be ok.

Published: Mon, 15 Feb 2021

http://ruthwrites.online/2021/02/15/like-little-pieces-of-the-sky/

Little tent in the big woods

Wed, 27 Jul 2011

When I was about 8, my cousins decided that we would pitch a tent in the woods behind our holiday home, and camp out overnight. During the day leading up to that, it seemed like a fun, adventurous idea, but by the time evening came, I wasn't so sure. I remember a growing knot in my stomach, and a heightening sense of dread as everyone else got increasingly excited. I smiled, and inwardly panicked. When bedtime came, I managed to get into the tent, but minutes later burst into tears and ran into the house again. Oh the relief! But I was disappointed in myself too.

Some things never change. It may not involve camping in the woods anymore, but my behaviour is the same. Every 'exciting' experience I ever have, I approach with the same mixture of dwindling excitement and growing apprehension. The only difference is that now, as a grown-up, I don't have the option of running away. On the whole, I am glad about that. If I had been able to run away, I would have never lived in France for a year, difficult as that was. I wouldn't have gone away to university. I wouldn't have had children. And oh so much more. There are many days when I face the temptation of hiding away in my safe home, and not venturing out to the big, scary woods. But, as I discovered a year on, camping out can be a lot of fun.

Published: Wed, 27 Jul 2011

http://ruthwrites.online/2011/07/27/little-tent-in-the-big-woods/

Look beyond

Mon, 24 Jul 2023

Your immediate needs and see what you have to give.

I was reading an article in Christianity Today that confirmed what I have been thinking about recently; life is more than the things you struggle with or the physical needs that are so easy to see. There is a greater purpose. For you and for me.

Since I got optic neuritis in 2001 I have lost the ability to notice people or things beside me. When I'm leaving anywhere I lift my hand to wave but never turn as I'm at risk of falling. Leading on from that, I recognise that my entire attention is on the next physical step I need to take, or the next challenge I must overcome, and never on the other things I have to offer others.

I don't think that this is a problem uniquely for me. Everyone has something that clouds their vision- it could be the baby you are caring for, the job that claims all your time, the absorbing vocation that narrows your vision, the hurt that fills up your thoughts, the anger that weighs you down, the physical pain that gives you no peace. We all have something, but my question is, what else?

What else do you have to offer? Who else has been blind sided by your pressing struggle? How can you be freed to see other people and additional uses in your life that are waiting in the sidelines to be seen again?

Never rule out what you can do for other people. Don't let your primary obsession push out all the other purposes you have. I'm off to have a think about the world and the needs around me, and the things I have to offer that I've long forgotten about. I think low self-esteem may be what stops us, believing that we have nothing to offer. That's rubbish. Think of the seemingly tiny things that have been done for you, and how much they meant. Nothing is too small when it comes to kindness. Even you reading this is doing something for me.😊

Be defiant . Don't let your circumstances prevent you from recognising how you can impact the lives of those around you. Believe that you have something of value to offer and have the courage to do it. Of course, it might be that you are the one who needs help right now, not the other way round. I truly hope there is someone close by who sees that.

Published: Mon, 24 Jul 2023

http://ruthwrites.online/2023/07/24/look-beyond/

Look out for

Mon, 25 Sep 2023

The helicopters.

I'm sure you know the story about the drowning man who refuses offers of help, saying that God would rescue him, not realising that God had sent the boat and helicopter to save him. I wonder how much help we miss out on because we're looking in the wrong place?

Last week the pedal assist on my trike stopped working. I was at the bottom of a gradual hill in the park and could not move. A woman came past saying 'you look like you need a push' and got me going again. I didn't even have to ask.

Asking for help is hard. Being helped is also a challenge. But when it happens, it feels good. Even though I need help frequently, I am always hesitant to ask for it. It's a mixture of frustration and shame I suppose. Frustration that it is not me who is doing the helping. Shame that I need it. But if I had said no to that woman, I would still be there, foolishly thinking that I can somehow sort it by myself.

If you are struggling, look out for the rescue possibilities close by, and never be too proud to accept them. The best thing about it is that most times, it blesses the helper too.

If we believe, we can see that God is looking out for us, placing people in our way when we most need it. Sometimes we can feel abandoned; sometimes it can feel that there is no rescue coming. That is the time when we wait and we pray.

I really hope those helicopters come for you when you need them. Don't forget they might not look the way you expect!

Published: Mon, 25 Sep 2023

`http://ruthwrites.online/2023/09/25/look-out-for/`

Look up

Wed, 30 Oct 2013

This thought has been brewing in my head a long time, but today C.S.Lewis, one of my heroes, said it out loud for me: "of course, as long as you are looking down, you cannot see something that is above you" (Mere Christianity).

A few months ago, I started getting horrible bouts of vertigo. Every time I lifted my head, and then brought it down again, it took several dizzying seconds before my mind followed my body. Reporting this to the MS nurse, she said, helpfully, 'just don't look up'. So now, if I remember, when I've to put something on a high shelf, or hang something up, I keep my eyes down, and blindly reach. Just believe that there's a plane in the sky as your children tell you, but don't look to check. Just listen to the birds swooping and circling, and use your imagination. This, I suggest, is a life half-lived. Look up, face the world spinning for a moment, but be glad you did it. Better advice. What's the worst that can happen, really?

I do hate the sick weirdness though. However wise C.S.Lewis was, I think there's something else to be seen down here. Into the dark, and the muck of ground-living, Jesus, Light of the World, came. And, by His Spirit, He's still here. So ok, if I can't look up, I can look around me, and there's plenty of wonder in that too.

Published: Wed, 30 Oct 2013

http://ruthwrites.online/2013/10/30/look-up/

No longer a slave

Mon, 03 Jan 2022

To fear.

That line has been running round my head for a couple of days and started yet another reflection. I can't remember a time when I lay awake with no worry or dread about things that I can't control. It's a horrible treadmill of existence if we let it take over.

If.

There is always a choice. Often it's so hard, nearly impossible, to set our minds to positive. I chose the photo here because I saw there was light trying to shine through the chains. It reminded me that in every situation, no matter how dark or impossible it may seem, there is, at least sometimes, light to be found.

Maybe, like me, you are afraid of a lot, because a lot has happened to you in the past. What can we do? The second line to that song is 'I am a child of God.' I can step out of the front door or start this new year, still pretty anxious, but knowing that my heavenly

Father is holding me fast. That doesn't mean that life is easy all of a sudden but it does mean that I am never facing anything alone.

I really hope that you are able to spot the chinks of light in your life, however overwhelmed you might feel. I hope that you are surrounded by people who know you and love you. Remember, as you face your battles, that you are held by people who love you.

Best of all, remember your Father God, who holds you better than anyone.

Published: Mon, 03 Jan 2022

http://ruthwrites.online/2022/01/03/no-longer-a-slave/

No tapestries or crutches here

Tue, 21 Jan 2014

I've been thinking about the word 'twee' today, and how frequently it is associated with all things Christian. It started when I was looking over my longer story (I won't give it the grand name of novel yet), checking for anything too frothy or florally, wanting to make sure it was real enough. It's a challenge for the Christian writer I suppose: not wanting to be in the league of 'novels for the Christian lady', but also needing to be true to the core of who you are.

When did Christianity become decorated over with fine tapestries and cute images? A work colleague of mine talking about faith quipped 'I suppose everyone needs a crutch.' I was caught off guard, and said nothing, For years now, I have wished I had responded: at the centre of my faith, there is a cross, not a crutch. Life with Jesus is a true life, but often not an easy one. Look into the Bible and see more wars than flowers, more poverty than riches, more suffering than luxury. But examine it closer and discover real peace, eternal wealth, and the certain promise of heaven. It tells the ultimate story, the story that can look the starving, the terminally ill, the depressed or the lost straight in the eye. This lasting truth is not twee; it is the only reality that stands when everything else collapses. Try cross-stitching that.

Published: Tue, 21 Jan 2014

http://ruthwrites.online/2014/01/21/no-tapestries-or-crutches-here/

Oh to be able to know for certain

Fri, 24 Jul 2015

Life is so full of difficult choices - to go for that job, or to stay put, to try that new treatment, or to stick with the old one, to move to the country, or pick a town house. I don't have that advantage some people talk about - 'God told me to' are words that I don't think I will ever be able to say. Sometimes I wish I could.

But then, I've seen how dangerous that can be - if one person drags others along a mistaken path, telling them God has clearly told them to do it. The one example I can recall did not end well. I have sat with an open Bible, asking for guidance. But I've often caught myself scanning the pages for words that will back up a decision I've actually already made. That is a self-focused kind of Bible bingo.

At the minute, we're going through that very stressful process of selling our house and looking for another. We were convinced we'd found 'the one', but it didn't work out. I've yet to understand why. I know I will in time.

In fact, every life event that has happened to me has had its reasons, when I look back over the years. Not all have been good experiences. Some have been horrific. I will never say that the bad ones have had anything to do with my good God, but He always brings some good, even in the darkest times.

I really don't want to make the wrong decision about a house, but I have a feeling that there is always a way to re-set, even when we might take the wrong path. That way, there is nothing to fear.

So, I'll take a deep breath, say a prayer, and step out. He'll still be there, even if it's in the mistakes.

Published: Fri, 24 Jul 2015

http://ruthwrites.online/2015/07/24/oh-to-be-able-to-know-for-certain/

One hundred candles

Mon, 09 Dec 2024

Have you ever said yes to something that realistically you can't do? Two weeks ago, I said 'of course I could write something about light on one hundred candles'. It didn't take long for me to realise that there was no way I could write on tiny candles with my shaky hands. I did find a solution and now I've one hundred candles with different quotes about light stuck on them. For the first time in a long time I have achieved something of note, so ha ha MS, I did it!

There is something wonderful in achieving a target. If you are feeling defeated, think of one thing you can do right now and do it! Self-fulfilment is a brilliant thing.

Thinking in tandem with that, I was reminded about the little lights I come across every day. I struggled into the park over a week ago, but I was so glad I had because I saw the most cheerful man waving at me. I am still thinking about it. Cast your mind back over your week, what lights have sparkled for you?

This morning my cleaner folded up the blankets beside me and we both agreed that being in a tidy space helps us tremendously. I always tidied before I lost my stability but seeing somebody doing it for me is a joy.

You don't know what impact you have on people round you. Even a wave or a smile can bless them. So, believe that you have something to give and let your light shine. It is nearly Christmas after all.

Published: Mon, 09 Dec 2024

http://ruthwrites.online/2024/12/09/one-hundred-candles/

Precious secret things

Thu, 19 May 2016

Do you ever re-discover something you haven't thought of for years? Last week I spied something through the clear plastic cover of a box of books I had taken from my old bedroom. It was the maroon NIV Bible my parents had given me when I was fourteen. I pulled it out and opened it to find the front and back pages covered in the handwritten, heartfelt messages of young people I had once done a summer scheme with. As I read them again after nearly twenty years, I was close to tears.

Then this week as I looked through it again with my daughter, a fragile pressed wild flower fell out. I can't remember when I picked it in Donegal, or why, but when it was suggested to me that I put it in the bin (sadly a question I frequently put to her), I couldn't do it.

Yesterday my wee girl brought in a crumbling, pale blue egg shell she had found on our front step. I opened my mouth to say, throw that out, but then I stopped myself. To her, it was a wonderful discovery, a thing to be treasured. So it's annoying me on the kitchen window-sill now.

We too often think that we can just bin things and buy a replacement. Something's broken? Don't worry, don't waste your time trying to mend it, just get another one. But there are some things that should not be consigned to landfill, things that cannot ever be replaced, and these are the most valuable of all- these crumbling, broken objects that hold a memory of happy moments, gifts given with love.

So go on, have a hoke through your own boxes, your roof-space or the back of your cupboards and see what you find. And whatever you do, don't bring a bin-bag.

Published: Thu, 19 May 2016

http://ruthwrites.online/2016/05/19/precious-secret-things/

Sit down next to me

Mon, 21 Oct 2024

I watched a dove sitting by itself on a lamp post for at least fifteen minutes. Eventually it flew off, clearly giving up on another dove coming to perch beside it. Do you ever wish that someone would come sit with you when you're at a low moment?

In my more able past, I used to look out for people sitting by themselves in my church. One time I sat with an elderly woman for what turned out to be her last Sunday. I am so glad I did that. Never doubt yourself, just have courage and be kind.

Now, I think my disability puts people off. Don't ever think that using a rollator or a wheelchair speaks of self-sufficiency. Everyone needs a friend. Someone to sit beside them to say 'I see you.' 'I am with you'. Do you have a friend like that? Are you willing to be that friend no matter what?

Self-dependency can tell a false story. Leaving a person to fend for themselves will not make them stronger. Pairing two people together will. It says in Ecclesiastes, 'Though one may be overpowered, two can defend themselves. A cord of three strands is not quickly broken.'*

So take heart, you never need to summon up the strength to face hard things alone. You've got a friend, just ask for their help. Hard to do, but always worth it.

Remember the times you were alone and make a promise to yourself that the person you see struggling will never be by themselves, if it is within your power to sit with them. Compassion is not expensive, it just takes a momentary ounce of courage. Look out for those precious chances today.

A lot of people are also walking a lonely road. Most times I go round the park I see someone by themselves. It might be by choice, but I'm not sure. My poor brother had to carry his collapsed dog for a kilometer yesterday. Someone to be beside him for that gruelling journey might have been a comfort. Many struggle alone with horrible things. Are you in a position to help them shoulder that burden? Jesus put it perfectly when He said, 'my yoke is easy and my burden is light'*. Getting alongside that would make a huge difference to anyone.

*Matthew 11:30

*Ecclesiastes 4:12

Published: Mon, 21 Oct 2024

`http://ruthwrites.online/2024/10/21/sit-down-next-to-me/`

Stand-fast

Mon, 18 Jan 2021

I finished The Pilgrim's Progress last night. While it was tough going, I met a few characters that I admire, and wanted to tell you a little bit about one of them today.

His name is Stand-fast. He's almost a reward for the reader who sticks with the story as he only appears in the final pages. Stand-fast has withstood many fears, temptations and trials before the group of pilgrims meet him. He sees the downfall of some pilgrims as he passes them and has to resist the lure of Madame Bubble. And yet, by the end, he is still known as Stand-fast. It made me think, how can we be like that?

Right now, the waves of pandemic seem to be constantly breaking nearer to us. The pull out is harder to withstand. We hear of so many, too many who have been dragged down beneath the waves. The people tasked with holding them up are getting weaker too. We need to find ways to dig our feet in, widen our stance and stand fast. I'm wondering how...

Thinking about my own survival strategies, one quality (that can sometimes teeter over into a negative thing) is doggedness. When I'm looking ahead to the distance I still have to walk, that tight-lipped refusal to give up helps me to keep going. If you're angry about the status quo, use that anger to fuel your commitment to do your bit. It doesn't take a lot of strength to stay home or wear a mask after all.

Another thing that helps is to think about who you are staying strong for. I always think of myself as unassertive but when it comes to my children or someone in greater need than me, strength rises up.

Sometimes, we need balustrades beside us to keep us upright. When we meet Stand-fast he is not standing fast at all. He is at his last ebb with his hands outstretched. I know this stance very well but am often reluctant to show it. Stand- fast is surprised and embarrassed that the others noticed him being like that. I wonder do we fail to see the outstretched hands of people around us either because they are too frightened to show us how they really feel, or our eyes are too firmly fixed on ourselves?

Sometimes we can stand fast when we're sitting down. (Contradictory I know). When I'm on a chair I'm able to reach out to others, write encouragement and also store up standing energy for later. There is no shame in taking a break from standing, fulfilling our duties or fighting our battles. It brings us to the same level as the falling, struggling, weaker ones beside us.

When we first see Stand-fast he is on his knees with his face raised heavenwards. You see? The best heroes know that there's something, Someone that they need, to keep on standing fast. As the character says, "He has held me, and hath kept me from my sins; yea, my steps hath He strengthened in His way."

What keeps you upright these stormy days? Is it a steel thread of determination? People standing alongside you? Or a strength that goes beyond all of that?

And who will you help up to their feet today?

Published: Mon, 18 Jan 2021

http://ruthwrites.online/2021/01/18/stand-fast/

Take hold of the blessing

Mon, 03 May 2021

With both hands.

Last week I was struggling to stand up and get things done. When my two washed and dried the dishes, when my other half did countless tasks for me, I was overcome with a feeling of being cared for.

That feeling can be an uneasy one, as we struggle with the frustration of not being able to do it all ourselves. Most of the time, that's the place I stay in- wishing I could do it all myself, embarrassed that yet again I have to concede defeat.

This time, however, it struck me that if I turned away from those negative feelings and stepped towards gratitude, life would be a little easier. Coming to terms with an inability to do things is really tough. But if we can push away our pride, we will see other people standing by to help us.

It nearly always brings me to tears when someone steps forward because I'm falling back. Before my second vaccine, I had just walked in to the hall and someone asked me if I had difficulty standing for long periods. Is it that obvious?! Then at the end another person wondered if there was anything he could do to help. I left feeling sad I was so easily found out, but also beautifully cared for.

I'm learning to be grateful for every kindness I'm shown. It's hard to accept help but we shouldn't push it away, making light of something to be cherished.

The place I am stumbling to is one of privilege and blessing. Any darkness in it is down to me.

The best thing is, when we open up to kindness, we may find that we have enough to share with other people.

So take hold of this blessing, lift it up and let it spread to the people next to you. Once they have opened themselves up to it, they'll hopefully pass it on to someone else.

Published: Mon, 03 May 2021

`http://ruthwrites.online/2021/05/03/take-hold-of-the-blessing/`

Thank God for Christmas

Sun, 11 Dec 2022

Now I'm not talking about the parties, the terrible traffic, the shopping, the financial pressure, the difficult family relationships. I'm talking about the light-filled real start of it all; when God Himself came here to show us we are not alone in this dark world.

I know the events of the Nativity most likely took place in a warmer month of the year, but I think December is perfect now- when the daylight is brief and the cold is bitter. What better time to drink warm wine and contemplate a big sparkling tree in the middle of our living room!

I know some hate this time of year because of the pain or memories it stirs up, the pressure of gift buying, the nonsense of it all. But beneath and beyond all of that, there's God in human form, showing us that there is so much more for us than we realise. Evidence that someone has been here who understands everything that is tough about this life and chose a horrible death to prove it. And to save us all.

So when you are pushing through crowds of shoppers or sighing in traffic jams, think about the Light of the world who faced the darkness for you.

Now that is some gift, isn't it

Published: Sun, 11 Dec 2022

http://ruthwrites.online/2022/12/11/thank-god-for-christmas/

The intangibles

Mon, 28 Aug 2023

I have discovered a great secret. To live without tangible strength is to exist among the intangible things: like inner strength, unseen miracles and quiet victories.

Sounds a bit mystical, doesn't it? So many people have told me they are praying for my healing. I know they mean visibly renewed health and strength. I would truly love that to be a reality for me. But in the meantime, I am discovering the life of opposites. When you think about a person walking unsteadily with a stick did it ever occur to you that they are strong? When a child says they are sorry, have you ever noticed they are teaching you an age-old wisdom? What is better: strength on the surface of things or inner power that will never leave you?

Of course, everyone wants recognition right now. An immediate acknowledgement that they are winners. I understand that. But I'm here to remind you about the unseen things you have. For the frightened, I say every time you step out your front door, you are brave. Every appointment you keep is a victory. If you feel shaky, remember that you are strong. If you are terrified by many things, you are courageous when you face even one. Turn away from the mirror and know you are beautiful. Believe you are precious and treat yourself like that.

I may not be striding along, but if anyone asks, I am running a race that takes me from here to eternity. And it is open for you too.

Published: Mon, 28 Aug 2023

http://ruthwrites.online/2023/08/28/the-intangibles/

The lifeboat is there

Mon, 18 Mar 2024

When you are facing stormy seas in your life, never forget to look out for lifeboats.

I was looking through all the many titles I've written that haven't ever published and I noticed that the last few have been entitled things like 'wilderness' or 'the desert place'. Not good, is it? But today, I want to focus on how we can be rescued from hard situations, or find the tools to survive them. The most important word to anyone facing storms or hardship has got to be 'hope'. How can you look for what you don't believe will ever come? I'm here, speaking out of a time where nothing is happening that should be. I am waiting for things to change, but in the meantime my hand is over my eyes as I watch for lifeboats. They mightn't look like the one in the picture; they might be a friend making you dinner, a son carrying you up tea, a daughter cleaning the oven for you, an unexpected call with an old friend or your parents coming to visit.

You see? Rescues are everywhere. Sometimes you need to call for them, sometimes you need to admit you need help. If you believe, God is there, waiting to lift you up. But in my experience, it is the people around you who can be His hands and feet. The greatest thing is that around you, beside you is Jesus Christ, who holds all of your hope. That is, for all of us, the hardest but greatest thing to live for.

If you can't see that yet, remember lifeboats are bouncing across your stormy seas and soon, they will reach you. Don't lose hope. Keep a look out because they will come.

Published: Mon, 18 Mar 2024

http://ruthwrites.online/2024/03/18/the-lifeboat-is-there/

The one hundredth sheep

Mon, 26 Apr 2021

In my last book, The Lost Things, one of my characters uses the ideology of the hundredth sheep to inform her attitude towards every individual that crosses her path. In the New Testament parable, the shepherd leaves his other 99 sheep to search for the lost one. It's the idea that each person is worth dropping everything for. The value of the one is more than a nameless multitude.

Maybe it's because my social media followers are low in number or I'm having difficulties 'increasing my audience' but the awareness that every individual counts is what keeps me writing these blog posts. If one person is helped by what I say, then that makes my day. I write as though I'm speaking to someone who is struggling and needs encouragement. I don't write to change the world. I write to help the one hundredth sheep who has lost their way.

Some days, most days, we can all feel that we're making little difference in the world. But think about the times when you gave someone a smile or a hello, the moments when you waved thank-you or go ahead when you were driving. Now think about how it made you feel when someone did the same for you.

Most of us are not in the business of shifting the earth or transforming communities every day of our lives. But if we live like every life matters, we can change the world, one sheep at a time.

As I've said before, we don't know the struggles other people are going through and so, we don't know how much a kind word or a friendly smile will change their day.

And you never know, it might even rescue them.

Published: Mon, 26 Apr 2021

http://ruthwrites.online/2021/04/26/the-one-hundredth-sheep/

The other side of it

Mon, 21 Mar 2022

At the end of another unremarkable day this week I got to thinking about tapestries, as you do!

I realised that if we just viewed things from another angle, they might not seem so terrible. I forced myself to look beyond another embarrassing day of walking unsteadily and spot the number of positive things that had happened that could easily have been missed. I remembered then; the man behind the till asking for my bag so he could pack it for me, the woman who asked me if I was alright when I was slow putting the trolley back and the other one who had asked for my help to get something she couldn't reach herself.

We might just see the tangles but someone else can pick out the beauty. It is easy to feel that everyone can only see the flaws we struggle with every day but the truth is, most barely notice that part of you. What they recognise is what else you do or say that helps them too. I was so taken aback that someone looked past my stick to find a person who could help her. She will never know how much it meant for someone to ask shaky me to give them a hand.

Like swans, most admire their gracefulness and forget about their frantic padding beneath the surface. Of course sometimes we need acknowledgement that life is a huge challenge for us, but other times it is so good to realise that when people look at us, they don't see our frailty first.

There is so much more to you than the burdens you carry. When people look at you they may notice your struggles, but I'm almost certain the first thing they will take note of is your strength.

Published: Mon, 21 Mar 2022

http://ruthwrites.online/2022/03/21/the-other-side-of-it/

The power of gratitude

Mon, 22 May 2023

When was the last time we were truly thankful for something or someone? It is easy to let troubles fill up our lives so there is no room, no thought of all we have been given. All that we have right now.

Last week I listened to Max Lucado saying 'gratitude pushes out anxiety'*. So when I am alone, just as the usual panic starts to build, I distract myself by listing all the things I'm thankful for. It's like changing your mind- from clamouring worry to measured thankfulness.

It is a surprise to me that I am still writing this when my legs are bad and my dog is constantly barking at our house painter. I could give in to irritation and frustration, but I won't. The sun is shining, I've spent a lovely morning with my parents and the house is steadily changing from cement colour to a clean white, not too dissimilar to my mood!

How would you say your state of mind is today? Like cement? Listless? Could you put on a metaphorical coat of paint as you assess yourself and see that you and you alone are in charge of how you colour your life.

Make a decision and stick with it. I'm opting for a bright day today. How about you?

Anxious for Nothing Max Lucado

Published: Mon, 22 May 2023

http://ruthwrites.online/2023/05/22/the-power-of/

The rock

Sat, 04 May 2024

Do you ever feel everything in your world is moving too fast? And you are left searching for something solid to hold onto?

Sometimes I put the brakes on my rollator because I don't like the way it rolls away from me. Years ago when my son was having dizzy spells, his dad encouraged him to put his hand on the wall, for something unmoving to lean against. When I'm getting back to the house, I often put my hand out to the very unattractive metal rail beside the step because it doesn't move.

The one problem with searching for something immoveable is that eventually you will have to move away from it. It feels safer to stand still but can get lonely when everyone else leaves you behind. That's the challenge: do you stay in the safety or step into the unknown?

The one thing that helps me when things are moving too fast is rooting myself into the knowledge of an almighty, unchanging God who is holding me. When the world looks like it is crumbling, when your life is sinking, when the things you thought would never change suddenly slip away, remember that God is your safe place, your steadfast foothold. That certainty is such a help to me. In Psalm 18 v 2 it says 'The Lord is my rock, my fortress and my deliverer; my God is my rock, in whom I take refuge, my shield and the horn of my salvation, my stronghold.' Maybe that sounds like something you can't comprehend, but let it settle in your mind next time you feel the storms in your life are rising. It's the one true thing I know and I hope it becomes true for you too

Published: Sat, 04 May 2024

http://ruthwrites.online/2024/05/04/the-rock/

The things that stick

Mon, 21 Dec 2020

Do you remember doing Christmas crafts at school? My favourite was drawing a shape with glue then pouring glitter over and shaking the surplus off to reveal a perfect Christmas shape. All at once, mistakes and mess fell away and the best stuck.

This year everything has been stripped away. We've lost precious people, livelihoods and a lot of the freedoms we took for granted before. The after-picture is ragged, broken, unsightly. Far from perfect.

But, for me, something beautiful has stuck. This time last year I wrote Immanuel. I reread it this morning and realised that everything I said then still stands. What I believed then has stuck through all the pain and mess of this year.

When you shake your life what sticks? I really hope you find the things, the people that matter, still holding onto you.

You know, there is only One who defies hardship and loneliness. And He doesn't stand at a safe distance from you. He is always right there. At your side.

I hope that this Christmas you can feel that. That's what it's really about, when you shake off the surplus.

Published: Mon, 21 Dec 2020

http://ruthwrites.online/2020/12/21/the-things-that-stick/

The unnoticed ones

Tue, 16 May 2017

Last night I read something my grandfather had written many years ago, and it confirmed a pre-occupation I've had for some time. Reflecting on the healing of the man beside the pool of Siloam he wrote, 'I look for God's power in the smashing of the nations, I see it in Your healing of the one the world has forgotten. I see and I take hope...God is here and I know He is here for every broken soul, including me.'

This week I've been hearing people talk about 'stories of the forgotten'. Maybe it's the fashionable pre-occupation of the art world at the moment, maybe it's a genuine concern, who knows, but I like it. The idea that in this digital age when we can go anywhere, see anyone, learn anything and yet still be lost bothers me. And then it struck me: we now have the means to change that. Small acts done individually can build into something massive. That has only become possible in our time. Now, remembering forgotten souls, telling hitherto unheard stories, is truly within our reach. Each of us can come close to the 'uns' of this world - unreachable, unheard, untouchable, unnoticable, and we can help to change their seemingly impossible circumstances.

Now, the 'healing of the one the world has forgotten' can actually grow into that 'smashing of the nations' my papa dreamed of. Turn your phones on, open your laptops, contact your charities and watch your small acts do something great!

Published: Tue, 16 May 2017

http://ruthwrites.online/2017/05/16/the-unnoticed-ones/

There are blessings all around you

Mon, 27 Nov 2023

I'll be honest, I have heard and read some sad things this past week and I am only now getting to a point where I can find any goodness to write about. Maybe some weeks my posts don't resonate with you, I understand that. But here is something you can always hold onto: whatever you are feeling or facing or struggling with right now, there will always be good things in your life. Always.

Of course, when I was lying on a hospital bed in the middle of the night last year, I would not have agreed with the statement above. Even now, looking back, I am struggling to see any good moments there. But, there was a fellow patient who kept me company, there was a nurse who brought me warm water to wash, another who always smiled as he went about his business. Even if you are in a worst case scenario, blessings can be found.

Think about a bleak time you experienced recently, but now try and find even one blessing there. We bought a painting two days ago and the artist, Heather Byrne, talked about the 'accidental paint marks' in her drawing that caused 'unexpected movement'. So, in her own artistic way, she has found a blessing. I will never look at that random wave in our painting in the same way again.

I have said it before, and I'll say it now; life is full of imperfections. But is there a way of seeing some of them differently? It definitely doesn't work all the time, but occasionally it does. Right now I am sitting down because my legs are already tired and it's only half ten in the morning! But, the sun is shining on my head and I can see that most of the sky is blue. Like when you fly, the plane pushes through the dark cloud and soon you will see the sun again. Wade through the quagmire of hardship and there will be a view from a higher point that shows you how much you have overcome.

I know that it can be impossible at times to see blessings, but I truly hope that today you encounter at least one.

Published: Mon, 27 Nov 2023

http://ruthwrites.online/2023/11/27/there-are-blessings-all-around-you/

There is no time there

Mon, 20 Mar 2017

That must be one of my favourite speeches ever; the one that Sydney Carton makes in A Tale of Two Cities before he is killed. My heart always lifts with the promise that the drudgery of this life will be left behind forever. I love the idea of eternal rest when most days I'm plain worn out.

But yesterday, after a conversation about heaven divided the parties over whether there would be a permanent, unchanged state, or a certain amount of movement and transformation. Honestly, the prospect of singing endless hymns on repeat does not fill me with a huge amount of happy anticipation, much as I love singing.

Of course, the idea of there being no time also leads to the idea that when you go to heaven, everyone you love will already be there. I like that notion. And Sydney must have too. What I just can't get my head round is this 'permanent state of bliss' association with heaven.

I know I've shared my dislike of change before, but here's what I'm realising - change is built in to the astounding planet we live on - the tides sweeping in and out, the rain showers starting and stopping, the clouds chasing across the sky, the small bulbs bursting out of darkness into magnificent colour, the baby taking her first uncertain steps...and so much more - an infinity of constant movement.

A heaven of changing seasons?

I'll tell you when I get there.

Published: Mon, 20 Mar 2017

http://ruthwrites.online/2017/03/20/there-is-no-time-there/

There's another in the fire

Mon, 08 Mar 2021

For many years now, I've been reassured by the Bible story of Daniel's friends, Shadrach, Meshach and Abednego. They had an incredibly tough time, getting thrown into a blazing furnace. Before that happened, they said that they believed God would rescue them but even if he does not they would still believe. That even if he does not kind of belief has kept me going through many hard times.

A few months ago I was reminded about this story. Hillsong released a song with the title, 'There's another in the fire', another reference to my ancient friends. They were thrown into the furnace and returned unscathed. When they were in, the king who'd thrown them there saw a fourth figure walking round with them. We don't know if the three men saw he was there though.

Sometimes, it is impossible to see any comforting presence when we are in our own furnace. Sometimes, another person can reassure us that we were not alone. Sometimes we just need to cling onto our 'even if he does not'faith.

I was thinking about that at the weekend when I was in the MRI machine, my personal furnace. The radiographers did not speak to me as the machine roared, banged and shook. Once, they asked me to keep very still and I said, 'can you hear me?' No answer. I prayed. No answer. I reminded myself that help is near. Even when we don't see it. That day I did encounter 'fourth figures'. A man smoking by the entrance showed me how to get in. Afterwards another man walked me the whole way out when I got lost. My own man went in to get me, after me telling him I was very shaky. He came looking, without my knowledge. He was there when I didn't even know it.

What is your furnace right now? Do you know that you're not alone, even when you feel it? Who is your fourth person? Who can you be that fourth person for?

My prayer for you all is that you would know the Other in the fire. God isn't in the business of putting out our fires, but He makes very sure He is right there with us. It's a mystery that I find hard to accept sometimes, but that doesn't make it any less true.

Published: Mon, 08 Mar 2021

http://ruthwrites.online/2021/03/08/theres-another-in-the-fire/

Thin people, thin places

Thu, 03 May 2018

A few weeks ago, a friend (thankyou Aileen!) reminded me of the phrase 'a thin place'. In other words, a place that is close to heaven. I'm sure you've all been somewhere like that, where you feel that you only need to stretch out your hand to touch something outside of your finite life. It could be a wide, open expanse of sky, a canopy of stars, a smashing sea, a mountain-top panorama...

Of course, my number one thin place is Donegal, a place that someone once said was just 'too beautiful to take in'. I could think of others too - the garden of the Nunnery in Iona, a church in St. Guillaume le Desert in the south of France, the living room of my husband's grandparents. Of course, for me, these places had significance because of all the prayers that had been uttered in them, but I think other people unaware of that depth would still be stopped in their tracks.

I wonder if, in the same way, we can encounter 'thin' people too? Perhaps it is a mercy of grief that I recognise this in some who have passed on. Or maybe when I think of them now, I see how at home they would be in heaven. It's a gentleness,a kindness, a preference for listening over speaking, a sense of peace. Thinking about my snappy presence as a mum, I'm not sure I've got that. Yet. But I'm sure going to spend time with people who can show me how.

I am so thankful, in this dark, filthy life, for the places and the people that point me to something beyond. Something eternal.

Published: Thu, 03 May 2018

http://ruthwrites.online/2018/05/03/thin-people-thin-places/

Think of yourself

Fri, 08 Apr 2022

Less.

I came across this quote from CS Lewis that I've been pondering: "Humility is not thinking less of yourself, it's thinking of yourself less."

I will confess something to you. Somewhere in my head as I feel embarrassment about how I walk and move, I have wrongly associated shame with humility. Being humble has absolutely nothing to do with feeling bad about yourself. As CS Lewis reminded me, it has everything to do with forgetting about yourself and focusing on how you see the people around you.

Of course, you can't help other people until you realise that you are of immense value first. Don't think less of yourself. Once you understand that you are worthy of all the love people have for you, you can love in return. Humility is not about feeling bad about yourself, it is about making other people feel good. You can't do that until you have a healthy opinion of yourself. It is only when your heart is filled up with love that you can let it spill over onto others.

I had an encounter with my ever kind green grocer that reinforced that this week. He always tells me to be careful, but this time when I looked at him I saw that his face was covered in cuts. He had fallen when he was training for the marathon and told me he hadn't had the courage to go out running since then. Now that is something I could relate to!

So if you're feeling low, don't think badly of yourself. Look around you and see that there are others in situations not unlike your own. And maybe you can use what you're going through to help them too.

Published: Fri, 08 Apr 2022

http://ruthwrites.online/2022/04/08/think-of-yourself/

What the birds teach me

Mon, 20 Nov 2023

Do you ever notice the lessons from the world around you? There is an abundance in nature for you to explore, and it's free!

I mentioned the little birds I saw last week, that someone else saw too. It made me realise again that we are not alone. Every time you look at the sky, remember that other people are seeing it as well. As the birds group together, so do the people who watch them.

Every morning I hear the brave first bird calling. It doesn't have a song, just a repeated chittering. It makes me smile; does it go first because it can't sing? Is it like a conductor tapping his baton before the orchestra starts to play? If you feel unremarkable, remember that the first brave step can start a miraculous cascade of others.

Recently I looked out as a large starling perched above the bird feeder, intimidating the others from approaching. One brave little blue tit flew in and got a few seeds. Another one followed shortly after. The dark bird sat on. It got me thinking. Is there anything in your life like that bird? A fear, worry, sadness or dread? Can you escape it, or does it cast a shadow over everything?

Without a doubt, there are moments every day where my 'dark bird' looms over me. Some days I have the strength to be like that little bird and carry on regardless, but other days, tiredness lets darkness win. What we need is someone else to brave the dark bird with us. A friend perhaps, or a faith that the Father we trust is so much brighter and stronger than any black feeling we battle against.

Eventually, the starling flew away and there was a feeding frenzy for the other birds. When you have a better day, celebrate it. And remember, especially when you're under the shadow, that there will always be better times.

I hope you can find the strength to carry on, despite the darkness you face. Look up at the sky and see the birds soaring, dipping and diving.

I hope you can let your heart join them.

Published: Mon, 20 Nov 2023

`http://ruthwrites.online/2023/11/20/what-the-birds-teach-me/`

You are never alone

Mon, 07 Oct 2024

I have faced a number of lonely moments, as you all have. Last Friday morning I was having an MRI and although I could sometimes glimpse the tops of the radiographers' heads behind the glass, I was by myself. But! I reminded myself that, if we believe, God is always with us I forgot that for half of the scan and then was calmed by the steadying truth that I am not ever going through anything alone.

I often put my hands together when I'm facing a stressful situation because I think about the idea that God is there, holding my hand as well. You never have to face anything alone. Of course, there are many times when I still panic and don't feel that God is with me. But I try to tell myself He promised He would never leave or forsake me.

Do you feel abandoned or alone? I know that feeling, but sometimes a true fact can be held onto. Sometimes it's the good people near us who help us. The radiology team last Friday were a solid reminder that God was right there beside me. I know you might find that hard to accept but I really hope you know it's true one day.

If I didn't know that I was not alone, there is so much I would hide from. I was holding tight to the cable with the panic button I could push at any moment, but the main thing I was holding onto was the knowledge that God was holding tightly onto me.

Maybe one day you'll know that too.

Published: Mon, 07 Oct 2024

http://ruthwrites.online/2024/10/07/you-are-never-alone/

Health

A difficult answer to a difficult question

Fri, 11 Apr 2014

Another very tough week has come my way - the part when I couldn't finish the nursery's 4 year old-friendly sponsor walk wins the prize for one of the worst, most humiliating moments of my life so far. So, you can understand how the words 'His eyes are always upon us' were not particularly helpful. If God could see me, why didn't He help. Did He just look on for some higher purpose?

No, no. He saw a world in pain and He sent His only Son right into it. And the answer to that 'where was God' cry was given. It was terrifying. It was heartbreaking. It was lonely. It was excruciatingly painful. To say that God is just an indifferent onlooker is to deny His Son, and the cross. He's given His answer in person, but we keep forgetting that. We also forget that He defeated all the terror and finality of death. For now, sometimes, all I have is the promise of that, and I know that I need the faith to hold onto it. This life is only an imperfect, (often very) frayed introduction to the unending, majestic story. Sometimes, life can get better in the present. But sometimes, all we can know is that God has the ultimate first-hand experience of what it means to suffer. That is the answer I need to accept. And actually, it is incontestable.

Published: Fri, 11 Apr 2014

http://ruthwrites.online/2014/04/11/a-difficult-answer-to-a-difficult-question/

By your side

Mon, 08 Aug 2022

For the past few months I have not been able to walk without the support of someone else. I tried with just my trekking poles at the weekend but had to concede that right now, I still need someone to keep me from falling.

Do you ever wish you could do it all by yourself? In your own time? The way you prefer? Me too. But sometimes life takes us down a different path. And there are lessons to be learnt there too.

When we are dependent on another person we learn to be patient. We learn to follow the rhythm of their steps. We learn to trust. I have never been good at any of those. I would always choose working alone over as part of a team. I always thought the result would be better in the end. Even now I find fault with how my family are walking with me and the way they set me down. However, only today my neighbour remarked on how fast I was walking. When someone else is holding onto me, I never fall.

Being independent is lauded as the way to be. Fleetwood Mac tells us to 'go your own way' and Frank Sinatra boasted 'I did it my way'. But if we can't, if stepping out leads to falling over, then having someone by your side is better.

Nicky Gumbel recently reminded me that when no-one else is around, God always is; 'That the God who created the universe should be with you is not something to be taken lightly. It is an extraordinary and wonderful promise. To experience God with you by his Spirit is life changing.' Knowing that we are never alone is immensely comforting.

Is your arm ready to be held onto? Are you strong enough to admit you need somebody else's?

I think that is a lifelong lesson for all of us, don't you?

Published: Mon, 08 Aug 2022

http://ruthwrites.online/2022/08/08/by-your-side/

Dare to believe

Mon, 06 Jun 2022

That good things will happen.

In 2005 I told my husband I'd be fine without him, 'it was just a routine appointment' I said. I had no idea that bad things could happen to me the way they did with other people. That day my tendency towards optimism got a horrible knock. Since then I always fear the worst

It's a terrible way to live.

We drove up to Horn Head a few days ago to see the sunset. As I had to wait in the car while the others walked out to catch it, all I could do was look for a change in colour in the landscape in front of me. It didn't seem to get golden or pink so I thought it had not been a good one. Until my son came back and told me he had taken hundreds of photos and we drove round so I could see it too. It was far from disappointing.

Once you get hooked on the 'I knew that would happen's and the smug 'i told you so's it's hard to remember how to practise hope. Believing that even now, sometimes, life will pleasantly surprise you. Every time your child walks to school, they're more likely to be happy than run over. Every time you phone for results from those blood tests they're more likely to be normal than concerning. Every time you look at the calendar and tentatively make plans you fear you won't manage and then you do it anyway, that's believing good things are still possible.

This very day I'm deciding that life will improve. Sometimes the expectation of that can make a big difference. I was told that the treatment I received would help, I was assured that this current state I'm struggling with will pass. I have forgotten to believe that. If you feel like nothing is ever going to change, then try to imagine how you would feel if something did. I will be prepared for something good to happen, if you promise to join me in believing that too.

Try and push back all the 'last time's and the 'what if's and get ready for a good surprise. What will happen today that you never expected? Be prepared for your catastrophising to be proven wrong.

It's an overlooked notion, but things can actually turn out all right sometimes

Published: Mon, 06 Jun 2022

http://ruthwrites.online/2022/06/06/dare-to-believe/

Dig deep!

Mon, 03 Aug 2020

What does that mean anyway? What if you search around inside yourself and come up empty?

It's usually sports coaches prepping their teams at half-time or personalities reflecting on their recent performances who talk about finding the last power surge that took them over the finish line or helped them with the winning point.

I've read about and watched fictional characters who are lacking and then suddenly, miraculously, they are able to put the magic into their ballet steps, the distance into their throws, the inspiration into their writing. Tell me if that's ever happened to you in real life?!

To be honest, second wind is nothing but a fairy tale to me. Every time I stop at the gate on my way out of the park, I hope for a surprising rocket boost but every time, I just have to fix my eyes on my next step, knuckle down and get home.

How many of us are just surviving life like that and not really living it? How many are scrabbling around in the gravel without a spade hoping for something better?

In my experience, if you can't 'dig deep' then look about and see the friends beside you who can. These days I'm so thankful for my husband who always picks up things I've started and finishes them for me when I can't do any more. Do you need someone like that? Or can you be that person for somebody else?

We're not built to be stand alone, self-sufficient people. We're designed for community. Sometimes, achieving things by ourselves is pleasing. Sometimes it is impossibly lonely.

I'll never forget the image of a woman collapsing just metres from the finish line of a marathon and being carried to the end by two other participants.

Being helped on your journey, that's real life. Maybe when we rest, we'll plumb greater depths. Maybe when we wait, somebody else will do that for us.

Maybe there'll even be treasure!

Published: Mon, 03 Aug 2020

http://ruthwrites.online/2020/08/03/dig-deep/

Disability, or defeat

Fri, 10 Dec 2010

Something has happened to me over the past few months. I seem to have gone from living in denial about having MS, to letting it cloud everything that I do. I remember distinctly the day I was told I had it. I stood at the front door about to put the key in the lock, and suddenly got a vivid thought: I had a clear choice - I could either respond to my diagnosis with a lifetime of bitterness and despair, OR, I could watch and see what good things God was going to bring out of it. That is a choice, I see now, that I have to make every day. Sadly it's not a straight-forward one-off thing.

Going to counseling recently has helped me see that I was far from ok with having MS - all I'd done was to deny it, or push down my experiences of it as deep as I possibly could. That kind of worked, but surprising anger and tears would come, for no apparent reason, and I realised that denial was not going to hold all that at bay forever. Now, though, I have started to let myself be angry and sad for the real reasons, and it's a terrifying place to be. I hope that this is a process, and that my slow acceptance does not turn into a permanent feeling of defeat.

I have encountered many people with health issues, and an interesting pattern has emerged. Seemingly with a stamped on disability, you can either be a hero, or you can be a victim. You can either defy your disability, or you can be destroyed by it - allowing it to map out your life, blind you to the needs of others, and invade all your conversations. Hence this blog: I can let myself be the self-absorbed victim here. But oh how I would love to be a hero.

Published: Fri, 10 Dec 2010

http://ruthwrites.online/2010/12/10/disability-or-defeat/

"Do you think you could very kindly lean against me,'

Mon, 20 Jul 2020

cos I keep pulling so hard that I fall over backwards."

I was reminded of that Winnie the Pooh quote when I saw the other mugs on the shelf in my parents' holiday house. My siblings had different ones, but that one was mine. Now, I can see how apt it was.

Everyone needs someone to lean against don't they? A lot of the time I struggle to walk without someone to hold onto, physically speaking. My children have got into the way of offering me a hand and my husband often crooks his arm for me to slide mine into. When they forget, I feel panic rising as I calculate how long I can go on my own.

Thinking beyond that, I'm wondering how good I am at making my own mind up, forming my own opinions without turning to someone beside me to think how they think, follow their lead.

For most of my life I have simply followed the lead of people I respect. When I left home for university, I had an opportunity to own my faith and life choices for the first time. Lifted further away from the familiar when I lived in France was the real deal-breaker I suppose. But still, I waited to hear what other people thought before I said anything myself.

My health struggles have given me something that most others can't offer guidance on. It's been time to carve my own path and not a pleasant one at that.

Independence is a laudable trait, but I would argue that the ability to lean on other people has to go alongside it. To look to others for help is not a sign of weakness. I'm not sure that many people truly understand that.

If you ask someone for help or advice, you are acknowledging that you need more than just yourself. Knowing our own mind is really important, but recognising that we can't make it alone is too.

I want to make sure I can defend my own opinions, make my own decisions and step out by myself if need be.

But I will never move so far away from other people that I've nobody's back to lean against. Everybody needs somebody after all.

Published: Mon, 20 Jul 2020

http://ruthwrites.online/2020/07/20/do-you-think-you-could-very-kindly-lean-against-me/

Doing less does not mean

Mon, 08 Jun 2020

Being less.

When I commented that I was late this morning my son said, 'sure you've got nothing to do anyway'. Before that my husband had encouraged me to stay in bed as I didn't have anything in particular to get up for. As you can imagine, neither comment helped with my sense of purpose for this day.

During lockdown two types of people have emerged: those who are defying circumstances and achieving an awful lot, and those who are mainly sitting around feeling lost.

Sadly, I would relate most to the latter group. I walk in to my children sitting with their school books out, check they're on track and leave the room again. When I try to involve myself they seem a little frustrated with me, so on the whole, home schooling looks after itself, much to their credit.

Years ago we read Richard Scarry's What do people do all day?. Both my children decided separately that the answer to the question, 'what does your mummy do?' was 'she cooks the dinner'.

I have always bumbled my answer to that question anyway. Inside I'm scrambling for the best response like a proud 'I'm a stay-at-home mum', a half-hearted 'I used to work in adult education' or a whispered 'I'm an author'. Maybe it's time to put all those half-hearted self-definitions aside...

Here's the truth: over these recent years, I have learned more about sitting than anything else. If I have to sit in a public place, I still take my phone out to look more purposeful.

The challenge for me is to sit empty-handed and just be.

If you are feeling lost at the minute, whether because of furlough, unemployment, illness or just lockdown-itis, let me encourage you to enjoy just being for a while. It doesn't matter if you don't have anything to tweet about or take photos of. You are worth more than your job title or your Facebook status. Much more. And you know what?

Sometimes being is more important than doing.

Published: Mon, 08 Jun 2020

http://ruthwrites.online/2020/06/08/doing-less-does-not-mean/

Everybody has something

Wed, 27 Jan 2016

Or so I say when I tell someone I have MS. It's a kind of turning the attention away from me/filling the awkward silence kind of a thing. Mostly, they then try to argue that they've got it easy compared to me, and I say again, 'things could be worse.' I know that to be true, but sadly me saying that leads to people telling me how rubbish things are for me. But actually they're not so bad.

That awareness of how fortunate I am came to the fore again this morning. I was sitting in the hospital waiting for my run-of-the-mill review, and watching all the other outpatients as they made their way to the end of the corridor to the MS clinic. Ridiculous really, putting a clinic for people who often have mobility issues at the very back of the hospital! A few were like me, walking unaided, but several were dragging themselves along between two crutches, or being pushed in wheelchairs. There was one man, probably about my age, who had dropped one of his crutches and he had to get right down on his knees to retrieve it. It was so excruciating to watch, and yet to offer help might have humiliated him further. Another lady struggled the whole way over, checked in and then went back to get a coffee. She came back again saying she shouldn't have taken both crutches as she'd no hands free to carry her drink. This time the receptionist offered to go for her, but she shook her head and set off again, one crutch left behind. The lady sitting beside me told me that her dad had died only two weeks ago. He'd had MS for 65 years, and his wife had become his full-time carer at least ten years ago. Now his daughter has it too.

So you see, you don't have to go far before finding that there is always someone else facing something that overwhelms them. It's not just in the hospital either. I remember my mum used to always tell us that the most problem-filled area in her elder's district was also the most wealthy.

Everybody has something, and knowing that changes how you treat people I think. Right now, today's experience makes me feel utterly heartbroken, but also deeply thankful for all the somethings that I have that are good, and filled with love. And that's a something worth smiling about.

Published: Wed, 27 Jan 2016

http://ruthwrites.online/2016/01/27/everybody-has-something/

Find your audience

Mon, 30 Oct 2023

Going on my trike and also in the wheelchair has taught me a precious lesson. Now, all those people that we look beyond or above have become the eyes that I meet. There is an invisible, often unseen group of people that I now see and share smiles with. I can't believe it's taken this long for me to see them.

In the past I have always tried to look at people in wheelchairs but very few smiled back. Now, as I am in their world, they connect with me.

I wonder who your crowd is; who are the people you best relate to? It might be your colleagues at work, the people commiserating with you as you meet eyes across shopping trolleys or pushchairs, the fellow supporters watching a sports match, the singers sitting behind or beside you in a choir. These are your people; this is your audience.

I got the best smile this weekend from an elderly woman being pushed along in a wheelchair. It was like she was saying, 'I see you, you see me.' What a joy. Getting alongside someone can be the best gift you can give them. If it's a child, crouch down to their level. If it's a colleague, listen to their problems over a cup of tea. If it's a fellow music or sports lover, meet their eye and join their applause

I do hope that if I'm ever on my feet again, I'll remember how much my waist-level audience appreciated being shown that they are not alone, and never forgotten. I read this morning about 'participatory suffering'. Can you find someone who you can share that with? To know that someone else has been where you are is a comfort in itself.

Now my question for you is, who is your audience?

Are you looking in the right place for it?

Published: Mon, 30 Oct 2023

http://ruthwrites.online/2023/10/30/find-your-audience/

Giving away nostalgia

Wed, 16 Jul 2014

I did something yesterday that really was a long time coming, but I never seemed to be able to face it before. I flung open an over-stuffed wardrobe, and pulled out all my shoes. The ones I had no chance of walking or even standing in anymore. I'd kept them in this wild hope that one day it would be possible again, but last night I faced up to the harsh reality that it might never happen.

Maybe I expected to be tearful about it, but that was helped by the disturbing sight of my seven year old son walking around in pointy black heels. And my sweet little girl pushing her perfect wee feet into ridiculous silver wedges. As it turns out, I felt unusually pragmatic - the whole 'that was then, but this is now' philosophy. And in fact, as I was thinking back, I realised that there were a lot of bad memories attached to those shoes - like the time I griped at my husband when he suggested walking/hobbling until a never-to-be-seen taxi appeared, or standing at a wedding reception dreaming of slippers, or having to ditch them and walk barefoot into the church. Not a high point - in either sense...

Looking back at old photos recently, it struck me that if you put a smile on for the camera, you paint over the true story. There is something almost redemptive about that I suppose. But I won't paint over the stories around my shoes any longer - they looked nice, and sometimes made me feel nice, but now they're an unassailable cliff to me, and I'm choosing solid ground. (With maybe a few sparkly flats thrown in.)

Published: Wed, 16 Jul 2014

http://ruthwrites.online/2014/07/16/giving-away-nostalgia/

Head like a sieve

Mon, 30 Sep 2019

Absolutely doolally. That's me.

I'll give you an example: last week I was on my phone talking to my husband. After a few minutes I said into my phone, 'I have no idea where my phone is.' It didn't dawn on me until he pointed out that I was holding the blinking thing to my ear.

I don't think I was as much of a scatterbrain before children, but then, I can't remember that either. The trouble is, my head is now mostly full of the things the children have to do, a little full of my own worries and slightly cloudy with MS stuff. I forget names frequently and I double-book myself constantly. If the thing isn't in the calendar hanging on the kitchen wall then you can forget it, because I certainly will.

It seems slightly endearing when I'm telling you funny stories about phantom phones, but it can be very stressful.

I have discovered a few useful ways of setting reminders -I tell Alexa (you know her) to set alarms, I use the oven timer, I put things in my phone calendar. That's worked so far, but I'm sure there'll be a day when the alarms go off or the reminder pings and I have no idea why! When I was growing up my mum used to pull out her hanky and frown at the knot in it, asking us all, 'what's that for?!'

There's a popular reminder method where you put a poka yoke into your day to trigger your memory. Poka-yoke is a Japanese term that means "mistake-proofing" or "inadvertent error prevention". It is used in factories to help equipment operators avoid mistakes (poka). In my house, it helps us to go to sleep, safe in the knowledge that a reminder is there for us in the morning. Sometimes I'm already in bed when I remember I need a poka-yoke, so I just change round the books on my bedside table or fling a random thing on the floor (not my husband!) that I'll trip over in the morning.

When you think about it, all the things that fly around our heads and make our hearts flip over are usually insignificant. It's the bigger stuff that matters and that sticks. Like a sieve, the tiny things can fall through, but the more substantial things stay put. You know who you are, you never forget the people that matter to you, you treasure the precious things. So what if I burn the dinner, miss a hair-cut, call someone Jane for a year when their name's actually Louise or walk around the house searching for the phone in my hand!

I don't mind being a sieve-head if I still hold onto and love the most important parts of my life.

Now, why on earth is there a mop handle propped up against the door?

It'll come to me...

Published: Mon, 30 Sep 2019

http://ruthwrites.online/2019/09/30/head-like-a/

In my papa's chair

Wed, 11 May 2011

children wondering why papa

cannot

Or will not play;

His heart joins them

While his body cannot respond

Those are the lines of a poem that my grandfather wrote towards the end of his life. Out of a whole book of poetry, I have always remembered those particular words - mainly because they gave me a connection to someone who went out of my life when I was only eleven years old. But now, I am recalling them because I am beginning to truly understand the struggle behind them.

A few weeks ago, I was sitting in a chair in Donegal, affectionately known as 'papa's chair', forced off my feet with a bout of MS fatigue, and watching my husband and two children play hide and seek in the garden. I suddenly caught a glimpse of how my papa must have felt, sitting in that very chair, watching me, my siblings and cousins play outside, and looking beyond to the fields he worked hard in when he was young.

And yet, it struck me that it was most likely when papa was in that chair, often not out of choice. that he plumbed deeper depths of thought and feeling than he ever had before. In the closing lines of the poem, he writes:

Maybe I'm missing a lot;

Sunset is always

The most beautiful part

Of the day

I have hoped that in my struggles with MS, the same deepening of insight will be brought to me too. I never really knew papa, but strangely now, taking a few small steps in his huge ones, I feel like I am closer to him.

Published: Wed, 11 May 2011

`http://ruthwrites.online/2011/05/11/in-my-papas-chair/`

In need of

Mon, 22 Mar 2021

A boost. Most days I feel like Mr Smallwood in Bleak House who tells his daughter repeatedly, 'shake me up Judy'. Most days it seems that my energy connection has been pulled out. Most days I need back-up.

When I was watching the rugby last weekend I spotted something... When a forward has the ball and is attacking, other forwards latch onto him to increase his momentum. It made me wonder, where are my forwards right now? Who or maybe what are they?

Sometimes we have to create our own help. If two rugby players crashed into my back I'd hilariously end up on the floor, not propelled forwards. I'd rather hold on to my trekking poles than someone else's arm. I like to set my own pace. Most of the time. Other times I want an outside strength to get beside me and lift me up.

Boosts can exist in the world around us too. Crocuses to herald the end of winter, bird song after a sleepless night or sun over our shivering bodies. A tiny hand learning to wave. A remembered song. An encouraging word from a friend.

The forward didn't have to look behind him to know help was at hand. In real life, we do need to search for the things that will lift us. When struggles blind us, it might take a friend to find them for us. My daughter yesterday looked at a leafless tree and shouted 'bud!' I hadn't noticed them. My son stationed himself close by when he knew I would need him to haul me up. His dad is always asking me if I want to 'hook on'.

These things in nature, this family are my forwards. What are yours?

Published: Mon, 22 Mar 2021

http://ruthwrites.online/2021/03/22/in-need-of/

In the woods

Mon, 16 Jan 2023

At least three times, every time he has seen me in fact, my surgeon has uttered those pessimistic words: 'you're not out of the woods yet'. He hasn't told me how to get out, or how to survive while I'm in there. Not great for a Wind in the Willows aficionado that's for sure. The only way that terrified Mole could cope when he was in the wild woods was by running out of them. I'm trapped here for two years apparently.

Has anyone ever said something to you that keeps you in fear? It could be a horrible health diagnosis, an addiction that's always threatening to come back, a damning description of who people say you are, or worse still, the negative things you believe about yourself. All those things are your woods. Not beautiful trees dappled with sunshine surrounding a peaceful lake, but dark, enclosing spaces that swallow up the light and block your path out. The problem is, the further you are pushed in, the harder it is to escape.

What do we do when we're stuck in a place that makes us miserable? Right now I'm cutting myself some slack and accepting that now is the time to hibernate. To rest. And luckily for me, to get better. Something that sadly is not possible for everyone.

So, when you feel trapped in your situation, pull together things that make you feel more safe and comfortable. Invite people in who can keep you company and even cut back some of the branches to let in more light, helping you to find a path through. The sun is waiting to shine on you again. The birds are ready to sing.

The God of deep forests created a garden. The Lord of storms also calmed them. The Father sent His Son to walk through dark wildness and die on a rugged tree so we would never be alone in the woods again.

Don't feel doomed or stuck.

You are seen and saved, always.

Published: Mon, 16 Jan 2023

`http://ruthwrites.online/2023/01/16/in-the-woods/`

It's not a forever thing

Mon, 05 Dec 2022

Right this minute, I am dosed up on painkillers sitting on bed thinking, how did this get so bad? You might think I'm always full of positivity. That's not necessarily the case.

I'm sure that there is no-one who can say they are problem-free. And so, this slightly grumpy post is for anyone who is plain fed up. For those who live with pain day in day out, I understand you a little more now. For those who look at the rain and the rainbow is nowhere to be seen, I'm with you. For those who have run out of hope, I am sitting alongside you.

Sometimes, nobody needs a Pollyanna. Sometimes you just need to sit in your doldrums for a while. And that's ok. Life can be hard, and then gets harder still. When you think you've hit the bottom, it can give way.

You know I can't leave you down there though. I have to find a way to lift us out. For both our sakes. Looking out at the dark at half four in the afternoon I am remembering something that always helps me: this darkness is not a forever thing. I will say it, I have to; change is on its way. My bones are going to behave the way they should. I will walk again, albeit not like a normal person but in my own wobbly way. Whatever you are facing right now, there are people who can help you. However impossible the situation, there is a way out.

Every year my granny bemoaned the shortening of daylight. Every year someone else would point out the longer daylight hours. Thank God for seasons and the passing of time. Even in the depths of winter we can say spring is on its way.

Light is coming.

Let's watch for it and hold tight to each other.

Published: Mon, 05 Dec 2022

`http://ruthwrites.online/2022/12/05/its-not-a-forever-thing/`

Laurels and if onlys

Thu, 02 Aug 2012

I was good once, I was clever once, back then I was better. Now I am not what I was, and my hopes for what I will be are shaky. The middle one is the worst out of the past, present and future me. Or is it.

The past is now an air-brushed version of reality, full of successes which were straight-forward to achieve, and clearly laid-out milestones. I ran through all of them with the certainty that this is where I was supposed to be, what I was meant to do. It wasn't all easy, but the hard parts have gone into soft-focus now, and most make sense too.

Now is different. Now is full of routines, some that I have created to re-make a day-sized version of the road map I had before. I miss the frequent recognition of my worth, the praise for my regular achievements, the salary too. I miss adults. Children's conversations are of another world, and another vocabulary. I'm getting more fluent, but miss my own words.

There's a true wisdom about savouring the present, living for the moment, watching you don't let it pass by un-noticed. It is a cruel truth though, that you only savour what is passed, you only value what you miss.

The future is unknown. I've already kitted it out with a city's worth full of worry and pessimism. Do I look back on the past, focus on the present and anticipate good things amongst the bad? Rarely. For some reason, fear always seems more concrete than hope. And yet I want to get better at that. It's my non-SMART goal.

Standing back from past, present and future, I think I can see 3 versions of myself, and, funnily enough, they all look like me.

Published: Thu, 02 Aug 2012

http://ruthwrites.online/2012/08/02/laurels-and-if-onlys/

My 500 miles

Tue, 10 Jun 2014

If you didn't know, you'd think I was a pretty lazy person - always parking as close as possible to my destination, sitting on whatever bench is available, griping about the long standing wait at the end of school. It does look bad, I know that painfully well.

You have no idea how much I wish things weren't like that for me. I wish I could stand for the whole time at my kids' sports' days, maybe even jump up and down when they're on. I wish I could hold my wee girl's hand and finish her sponsored walk, instead of being halted by my weak legs. I wish I could smile and say 'we're walking home today', and hear my son cheering. I wish I could just wander about the shops, browsing, picking things up and thinking I'll maybe go back to them later. I wish I could be active with my children, and take them to parks in the afternoon like I used to. I wish when my husband wants to wander around a city, I could say yes. I wish I could scramble down the sand dunes to my favourite beach, and know that I'll be able to climb back up. Climbing a mountain or even a hill is a distant memory now, possibly never to be re-lived.

Right now, getting up the stairs is my mountain, and walking across the playground my marathon. I hope with all my heart that my children will understand all this one day. I am doing all I can, I am trying to be all I should be.

If, at first glance, you think I am achieving nothing, consider my hidden story, and realise that all this is my 500 miles. Struggled through because I want to show my people I'm there for them, and I love them. Nothing can ever rival that.

Published: Tue, 10 Jun 2014

http://ruthwrites.online/2014/06/10/my-500-miles/

My monster

Tue, 25 Sep 2012

They say, if you name your fear, you can defeat it. Not sure it's that easy, and I do wish I was in the "they" all-knowing group, but at this point, I'll try anything.

My monster used to be invisible, dormant, easy to ignore. First, it was because I didn't know it even existed. I miss those oblivious days now. I hate ruining them with informed retrospect too, weighing down innocent memories with heavy explanations for how I felt, what I did that time.

Then, it was like a vague whisper, flitting about my mind from time to time, but quickly suppressed. "It's mild", I happily reassured my listeners. And myself. How can something mild ever become monstrous?

But it did. It is. It hangs onto my legs, rides on my back, pushing me towards the ground. It nudges me this way and that, turning balance and light footedness into a fantasy. It's not happy to simply cling onto me, it seeps inside as well, bringing prickles and numbness to random points, always keeping up the panic by going somewhere new. It makes me hope for rain, so I can drive, not walk to school. It turns me into a nag, giving orders from a sitting position to do things that I've always done, things that I see as 'my job' to do. It steals my identity, takes away all the things that I use to define myself, and bring meaning to my existence.

But my head, in my head is the worst. The physical stuff is one thing, but the mental disabling is the part that I hate the most. Flashes of inexplicable anger, waves of worry and fear over the future, and tears, many, many tears. Some shed, most pushed down. The monster is not dormant any more. It is active, and terrifying.

But now, I know it. Now, I've named it, described it, and one day, in my mind at least (I hope), I will defeat it.

Published: Tue, 25 Sep 2012

http://ruthwrites.online/2012/09/25/my-monster/

One wobbly stone at a time

Mon, 05 Aug 2019

Last week I was stuck between a rock and a hard place. Quite literally. I'd done the too long walk across the rippled sand and now I didn't have the strength to get home.

My mum phoned dad and he drove his 4x4 over the rough hill road to get me. Problem was, there were a lot of rocks between me and the car. My mum and my sister coaxed me, one stone at a time, until I reached the slope going up to the field where dad was. It was slightly hilarious (my sister was laughing at the thought of me using it for a blog.) The final push was blocked by brambles so dad, Prince Charming style, hacked at them to clear the path. Meanwhile my two were cheering me on from the shore.

Not exactly my most dignified moment, but up there as one of the best family memories. You see, yet again, I've encountered love when I was at my worst.

Life is overwhelming, and often seems impossible to get through, like that heap of rocks. But if you just lift your hand, acknowledge you're not able to do it by yourself, then help comes. I've tried it a lot over these past years and I can promise you, it works. You might embarrass yourself along the way but who's going to remember that?

Like I always say, if I can walk into a wedding in my socks without being laughed at, then you can get away with pretty much anything!

Published: Mon, 05 Aug 2019

http://ruthwrites.online/2019/08/05/one-wobbly-stone-at-a-time/

Spring in your step

Mon, 27 Apr 2020

It's been a long time since I walked with light footsteps. I haven't been able to skip, dance, jog or jump for years.

Last week when I was doing the MS version (ie very little) of Joe Wicks with my two, I shocked them and myself by giving a little jump. With both my heavy feet off the floor. That may seem a nothing to most, but it was something to celebrate for me.

These Covid days, I'm certain that most of us are taking heavier steps as the anxiety, uncertainty and grief push down on our shoulders. When will it end? No-one knows. So, do we just endure indefinitely or...

Do we search for a way to lift our heavy feet off the ground, even just once a day? Of course, treat that metaphorically and the world's your oyster.

I haven't been able to lift my feet high since that one time, but I have found many ways to experience lightness of heart; my husband got a bird bath for his birthday and I spend a lot of time watching it, waiting for a bird to skid in and splash around, not a heavy boot in sight. My children are constantly giggling which is a joyful sound. Watching my dog tear in crazy circles round the garden is exhilarating too.

If you can't find anything to make you skip, remember that there is a spring right here, all around you. If you don't have the energy to muster it up by yourself, look for the flowers blooming for you outside. No darkness, no pain, no heaviness of step or heart can stop them from springing up in all their blue, red, yellow, purple, rainbow glory.

There may not be a spring in your step, but there's one outside your door, just waiting for you!

Published: Mon, 27 Apr 2020

http://ruthwrites.online/2020/04/27/spring-in-your-step/

Starting at the very beginning

Mon, 26 Aug 2024

I know it's hard, but sometimes you have to go over the things you used to know, that you haven't been able to do for some time. Take heart and trust it will come back again.

I sat down at the piano this week, for the first time in two years. You know what I discovered? My fingers had not forgotten all the scales I used to practice when I was in my teens. Before I could get my brain in order, my fingers were already working. So be encouraged, the things you used to do or know can come back. Shut out the naysayer part of your head and believe you can do whatever you set out to do.

After many years looking after her growing family, my mum went back to work as a doctor. She was left in a room to see patients on her first day back! And it all passed without a hitch

There are some things that we need to accept are not within our power to do anymore. My bike is sitting in the garage, left behind. But now I can cycle a different way. Maybe you can't imagine starting over with anything, but think again, there might be another way.

As for me, I need to walk away from certain things but, I will head towards the activities I can do. Set your sights on the other ways, or trust in the faithful practice you did in the past. Like playing the piano, it does come back!

Published: Mon, 26 Aug 2024

http://ruthwrites.online/2024/08/26/starting-at-the-very-beginning/

Struggles with benefits

Tue, 09 Jul 2019

Don't get me wrong, I would love to not have MS. More than anything. I would love to be able to walk beside my family wherever they go, to move with grace, to wear nice shoes, to not have this imprisoning, wretched, sometimes terrifying disease.

BUT yet again I'm discovering an amazing capacity for kindness in the people around me.

I was always the type of person who just wanted to blend in, but with this, I'm out there exposed. We went on a boat to an island off Dingle yesterday. Stupidly I thought I'd just walk smoothly up a gang plank from a flat jetty. What I actually encountered was a very steep hill leading down to rocks with a little dinghy waiting to take us to a slightly bigger boat. I put my sunglasses on to hide the tears as I slowly, one trekking pole in front of the other, struggled behind my family. As we put on life jackets I thought, I can't do this.

But then I saw the men in the boat, hands reaching out to help me on. I can't tell you how thankful I was for them, with their strong hand grip, their reassuring words. (Slightly in love with them now). When I was struggling to juggle poles and life jacket, a woman stepped down to help. The sunglasses were definitely a good plan. The man sitting beside me spoke encouragement to me as well.

All this got me thinking, if I had not needed anyone or anything I would never have summoned up all this goodness. So, either I skip in heels oblivious, or I stagger, fall into blessing. It is humiliating to be helped, but so, so beautiful.

I really hope that one day I'll be somebody else's angel the way all those people were to me.

Published: Tue, 09 Jul 2019

http://ruthwrites.online/2019/07/09/struggles-with-benefits/

Swimming to be

Fri, 20 Sep 2013

...more than somebody who walks like they're permanently on a wobble-board. Somebody who, all of a sudden, sheds the image of mild disability to become like anybody else. I can speak of the lengths I have done, and not the length of naps I've had or how hard I've found the day.

Nobody knows, in the pool, who I am or what's wrong with me. I'm just this dark-haired girl in a navy swimsuit who smiles and makes standard comments about the temperature of the water, or how busy it is. As I swim, I don't think about anything. Not how weary I'll be, or what other things I have to exert myself to do. I don't notice the weakness of my legs, or the imbalance of my body. I just keep the number of the length I'm on in my head. I just swim.

It's the only time that I forget about my troubles, and assert my right to physical fitness. In the water, I am graceful. Not like the way I feel on land, that's for sure. I can do as much, sometimes more, than other people I know, and that is a rare occurrence for me now. Of course it's a hard slog too, but it's a precious time to me. During those 30 minutes, my monster sleeps forgotten. It will return, but when I swim, I'm in a blissful, watery state of oblivion. And that feels to me like a very real glimpse of heaven.

Published: Fri, 20 Sep 2013

http://ruthwrites.online/2013/09/20/swimming-to-be/

Take your time

Mon, 10 Jan 2022

I have heard those three words a lot, especially in recent times when my balance is completely off. They have never annoyed me; quite the opposite.

There is a part of me that is ashamed of the way I stumble and panic people watching me but tonight, as I set to writing this, I have decided to turn away from shame and focus on gratitude. When people ask me to take my time they are not showing impatience, just beautiful kindness. In this world of every man or woman for themselves, I give you the countless people who have been considerate of me. So no, the world has not entirely gone to pot.

I wasted time today trying to justify my indignation about something. Now, I'm spending time remembering the smiles, the concern and the offers of help. I'm celebrating that in fact.

Which leads me to ask, when was the last time I took my eyes off myself and shown kindness to someone else? Every time someone comes into my head, I need to let them know. I can't physically do anything, but, remembering how much a card or a message means to me, I can do that.

How can you help someone else take it slower, how can you lighten their load? Even if it's just speaking three words to them?

'Take your time'.

Published: Mon, 10 Jan 2022

http://ruthwrites.online/2022/01/10/take-your-time/

The blankets

Fri, 02 Oct 2020

When I was pondering what I would write about last week I was thinking about blankets. At the time I was walking with heavy steps along my street, fighting against a horrible sense of fatigue. Quite often, when I try to explain fatigue I talk about having a wet woollen blanket dropped over my head, my shoulders, my arms and legs.

Thankfully, I'm not going to dwell on that horrible image today.

Not long after that misguided, terrible decision to tell you all about fatigue, something lovely happened. I was sitting in my armchair with a cosy blanket over my knees. The sun was drawing bright lines across the room and my dog was seeking out the best spot for her morning doze. Very gently, without me even noticing, she lay down on the edge of the fleecy cover. I didn't ever want to stand up and wreck the comfort she was unintentionally bringing both to herself and to me.

Whenever times are hard, we need to be more like my dog Hazel; looking in every corner for a tiny scrap of comfort and luxuriating in it. Every time something that I used to take for granted appears in my day, I feel an overwhelming, joyful rush of gratitude. Now, sitting out in the cold but sunny garden with my parents makes me so so happy. Hours later, I still feel the edge of that happiness. I'm blogging about it to make it last even longer!

Interestingly, the Ruth of the Bible also sought out the edge of a blanket and it changed her life. When she lay at Boaz's feet, she asked him to take her 'under your protecting wing' (Ruth 3v9, The Message).

There are two thoughts here: learn to luxuriate in the little things, and, share them with someone else.

You never know, that insignificant act might change a life!

Published: Fri, 02 Oct 2020

http://ruthwrites.online/2020/10/02/the-blankets/

The dream

Tue, 31 May 2016

Two things happened recently which made me feel sad. The first was yet another familiar instance of wanting to be able to walk faster and further than I could. It's like that common nightmare of needing to be somewhere and not being able to run to make it on time. Your head is telling you to run, and you just end up walking through treacle.

I'm afraid to tell you, for me, that nightmare is my day-to-day waking life. My kids were on their bikes in the park, but the arrangement of me meeting them on a bench half-way fell through, so I ended up walking as quickly as I could, knowing with every step that they were waiting for me further along the path, hoping they would have the sense to stay there, and not try to cross the road. In that moment, right then, I wished I could fly. People walked quickly past my struggling self - one suggested a skateboard, one roller-skates when I told them I had been left behind, two options which were so impossible, they made me laugh. Happy ending though: the children had waited, and didn't complain or criticise, they just carried on beside me, happy I was there.

The other thing was harder - I was standing at our front door seeing my two aging parents struggle to get to their car, my dad hit by another wave of Lime's disease, my mum in agony with one hip, and unsteady with the other one, a recent replacement. She has had to say goodbye to many beloved past-times - kneeling to garden, swimming in the waves of Donegal, riding her bike. That is a stuck place that many, many people, most of us actually, will have to live in as the years pass by.

I'm remembering two photos of my children - one is my son holding on to the bars of his playpen, screaming blue murder to get out, desperate to move beyond the square metre space he's been restricted too. That is like everyone who has been forced to exist in ever-shrinking spaces. The other picture, however, is of my little girl, plonked down on a rug in my parent's garden, playing with all the toys within her reach. She couldn't even crawl then, but she just sat happily for over an hour, pleased with what was nearby.

So, what are the things that bring us contentment when the dream of flying is only ever going to be just that - a dream? I don't know about you, but I intend to seek those things out.

And possibly buy a bike.

Published: Tue, 31 May 2016

http://ruthwrites.online/2016/05/31/the-dream/

There is no beauty

Mon, 22 Jan 2024

Every week I try to put a positive spin on life, but I have to tell you that sometimes it is so so hard. People often, almost rightly, think that disability goes hand in hand with courage. But I'm here to tell you that sometimes that image slips and the hard truth comes out.

This week I have struggled to lift one of my feet which makes getting places almost impossible. The two men in my life try to help, but it is a frustrating process. MS is ugly, and can easily make the people impacted by it downhearted too.

I was thinking about this today, and the image of the cross came to mind. Don't ever think that there was anything beautiful about that. BUT, because of the cross we have a chance to live forever, to have everything we regret wiped out. We are offered a new start. Because of my hateful MS I get to see the best of my children, my husband and my family. I must never forget that all the ugliness of the cross bought us everything and all the ugliness of my sickness bought me indescribable kindness.

If you are in your own kind of hell today, reach out your hands and take the blessings that are waiting for you . I will not let the darkness win, and I know the cross has already dealt with it all. Live your life knowing that and somehow, things will feel a little more bearable.

Published: Mon, 22 Jan 2024

http://ruthwrites.online/2024/01/22/there-is-no-beauty/

Ways around

Tue, 04 Jun 2019

Sitting here watching my daughter in her ballet class, I'm reminded that even though I've lost grace myself, I can take delight in hers.

Even though I can't make it to the top of a mountain, my family can phone me from one and share a panorama of the view. Even though I can't walk the dog at the moment, she still shows me love and devotion.

When you can't do a thing, for a multitude of reasons, there is almost always a way round it. Don't lose heart. Some amazing people do things in spite of the odds stacked against them. I have hugely optimistic days like that sometimes.

But for the rest of the time, I'm discovering that I just need to be clever about stuff, and take a longer view.

Right now my son is coping with a broken finger which happened only a couple of weeks after he discovered a love for sailing. He's coming to terms with it now, knowing that one day soon he'll be back out on the water again. In the meantime, he opens his wardrobe, breathes in the smell of his new wet suit and feels happy anticipation. I hate it that he's learning the horrible lesson I've been taught, but I'm thankful he's found a way round.

The other alternative route I have is found in writing. When I write, I can go anywhere, help anyone, do anything. And always guarantee a happy ending too.

It struck me recently that perhaps that's why I started to do it in the first place.

Is there something blocking you at the minute? Can you see a solution? Look about you, maybe there's someone else who can do it for you, or maybe there's another way.

I really hope you can find it.

Published: Tue, 04 Jun 2019

`http://ruthwrites.online/2019/06/04/ways-around/`

When the pain comes down,

Mon, 28 Nov 2022

Floods of kindness rise up.

Of course I never want to learn this lesson, but it happens to all of us whether we want it or not. I would guess that you probably know what it feels like to be washed up in a tough place, looking round for some kind of rescue.

A few days ago I fell on the kitchen floor and broke my hip. It wasn't long before people arrived to help whatever way they could. Even fellow-sufferers on the ward tried their best to spur each other on. When the chaplain arrived she found herself having to pray for me and then the other two women there! Funny how, when we're at our lowest point, thoughts of the highest power become more vital.

I was thinking that it was easy for people to help me when I was so obviously in need. But what about those who are secretly in pain, when it isn't as clear that they need help? Someone approached me in hospital who was grieving for her friend. Because she saw my clear suffering, she was able to tell me about hers. I suppose the rule is don't be afraid to show you are struggling because, in a strange kind of way, it might help someone else.

Of course I wish I didn't have to learn this particular lesson so frequently, but the overwhelming blessings I encounter along the way are so great.

I truly hope that, if you are stuck right now, somebody else will stop and see your pain.

I really hope that kindness rises up for you too, just like it did for me.

Published: Mon, 28 Nov 2022

http://ruthwrites.online/2022/11/28/when-the-pain-comes-down/

When the rhythm of your life changes,

Mon, 21 Sep 2020

Sing a different song.

Last month I discovered a trick for surviving the stress of an MRI. This one was the longest I've ever had and honestly, I was terrified. I remembered that the other times I'd been in that wretched, claustrophobic magnet I'd had moments where the panic nearly took me over. And those ones were about a third of the time.

For this one, however, I discovered that as the beating racket got louder and louder, I could find a tune that matched it. For some reason, Sunday school songs from years ago worked best. Even the ones I'd never liked. When the banging altered, I changed my tune to fit. (I wasn't singing out loud of course, that would have had the radiographers scratching their heads- is there something else wrong with that woman in there?!)

That approach carried me up until the last five minutes when it was so uncomfortable all I could do was pray and will it to be over. But I was so encouraged that I had found a new way of enduring. I suppose that is what resilience is- changing your tune to work with whatever life throws at you.

People talk about 'seasons' as if they are more easy to bear if you put a pretty name to them. I know some of you wouldn't even describe what you're going through as winter. It's much more relentless than that. But I wonder if wherever you are, whatever you are going through, you can find a song, something, to help you bear it.

I told you that approach worked up until the last stretch. Sometimes all we can do is brace ourselves, grit our teeth and hope for a relief.

As older, wiser people say, 'this too shall pass'. That has annoyed me in the past, but actually, I think they may well be right.

Published: Mon, 21 Sep 2020

http://ruthwrites.online/2020/09/21/when-the-rhythm-of-your-life-changes/

When truth got stuck up the chimney

Tue, 26 Nov 2013

It began to shout - you can't keep me here forever. And then, it pushed itself out.

So, here's what happened. We'd just unblocked our chimney, in preparation for getting a stove installed. There was a powerful draught, and on advice, we put a plastic bag in the bottom, to stop the wind howling down. The plastic bag was a sturdy blue one I was given when I last picked up my interfeon injection pack. Clearly labelled with my name, the hospital's name, and what it contained. It was a good draught-excluder. For a few days.

Then one night, one very windy night, I was sitting on the sofa, opposite the fire-to-be, when I heard an almighty sucking noise, and whoosh, the bag was gone. I've looked up, my husband's looked up, as have my dad, my son and even my 4 year old daughter. None of us can see any blue, only light. There's no sign on the roof or the garden either.

Initially, I was concerned about littering, but then I remembered what the bag was, and what information about me was on it. Information I had not shared with anyone on the street, anyone at the school gates, or almost anywhere really. When I put up my blue badge so I can get a closer space in the car park at Tesco's, I get out of the car and distance myself from it as quickly as possible. I don't know what that says about my own self-assurance, or my view of disability in general, but it's not good. What I do know is that I'm afraid. Afraid of only being seen and talked about as someone who is sick. Who's not your average girl.

Probably, that telling bag will never be found, or read, but if it does, I need to hold my head high, be myself, and let those that discover it draw their own conclusions.

The truth will out, but can you see all its colours, or is it still just monochrome?

Published: Tue, 26 Nov 2013

http://ruthwrites.online/2013/11/26/when-truth-got-stuck-up-the-chimney/

Nature

A secret streak of green

Mon, 24 Feb 2020

'When a thing is wick, it has a life about it Maybe not a life like you and me But somewhere there's a secret streak of green inside itNow come and let me show you what I mean'*

My sister reminded me about this meaning of the word 'wick' yesterday. To most of us, 'wick' means embarrassed, rubbish, under par. But there's another meaning that has long been forgotten. When Mary sees The Secret Garden, she declares it to be dead. It's only when Dickon looks and 'walks about softly' that he can recognise there's life, a 'wick' in the plants around him. Even the lifeless roses have tiny shoots of green when the grass and dead boughs that were choking it are cleared away.

As yet another rainy, windy day arrived this morning, I was making myself think of what's good about February that January doesn't have. It's got to be the bulbs. The snowdrops get to us earlier, but this month, the crocuses arrive. I can already see promises of daffodils in the garden as well. The days are getting longer again too. Spring is steadily approaching. It has been a hard, dark old time for many of us this winter, but the good news is, spring is coming.

I wonder if you have a Dickon in your life, or is that the part you play in someone else's? My Dickon insisted only yesterday that he could see green on the plant I said was too storm-damaged to survive. I didn't believe him and yet, I've let it be just in case I'm wrong.

Maybe, 'just in case you're wrong', you should try and look for the wick in your life. That is so so hard to do sometimes. I know. But there might be hope somewhere you didn't expect, somewhere you've never looked before.

And don't forget, there are always crocuses.

*The Secret Garden, Frances Hodgson Burnett

Published: Mon, 24 Feb 2020

http://ruthwrites.online/2020/02/24/a-secret-streak-of-green/

A tradition of imperfection

Fri, 16 Dec 2016

Every Christmas, bar possibly one, my father-in-law brings home a terrible tree. Either it's too tall, too skinny, too crooked, or, like this time, too wrong in every way. He bought (no idea why they charged him for it) his tree this year, and decided to split it with a friend. The outcome is a short bush with a wide bit close to the middle, and a long, relatively straight spike at the top. The greatest thing is, no-one makes him go out and get a better one. Everyone just laughs, happy that the legend of the worst tree ever is still alive. Even now, days after I first saw a picture of it, I'm still chuckling. What could be better than that, really?!

Life is full of imperfections and disappointments; we see them all the time. Mostly, we wish they could be brushed out, improved, or taken away. Mostly, that is not an option. The big ones are far from funny, but the little ones are best dealt with with laughter. When I'm remembering my frequent times of imbalance or leg weakness, I find it lifts me to laugh at my silliness. When I'm in the middle of it, I'll be honest, the funny side is not as easy to find.

The first Christmas was far from perfect either. I am certain that the stable (or whatever it actually was) was not clean and warmly lit, and I find it hard to believe that Jesus, both man and God, did not roar as much as any other baby. That line, 'But little Lord Jesus no crying He makes' is based on the golden ideals of Renaissance paintings, not on the harsh reality of a very gritty Nativity. God did not select a palace for His Son. He placed Him as close to the bottom of the social ladder as He could. And who were the first visitors? Shepherds. I love the picture of dazzling angels shining their light onto a group of filthy vagabonds. That was the mind-boggling moment when perfection bent down and embraced imperfection.

So, if your tree is a little on the ugly side, cover it in sparkle and remember we are celebrating the perfect God coming to this drastically imperfect earth as man.

What a wonder.

Published: Fri, 16 Dec 2016

http://ruthwrites.online/2016/12/16/a-tradition-of-imperfection/

All things bright and beautiful

Mon, 23 Sep 2024

A few evenings ago I was watching the sky, hoping for some inspiration. A flock of crows were filling the clouds, but then I spotted a smaller group of swallows flying above them in a smaller, tighter circle. It made me think of friendship and the way people can surround you and lift you up when dark things threaten to bring you down.

Then, as I listened to the clear, fresh birdsong the next morning, I was reminded that there are always bright and beautiful gifts if we watch and wait for them. You could call them mercies.

CS Lewis chose the title of his book about grief over losing his wife, Surprised by Joy. Maybe that is the secret- there will be times when you can't recognise anything good, but there are often friends near you who can bring it to you. Or perhaps you can take it to them.

When you're feeling low, it can be very difficult to see anything bright, but if you expect to be surprised, then it can happen. A bird, maybe two, has been singing a bright song to me every morning, and it cuts through the blackness I sometimes feel. Nothing is forced, nothing has been fabricated, it's just beautiful before I even ask it to be.

Have a think about ways you could surround and lift up people struggling beside you. Like the swallows, aim for greater heights and carry others with you. Search for bright and beautiful things and share them with others. It is a happy way of bringing light, even in the darkest of times. Blessing other people always has a blessing in it for you too.

Published: Mon, 23 Sep 2024

http://ruthwrites.online/2024/09/23/all-things-bright-and-beautiful/

And then there were birds

Wed, 16 Dec 2015

All week I have been telling the family that I have a dream of seeing a robin in our new garden. If I saw a robin, I said, it would make everything better. Of course, an empty bird-feeder and two warring cats did not help. I spent two days giving off about the cats, shooing them away and generally blaming them for everything. My failure to get bird seed had nothing to do with it. Of course.

But then, a couple of nights ago on another errand in Dobbies I walked past the bird seed aisle and finally put some bags in the trolley. The next morning I filled up the only feeder I could find with peanuts and scattered mixed seed on the bird table. I went inside and waited. Not long after, I saw a brown bird at the end of the garden. Like a mad woman I started telling it (out loud) to turn around, and there it was - a promising flash of red!

Word must have spread then because when I was at the kitchen sink later, at least seven tits and finches swooped down from the tree they were perched on above the bordering bushes. He was the last one to arrive, waiting until the others had gone, but then, to my great happiness, there he was, feeding to his heart's content. Our first robin. The first Christmas in our new house has begun!

Published: Wed, 16 Dec 2015

http://ruthwrites.online/2015/12/16/and-then-there-were-birds/

Behind the grey

Mon, 04 Jun 2018

I was at a place at the weekend that I've never been before. I can't describe it to you, because almost all off it was covered in sea mist. I can tell you there were dunes, sand, and a few metres of sea, but that's all. It was a gentle, mystical, forgiving seaside, and I delighted in that. I didn't need to be presented with mountains I could never climb, or a horizon I had no dream to reach. This small piece of beauty was enough for me that day.

It was only when we got back that I was shown what was actually there - a spectacular scene of blue ocean with green hills sweeping down to embrace it. It took a while for me to accept that this was not a joke - it was all there, behind the grey.

How often we are so swamped in the mist of stress, illness, grief and pain, that we don't realise there is something else there, just beyond our own experience. Someone. Sometimes it is almost laughable, that heaven is within our reach. But one day, the mists will part, and we will see - something beyond all our imaginings, so startling, so spectacular that we will wonder why we spent so much time doubting it was real.

Not understanding that it was there all along.

Published: Mon, 04 Jun 2018

http://ruthwrites.online/2018/06/04/behind-the-grey/

Belonging

Wed, 12 Aug 2015

Do you ever get to a place and think 'so this is where I'm meant to be'? Last week, when I'd managed to get down to Marble Hill beach, I had the most wonderful feeling. It was like taking a deep breath, and feeling like I'd crossed the finish line. I had thought that the beautiful Back Strand I described in my last post was more than enough, but sitting on the golden sand, looking across the breaking waves and the blue water, I realised that this place was more a part of me than anywhere else. All those summer days throughout my childhood and adolescence soaking in this view had woven this shore firmly into my consciousness. I have always found myself singing when I'm there.

Let's be clear: it's something, Someone within and beyond the beauty that rings true with me. And He is not confined to space or time. I can't pack up Marble Hill and take it with me. I can look at pictures, I can close my eyes and remember, but the fact is, I'm not there. I'm in my grey, tarmac life, and the blue sea is far away now. I would love to still be sitting on the sand, but my beige armchair is all I've got.

Here's the best thing though: the God of Marble Hill is here. He's sitting with the orphans in the slums. He's walking in the midst of the refugees in Syria, He is everywhere. That is a tricky one to believe, and I find it hard to say too. BUT, one day, we will all be given our own Marble Hill, and it will last forever.

Published: Wed, 12 Aug 2015

`http://ruthwrites.online/2015/08/12/belonging/`

Cold water

Mon, 26 Jul 2021

It has been chokingly hot this past fortnight. People have been opening all the windows and doors in their houses searching for the tiniest of draughts, scuttling into the darkest corners and hiding their dogs indoors lest they pass out from the heat. Gardens are yellow, filled with shriveled plants.

Some people haven't said it, but most have:

This time it's too hot.

We were away for the week and as we drove back towards our house, I saw my hanging basket. Or what was left of it. I had loved that basket this year. It was the only thing in the garden I was able to say I had done myself. It looked like the type you would see hanging beside the door of a quaint little cottage. But now, it was a scraggly mess. I submerged it in a full sink of water and went to bed, not really believing that would work. But the next morning I looked and the flowers I'd given up on were fighting their way back. The water had worked it's magic.

I have felt like that limp, dying basket through this heat. My legs have been like buckling, shaking plastic straws. My balance has gone. I spent the holiday doing as little as I could, shying away from being in the full sun for too long. As the end of the week drew near, my mum's cousin offered his car to get me down to the place I had given up on ever reaching again. With a deal of help, I was in the cold water I had been craving all week. Like my hanging basket, my limpness faded away and for the first time in ages I was able to feel strong as I walked away from the water. That moment was fleeting but I'll treasure it forever.

When you think about the people in your life, is there someone who needs you to bring them to the water, whatever that might mean for them? All I could do was immerse my plants, but another person with the means made my life better.

What do you need right now? Or what do you have that you could use to help someone else?

It can be as small as a cup of tea. Or a watering can.

Published: Mon, 26 Jul 2021

`http://ruthwrites.online/2021/07/26/cold-water/`

Don't give up too easily

Mon, 09 Sep 2019

One of the things I associate with my mum is the way she spies a broken flower, bends down and puts it in a vase of water. My dad sees a faulty thing, and works to fix it. My granny used to scrape jam jars until they were almost as clean as they had been before. My mother-in-law makes beautiful bags out of worn out jeans.

Why have we stopped doing that? Why do we just give up and throw things out when they need rescued?

I know this is a la mode these days with all the concern about waste, but it's still not as good as it once was.

Thinking beyond the material, there's a tendency to walk away from unsatisfactory relationships and people too. At my wedding 17 years ago last Friday, the minister talked about faithfulness, naming it as something that goes further than romantic love. We've lost the ability to determinedly stick at things. We're very good at rubbishing them instead.

I know sometimes it is too hard to do it, but most times it is possible. I'm often tempted to give up when things don't work in my faulty body but then I think about that rescued flower, the mended clock, the people who have pulled themselves up from the dirt... and I remember this: most things are worth rescuing.

Including you!

Published: Mon, 09 Sep 2019

http://ruthwrites.online/2019/09/09/dont-give-up-too-easily/

Fading flowers

Mon, 22 Jul 2024

The buddleia in our garden is bright purple at the minute, but it will fade soon. Maybe there is someone in your life who is not the vibrant person they once were. Watching President Biden struggle with his age is a case in point.

But here is a crucial thing: we have to hold onto the best of the person we see right now, not denying their struggles but treasuring the glimmers of their true self they still give to you. I love seeing the older people in my life laugh, or tell stories about themselves. So maybe they can't do the things physically they used to do, but they are still them.

If you feel like you are fading, think about the parts that still make you shine, or let a friend show you. Maybe you or someone close to you have slowed down. Sitting down actually gives you a chance to dwell with other people and move deeper in conversation with them. When you can't run past, asking 'how are you?'and missing the answer, you can wait and listen properly. Some of the best conversations I have had have been the ones where I am there beside a person for the duration, like it or not!

If your struggles are swamping you, remember you are deeply loved, and your Father sees you. For those who are finding it hard to watch the people close to them getting older or sicker, gently handle your fading flowers and never forget that they deserve to be cherished.

Published: Mon, 22 Jul 2024

http://ruthwrites.online/2024/07/22/fading-flowers/

Fight for your chances

Mon, 13 May 2024

Two nights ago, my husband and son told me to stand up and come down the stairs to see something amazing. I reluctantly struggled into the garden and looked up to see a faint version of what you see in the picture above. They were both so excited and all I could think about was how I would get inside. Shame on me.

I often write about seeing colours in the darkness and defying the odds to achieve something but last night I let my struggles win and the chance which might never happen again in my lifetime nearly passed me by. So today I'm encouraging you to seize every opportunity you are given to live life to the very best of your ability. It might take an effort, it might not happen the way you expect, but have courage and wait to be amazed. Unusually and fortuitously, I may get a second chance tonight*. And I will do it better. I will look up at the sky and treasure what it offers to me. The words 'ok' and 'not that spectacular' will not come out of my ungrateful lips. Because this is a second chance to take hold of something very special.

People talk about FOMO, the fear of missing out. Of course I live with that a lot. But not every time. If you are able, see if you can find a clever way to join in or have the courage to stand up with everyone else. Remember the times you achieved something before and believe you can again. The sky is literally the limit!

Do you remember the last time you felt excited? Try and feel it again today. There is always another chance to do something differently. Don't let the reasons not to do something win. There is something you wish you could do. Sit down and think about what that is and do it. I'm in if you are!

*unfortunately the lights did not appear the next night so I am very glad I caught them . Now I see that living life as though you have only one chance is the right way to do it.

Published: Mon, 13 May 2024

`http://ruthwrites.online/2024/05/13/fight-for-your-chances/`

Goodbye old friend

Sun, 13 Jul 2014

You were always there, standing tall when I was rushing around, going here and there. Sometimes I forgot to look at you, but you stayed the same, ready to be noticed but unaffected if you weren't. When I sat down with my tea most mornings, there you were, and then we faced each other.

You marked the seasons for me - each arresting in their own way - a waiting period, a space of promise, a celebration time, and then days of beautiful, colourful reflection. Up to last year, you had someone to care for you, to rake up the dead leaves and clear the stage for more. He's gone now - another of my beloved daily companions.

Maybe that's why they did it. If I had been here when they came, I think I would have stood in front of that chain-saw and pleaded for you. You looked healthy to me - your leaves were as luscious as ever. You were too small for your roots to be a problem. Maybe they pushed his widow into it, or maybe she was worried about the raking. But I would have done that, even on my weakest day, if it had meant you'd still be here.

What am I to look at now that you're gone? What is going to remind me that troubles come and go but that some things never change?

I'll have to plant one in my own garden, and hope that the lonely widow sees it and gets some of the comfort that you gave to me, my reassuring tree.

Published: Sun, 13 Jul 2014

http://ruthwrites.online/2014/07/13/goodbye-old-friend/

Lean on me,

Mon, 27 Sep 2021

Lean on each other.

Two days ago, after one of them snapped in two and in the absence of sufficiently tall canes, we put a long bit of string right round all of the sunflowers. It looks terrible but was necessary.

I hated looking at the broken sunflower and felt relief when I saw the rest would be fine, now that they were all supporting each other.

How many feel that they have been struggling to stand alone over the past year and a half? How many have been snapped in two? For some without families or adequate medical support, the only place they were beside someone, if ever, would have been in a socially distanced queue. The only time they were doing something with someone else would have been the NHS clap across the driveway, or the swift handover of groceries with the Tesco driver.

Hugs and handshakes are long gone.

Many have not been touched by anyone apart from the person giving them the vaccine. Mourners have lined the roads, unable to get properly close to the grieving.

My mum and I have been counting the days until we can hug again. The finish line on that one is still retreating into the distance.

This month I have been filling out forms to justify my need for disability support. One of the questions is, 'in minutes, how long can you walk alone, without aids?' The honest answer is, I can't go anywhere without help.

We all need our fellow sunflowers to lean on. What I love about that image is: the weakest ones are holding up the strongest.

That's the wonder of community; even the most broken and unattractive can be pulled into a circle of mutual support so that they can each play their part in strengthening the ones beside them. It becomes difficult to pick out the 'best' because they are all so close together.

Who are you standing beside right now? Is there anyone who is broken and needs lifted up? Anyone by themselves? Remember however weak you feel, you can help someone else if you can only have the courage to get alongside them.

We're all sunflowers after all.

Published: Mon, 27 Sep 2021

http://ruthwrites.online/2021/09/27/lean-on-me/

Let the sea

Mon, 18 Jul 2022

Come to you.

I've been sitting looking out at this tempting pool on the beach in Donegal the last three times I've been here. Watching other people swimming in it. Hearing how blue it looks and how warm it feels. But my legs have decided it is far from my reach. As I watched the high tide moving in yesterday evening it suddenly struck me: the pool might be too far, but when the tide comes in, places to swim are closer and almost possible. Changing your approach and letting go of the original plan is not giving up,

Is there anything that you can see but never reach? Do you dream of being able to do something that your mind tells you is impossible? Let's look at it from a different perspective. Let's believe in alternative ways of achieving what you feel right now will never happen.

I told you about the mobility scooter I nervously tried the other week. On it, I was able to reach places I hadn't been close to for years. It's not the way I wanted, but it brought so much within my mostly tiny world.

Can you see another way of achieving the dreams you feel are slipping away? It is a frustrating way of being, but maybe there is a different solution.

This evening, or maybe some time over the two week holiday, I am going to wait for the tide and try to catch it. So it's not the distant pool but something like it is coming within my reach.

Can you look at your impossible dream and find another way to get it? Or can you do that for the person you see who has given up? I really hope you find a way. Dreams are not only for the go-getters.

They are for everyone.

Published: Mon, 18 Jul 2022

http://ruthwrites.online/2022/07/18/let-the-sea/

Little signs of hope

Wed, 15 Apr 2015

I should be editing my book, or cooking the dinner, but I've been looking at something for the past half-hour, and listening to something since yesterday evening, which deserve to be written about. You possibly remember my blog last year about the tree that was cut down. Well, shortly after that, my mum came round with a tiny Rowan sapling, and we planted it, in the front garden. It's looked like an unpromising stick all winter, as you would expect, and Ryan at one point thought he'd killed it. But, lo and behold! A couple of weeks ago we saw something different at the top of this 'dead' stick, and now, there are three, possibly four, little green branches sprouting from it. The joy that brings to me is immense.

In January, a wise friend wrote to me about the bulbs in her garden - hidden and showing no promise. She said that it was the time to wait, and sent a picture of what they would become. I'm sure they are bursting into colour as I write this, rewarding her patience, and affirming her faith.

Last night when I went to bed early, the birds were still up, and I knew that when I woke this morning, they would be singing again. Of course they were. Another joyful gift.

I am not as grateful as I should be, or as observant of all the many messages God is giving me every day. Messages about waiting and hoping, calls to watch for Him, and listen, reminders that He is still there, and still faithful. So, just open your senses, and I know you'll find Him. Like the bulbs or the dead stick, it might be that He is waiting for you to turn your eyes to Him, and then, prepare to be amazed!

Published: Wed, 15 Apr 2015

http://ruthwrites.online/2015/04/15/little-signs-of-hope/

Nature interrupts

Mon, 12 Jun 2023

This is possibly easy to say when the season is right and the weather is gentle, but I have been enjoying the sound of the wind shaking the leaves around my house. It reminds me that I am not alone, that there are many things in life that are greater than me.

Of course, I am not extolling earthquakes, hurricanes or other life-threatening calamities. But in my tame part of the world, I am thankful for the way the changing seasons can help me with my seemingly static life. There are icy, snowy times when everyone is trapped indoors or days when the rain punishes us for venturing outside, but even then I have memories of teenage boys sliding along slippy pavements, children trying to make snowballs out of a scrape of white on the playground, and running through the streets of Rome under torrential rain. Even traditionally 'bad' weather can hold a lot of joy.

Most of the time we are bound to a list of commitments, but sometimes nature interrupts. Even if, like me, the climate can keep us from going out, there is happiness to be found in looking and listening to the world around us. My son sails in the spring and summer, but he can't when there is no wind. So now every Saturday we hope the weather will let him go. Another lesson in acceptance I suppose.

If you are stressed out, drowning in deadlines, or simply locked in, remember that seasons change and this time will too. Take a moment to watch or listen to the rain, the wind, the sun or the hail and remember that you are held by the One who made them all.

What's the weather like with you today? Whatever it is, I hope you can enjoy it!

Published: Mon, 12 Jun 2023

`http://ruthwrites.online/2023/06/12/nature-interrupts/`

Open up

Mon, 10 Oct 2022

There is one lily in my parents' pond. We have all been watching and waiting for it to show off its petals. One day it did, but since then the leaves are refusing to unfurl. It could be the cold weather, it could be the changing season, but nothing will get it to open.

Isn't that very like us? We dare to reveal part of who we are, and if the circumstances are not right, we retreat back into our shell. Maybe someone laughed or criticised, maybe something went wrong in our lives. But, whatever the reason, we are not taking any chances again.

I can see that in my family. My daughter used to be a lot more outgoing but then she changed school and got quiet. Someone pointed out my son was going red and he rarely does anything in public now. These things could be simply growing up, but I wonder...

It is funny how we remember the times we failed so much more clearly than our successes. Every time I put one foot in front of the other I need to push the memories of falling out of my mind and remind myself of all the uneventful walks I've done instead.

What about you? Does the bad seem to win out over the good when you make plans? Has pain become the only thing you can anticipate feeling now? Are your doors closed to outsiders, new chances or a new you? Or can you find the courage to show your true colours?

We have to be so mindful of others when you think about what happens when ridicule or neglect closes them up. When we want our nervy dog to come to us, we open our arms wide and call her name. Is there someone you know that needs you to do that for them? The benefit of that is, it can be so rewarding for you too.

Published: Mon, 10 Oct 2022

http://ruthwrites.online/2022/10/10/open-up/

Singing in the rain

Mon, 15 Jul 2024

It was mostly cloudy and rainy during our holiday in Donegal last week. As we travelled home yesterday I asked my usual question, 'what were the highlights?'. Silence. I realised I couldn't think of any either. Not a good sign. Then I heard that not only had my in-laws' flight home been cancelled but their luggage hadn't arrived back when they did

I'm sure everyone has tales of worse holiday disasters. On the wettest day, after me saying there was no point going anywhere, we found ourselves travelling through lashing rain and grey countryside to a deserted beach we'd never been to before. As I sat in the car, I watched my dog tearing around, having so much fun it took a while to get her back on the lead. Even though I didn't experience it, the rest had had a wet but enlivening time. That, now I think of it, was the best day.

I am well aware that sometimes it is impossible to see anything good when life can be so hard. Eventually my son said it was a relaxing holiday even though the weather wasn't good. I also remembered that sunny days mean realising I can't get down to the beach to swim so the rain actually meant everyone was inside with me.

So when the rain pours and you are stuck indoors, look around you and enjoy the company. Or a good book.

I challenge you to find something positive, even when life is bleak. That fight for positivity can bring sunlight to you, even on the rainiest of days.

'Even the darkness will not be dark to you; the night will shine like the day, for darkness is as light to you.'

Psalm 139v12.

Published: Mon, 15 Jul 2024

http://ruthwrites.online/2024/07/15/singing-in-the-rain-2/

Sit down a while, remember..

Thu, 17 Aug 2017

smile.

Those words were engraved into the top of a park bench in Ards Friary, Co Donegal. Now, you all know I'm partial to a bit of bench sitting, but I've never sat on one that had its own instructions.

To be honest, I was too distracted by the beautiful view of woodland, golden sand and clear water to do anything but the first part of that command, but for days later I thought about it.

Memories are tricky things - they can bring back a world of pain in an instant, they can feed bitterness, they can distort the truth of the past. This time, however, the line on the seat was careful to direct the sitter's thoughts towards happiness.

When somebody dies, those closest to them take a long time before they can truly smile at the thought of their loved one. But when that becomes possible, grief can occasionally subside a little to let in joy. And healing. My auntie reminded us all recently of a funny thing my granny did on the day she died, and every time I think about it, I'm laughing. She was a hilarious wee lady sometimes. My husband's granny passed away just last weekend, but already the grandchildren are remembering happy things about her, in the midst of their deep sadness.

I suppose the Irish wake provides that crucial opportunity to reminisce and have a chuckle over incidents or funny quirks of the life that has gone. There is something really special about shared remembering, and the shared laughter that results. Things that were unnoticed or forgotten are brought to mind, and all at once the person who has left this world is brought close again.

So here's to good memories, and the relief they can bring.

Give it a go - think of someone you miss, search your mind for something they did or said...and smile!

Published: Thu, 17 Aug 2017

http://ruthwrites.online/2017/08/17/sit-down-a-while-remember/

The best place

Tue, 04 Aug 2015

I'm sitting here with the most heavenly of views beside me. August has only just begun, but the winds are up already, alternately bringing light and shade, forcing the sea to turn a different blue every second. It was part turquoise last time I looked, but now it's dark, dark blue, with small tufts of white spray bouncing across the deeper bay. Cloud shadows chase each other along the mottled sand, over the green and rocky headland. The hills across the sea are almost hidden, telling the story of the rain we had earlier, and hopefully won't have again. I can't see Muckish mountain from here, or I would know what's coming. I can only crane to see the sky behind me, and it's a promising blue mixed with sprinting wisps. They could gang up and block the sun. They could make rain. But right now, it is dry and bright, and in Donegal, you take what you get.

I love the sound of the wind here - howling down the chimney, pushing against the trees, making them dance. Every once in a while, it drops, and there is respite, but never for long. There aren't many birds out now save a few darting, diving gulls. I can hear a couple chirping in the bushes, but they're not showing themselves. I don't blame them. The sleek-coated cows are back in the field below. I saw the farmer earlier, and thought they'd been moved. I was told once what it meant for the weather when they were lying down or standing up, but I have no idea which way is good. But then, every type of weather here holds its own beauty, and today I have the privilege of watching them all.

Published: Tue, 04 Aug 2015

http://ruthwrites.online/2015/08/04/the-best-place/

The blackbird's song

Mon, 30 Mar 2020

I couldn't write my usual blog last week because I saw so many people telling us how to think, feel and behave and I felt yet another one of the same would be too much.

I'm returning to my usual today because I miss the discipline of positive thinking I practise every Monday. I've partially replaced it with my daily candle-lighting tryst, but I do have another tiny thought to share with you now...

Last week on a sunny freezing afternoon I forced myself to sit outside without Twitter, Facebook, whatsApp or children (😬). I was expecting to hear more sounds of nature than usual, although not to the extent people in Wuhan experienced it. When there was a break in traffic- hopefully just our heroes racing towards Craigavon hospital- I did enjoy one birdsong very much. I think it was only last year that I traced the tuneful sound to the opened, uplifted yellow beak to a blackbird. You all probably knew this already, but out of that uncolourful, dark bird comes one of the most beautiful songs in the garden.

You know my inclination to find light in the darkness, good in the bad, or to 'stumble into grace' as I once put it. Maybe, while also acknowledging the seriousness, darkness, grief and pain of this time, we can keep ourselves going by finding a way to savour the short songs of joy and kindness that are offered to us every day. Like the blackbird's song.

My daughter made a gratitude jar today as class-work. The idea is that each day you write down three things you are grateful for. As I have heard a number of times in a number of places, gratitude fights anxiety. Right now, I am grateful for her reminder, and for the blackbird who sang me out of my doldrums last week.

I wonder what you're grateful for today? You never know, doing this might go a way flattening the curve of fear too.

Published: Mon, 30 Mar 2020

: http://ruthwrites.online/2020/03/30/the-blackbirds-song/

The importance of

Mon, 17 Jul 2023

A good view. Even if it's just a slit of blue sky or the branch of a tree, the presence of nature can do positive things for the soul.

There are many who don't have the luxury of leafy streets or broad expanses of sky. Maybe they are stuck in a hospital bed with only metal rungs and their own feet in front of them. Or the flap of their flimsy tent that was never meant to be a permanent home. Or the constraining corners of a tiny room where they desperately wait for a rescue. I can't speak for them, only to say when you can see more than that, be thankful.

Of course, even when the most heavenly of views is right in front of you, you can feel sad. Is it possible, I wonder, to carry beauty inside of yourself when you are in a hard, empty place? Can you put your imagination to work and bring sparkling seas into your dark world?

Two days ago I saw an elderly woman sitting on a bench looking out to the sea. She was there when I arrived and still there when I left. She seemed peaceful and happy. But who knows? Would I have said the same if she had been sitting opposite me in a doctor's waiting room?

What about you? Can you conjure up a memory of something good when you are sitting in darkness? I find it nearly impossible to do, but maybe that is an important skill to develop. Having something beautiful to look at is a blessing, but can we practice carrying that wherever we go, whatever the circumstance?

Tomorrow I will be sitting attached to a drip for my next treatment in a room that looks out onto a car park. Can I practice bringing the memories of a good view closer to me ? Can you?

Published: Mon, 17 Jul 2023

http://ruthwrites.online/2023/07/17/the-importance-of/

The louder voice

Mon, 24 Jun 2024

I was listening to the birds again this morning and the loudest ones (crows) were drowning out the others. I've been thinking about that today- how often do you notice when you or somebody else is talked over by a louder person? I have found that when you are below other people, it is easy to be unheard.

The smaller, quieter birds have beautiful songs but you need to focus on them to properly hear. It's like children too. My daughter has the quietest voice, but give her a microphone and she shines. Here's what I want you to do: think of someone in your life who is often unheard and give them your attention.

I love it when people pull up a chair and talk with me if I'm sitting down, which is pretty much all the time. Two different people on separate occasions got down on their knees to speak to me. I won't forget that.

So this week, remember the crows and listen for the pure song that quietly rises beneath them. Remember that unheard ones deserve your attention and if it's you that feels unnoticed think about the God who sees every sparrow that falls and most certainly, fixes His eye on you

Published: Mon, 24 Jun 2024

`http://ruthwrites.online/2024/06/24/the-louder-voice/`

The wild wood

Thu, 09 Aug 2018

It was a dark, terrifying place a fair walk away from the house in Donegal. My brother used to go there for an adventure. I never went, and perhaps for that reason, it became even wilder in my head. Foolishly I thought if I refused to go there, its skin-tearing brambles, suffocating bracken and dark shadows would stay safely out of reach.

But I learnt a tough lesson when I grew up: you may not want to go there, but the wild woods will, inevitably, come to you. For me they take the form of a disease. For others it's grief, or depression, or broken relationships, or abuse. I hate, hate those wild woods.

I was reading the brilliant chapter in The Wind in The Willows where mole ventures into the Wild Wood to find Badger. He gets lost but then Rat comes with his pistols and they eventually, accidentally, come upon Badger's house. At first I thought, we could all do with a Rat in our lives, but then I realised that it was Moley who was the hero. He braved the woods because he was deeply concerned about Badger being lonely.

When you think about it, we can all be brave, concerned Moles or experienced Rats seeking out Badgers.

And, unlike Mole, we've all been there before.

Published: Thu, 09 Aug 2018

http://ruthwrites.online/2018/08/09/the-wild-wood/

Tiny things

Mon, 20 Sep 2021

My mum sent this photo a few days ago, marvelling at how something so amazing came from a tiny seed, dropped by a bird as he flew over her garden. She welcomed it as a promise that one day she too will be given a new, lasting life to replace the old tired version she has right now.

On this rainy day I'm noticing how the smallest of gestures can turn your life around; someone stepping in to type in a code at the self-service aisle when you've lost your balance, the dog making the end of your blanket into her bed, a robin landing on the fence opposite, the persistent tweeting that starts before the light, an impossibly happy smile from a baby. For the giver, these things might go unnoticed but for the person on the receiving end, these tiny things can mean the world.

That bird who dropped the seed, the man who entered the code, the robin who perched and the baby who smiled may not have known the changes they brought about. But you do.

It cost them nothing, but to you it meant everything. So next time you lend a hand, open a door or even just smile, remember that you may have had a sunflower's impact on someone else's day.

Published: Mon, 20 Sep 2021

http://ruthwrites.online/2021/09/20/tiny-things/

Walls, prickles and hackles

Mon, 22 Oct 2018

I've been thinking about defences today. Our dog discovered a very foolish hedgehog in the garden this morning. It was the unknown intruder to her, the prickly thing she didn't understand. She danced menacingly round it, barking. My husband stood in front of the terrified creature, waiting for a chance to grab the dog. Her response was even more hysterical than when she encounters cats. Interestingly, her hackles were not up this time though. Maybe part of her realises that this animal was more frightened of her than she was of it. She got too close once, and got spiked for it. So much barking, but at a safe distance. The thing about our dog is, she's nervous of most things, and wants nothing as much as her safe bed in her house near her people. She has scared people before, but what they don't realise is, she's like the hedgehog - all prickle and bluster.

Thinking about people, I feel the same is true a lot of the time; the bullies were often once the bullied, the hurt pull up their security defences and the weak turn in on themselves. There's a face I see quite often, and I'm sure you know it too: the eyes are down, the jaw is set, the mouth is tight; nothing shown, nothing offered. Nearly always, the story behind that face is one of pain, and fear of getting hurt again. How can they uncurl and experience life, if the last time they laid themselves bare, they were almost destroyed? The only answer I have to that is patience and love.

We got the dog in and waited. After a while the hedgehog stuck out his head, dug a little escape route and left the garden, hopefully never to return. It took longer for the dog to come down from her fright. She's asleep now at last. If only she had realised the hedgehog needed space and time.

Are you playing the waiting game with any hedgehogs in your life? Just remember there are prickles and bide your time.

Mrs Tiggywinkle's in there somewhere.

Published: Mon, 22 Oct 2018

http://ruthwrites.online/2018/10/22/walls-prickles-and-hackles/

Pandemic

A pocket full of posies

Mon, 16 Mar 2020

That nursery rhyme has been stuck on repeat in my head for at least a week now. Did you know that it was only in the mid 20th century that people associated it with the Plague and Black Death? When it was originally sung or chanted in the 17th century, there was no such dark association. Fake news and misinformation again! Anyway, it was the title line that I've been fixating on. What do we do at a time like this, when fear, dread and isolation are pressing in on us? Apart from buying so many tins and toilet rolls that the basket-carrying few get nothing?

What I'm thinking about now is, do I have enough inner resources to keep me going? And what are they? What is in my metaphorical pocket? What's in yours?

Definitely, the ability to write down my thoughts and share them with you has become even more precious. The indulgence of creating fictional worlds is also a welcome escape. Memories of good times, sunny holidays, loved ones that have already gone before us, music we've played or sang, even a joke so funny it has us laughing years after its first telling. A couple of months ago I tried to write down the stories my dad used to tell about his childhood escapades. It utterly failed. Some stories are all in the telling sadly. And the telling requires gathering together by a crackling roaring fire. So, right now, the memory of that is all I have.

That's the thing though. This is 'right now' but not forever. Forever is a whole other story that lasts from this present moment and continues way beyond it. Forever gives us a perspective that both treasures the right now and points to something far, far better. I have a small, temporary pocketful of resources that help with the present moment, but I also have a shield of faith* in an eternal God that can hold fast against whatever the world throws at me. You can have that too, if you only ask.

The best thing is, there's an abundant, never-ending supply.

*Ephesians 6, 10-18

Published: Mon, 16 Mar 2020

http://ruthwrites.online/2020/03/16/a-pocket-full-of-posies/

Being one of the 'only's

Mon, 09 Mar 2020

Last week I read a tweet criticising the common tendency now to dismiss the coronavirus as something that will affect only the elderly and the vulnerable: the 'only's'.

Being an only myself I have been feeling increasingly angry about this celebration of the fittest. Boris Johnson is smugly preparing to 'take it on the chin'. Others wave the threat of it away with their hand and an eye-roll. "It won't be a problem."

This morning I spent twenty minutes driving round searching, praying for a parking space. I ended up in one too far away for me to walk the distance. As I staggered to my destination I passed a car park with tens of empty spaces. It was barricaded off with the sign 'staff only'. I could have wept. Walking back, people stepped down on the road to overtake me. Not one stopped and offered their help. I was an 'only' to them. Or that's the way I felt.

Just a gentle thought: one day, all of us will be shut out, pushed away and overtaken by someone fitter, smarter and younger than we are. Even Boris will not be able to defeat that with his inimitable chin.

Next time you're out somewhere, have a look around and see the 'only's. Walk beside them and cherish your time with them. Because one day, that will be you.

Published: Mon, 09 Mar 2020

http://ruthwrites.online/2020/03/09/being-one-of-the-onlys/

Complicating kindness

Mon, 11 May 2020

I've had this knot in my chest since Saturday. Why? I read a tweet by someone who, rightfully or not, was destroying the act of clapping for the NHS every Thursday night. Admittedly, she did work for the NHS and had a very valid argument for her objection, mainly to do with the Conservative party. She turned it into the notion of people clapping while medical staff walked, poorly protected, to their deaths. She was, unfairly in my opinion, muddying the waters of good intention. I shook my head throughout the whole critique. No, you are being unfair to so many good people here.

Speaking for myself, I am not clapping because I agree with Boris, or out of an ignorance that there has not been a deadly incompetence amongst our politicians. I am clapping for my friends, my cousins, my sister-in-law, my doctors because it's the only thing I can offer right now. It's neighbourly too.

If we always saw a hundred sides to every act of kindness and let them stop us, there wouldn't be anything left. Silent streets, closed doors, needy people passed by. There is too much pride wrapped up in not doing what may be the kindest thing. Is it not better to step out and offer our help, however many objections our arm-folded observers have?

Many years ago, I shrank away from kindness because I read too much into it. Now I welcome care, consideration, even love with a grateful smile. People just want to help sometimes, no ulterior motive whatsoever.

There have been so many acts of kindness during these dark times. Deliveries made to isolating vulnerable neighbours, stepping aside to allow people to pass by safely, carrying groceries, parcels, even plants to our doors to help reduce the spread of this virus, and clapping. Not to say we're Conservatives. Not to support the danger people are putting themselves in every day to care for others but just, with no agenda, very simply, to show kindness. I truly hope that it is accepted in that way too.

Published: Mon, 11 May 2020

http://ruthwrites.online/2020/05/11/complicating-kindness/

I see you

Mon, 13 Apr 2020

At the beginning of lock-down I persuaded my parents to have a Duo call with me. My mum said "peepo!" when she saw me. Last week we had a zoom church service. The first five minutes were filled with people seeing their friends and saying hi. Over and over. It was funny but also the most joyful thing I've seen in this dark time.

I keep trying to think of a way, something, to replace the precious hug or handshake. I haven't found any words that suffice. The closest thing we have is the chance to see one another. That's more than we could have even ten years ago. So it's awkward, clunky and slightly boring, but the chance to look into the face of someone you care about is a true gift.

I've been worrying about the people near and far who desperately long to be seen; the children trapped in a tiny house, trying to keep away from an abusive parent, people living alone, trying to keep themselves safe, those who are grieving with no grave, last moments or funeral to look back on, the medical staff who keep asking for more PPE and feeling no-one is hearing them, those who are far from home and unable to get a connection to speak to their loved ones. The list is endless. All we can do, all I'm trying to do, is to pray to the One who always sees and hears. We can't reach many of the unseen, but we can pray.

Of course, those of us who have the privilege, yes, you heard me home-schoolers, of being within touching distance of our family, let's not squander it. Hold your people close and thank God you have them.

Published: Mon, 13 Apr 2020

http://ruthwrites.online/2020/04/13/i-see-you/

If a picture paints a thousand words,

Mon, 06 Jul 2020

Then how many words for a hug?

Throughout this dark, socially distant lockdown, I've been trying to think of ways to compensate for not being able to hug my mum. At the beginning I thought surely, with all my words, I'll be able to construct something that's as good as a hug. An instant later, I realised nothing is ever going to suffice. Advertisers have often tried to sell something as being as good. Remember cupasoup's 'hug in a mug'? Hot chocolate, wine, bubble bath, slankets (where have they gone now?) all tried to do something that felt as warm and comforting as human arms. I'm not sure that any succeeded.

A couple of months ago I saw some people had fabricated a sheet with arms pegged to a washing line that you could use to "safely" embrace someone you weren't living with. Still looked too risky to me. You can post a creepy cut-out torso with arms to someone too. How do you get those paper arms round you?!

When I see selfies of people with their arms round each other, even if that's apologised for after the fact, I feel a little angry. The hug, to many of us, is a delicate, precious, risky thing. To casually do it is to say, this hug may cost a life, but hey ho.

So I'm stumped. And then there's the people who have been living alone. The elderly who have limited visits from their family, served tea by masked but amazingly brave care workers. The children returning to school, leaving their mums and dads behind. What happens when they fall in the playground or just miss being close to their friends?

Maybe it was easier to hug without thinking about it before all this.

Maybe it costs more to say those brave words, 'I love you.'

Maybe we need to hug better when we get the chance.

We definitely need to not forget what we missed when it returns again.

Published: Mon, 06 Jul 2020

http://ruthwrites.online/2020/07/06/if-a-picture-paints-a-thousand-words/

Living without applause

Mon, 31 Aug 2020

I caught some of the proms the other night. There was a glaring absence however. The diminished orchestra was there. The animated conductor was there. But the audience was not.

The music rose and fell as normal but when it stopped, there was silence. At the end of the performance, after a time of nothing, they applauded each other. It just didn't feel right.

These days, sports teams carry on behind closed doors with no supporters to cheer them on. Musicians are reduced to online concerts, authors are doing virtual launches for their new books, ministers are preaching to a screen instead of a room of faces. All these things are unavoidable in the current climate. All require new levels of self-assurance and a fair amount of staying power.

It got me thinking, how many achievements and performances do we manage that never get any acknowledgement or recognition? How do we keep going without it?

I think it's a 21st century requirement to be seen and congratulated on everything. With this digital age, there's no excuse I suppose. The downside is when you're putting yourself out there and still no-one is acknowledging you. I've been there many times friends.

So, what to do? I remember when I faced my fears and got on a bike for the first time in years. When I pushed it back into the garage I put my fist in the air and said 'yes!'. I published my first book and my husband ran up the stairs with it to 'get the author's signature'. I've leant against our house wall many times after a struggle from the park and thought 'I made it!' The audience of one is the most common one isn't it?

For most of us, being praised by ourselves or one other person is all we can hope for. For this reason, we have to keep our eyes peeled and every time we see someone achieving something that is small in the world's eyes but huge in their own, we have to congratulate them.

Lonely victories are seldom repeated. So take those hesitant hands out of your pockets and get better at praising other people. If we can all applaud our health workers, then surely we can tell a friend they're doing great.

So to all you sleep-deprived mothers struggling to get through the day and hiding your tears, to anyone searching for work or a new home, to any unseen child teaching themselves when no-one else has time for them, to anyone taking their first shaky steps after an operation or finishing their first cycle of treatment, to the lonely managing to do it all by themselves, for all the unnoticed, tiny yet massive achievements, I applaud you.

Keep it up. You are amazing!

Published: Mon, 31 Aug 2020

http://ruthwrites.online/2020/08/31/living-without-applause/

Look intently

Mon, 10 Jun 2019

I've been thinking about lost or disappearing people recently. Lost because illness or age are swallowing up who they once were, disappearing because few are noticing what is happening to them.

I remember one of the first blogs I ever wrote I continually asserted 'I am Ruth', as I battled to come to terms with being 'the person with MS' and nothing more. I still struggle with that. I've noticed that getting my walking stick out is the equivalent of Harry Potter's invisibility cloak. People often look away, and I have to paste an overly bright smile on my face to win them back. I don't blame them - they're just trying to keep me from embarrassment or shame.

Last week, a number of people came into my awareness who are not what they once were - heroic, vibrant, attractive souls who are a shadow of the person they used to be. As I thought about them, I felt so much sadness. But then I realised what I had to do: I had to assert their identity the way I did in that blog. Whatever has happened to people close to us, we've got to fight to keep the things that make them them. We've got to look intently, search hopefully and take hold of the precious parts of them, never giving up or letting them go.

I gave pink flowers to one of those people last week because they reminded me of her. When she saw them she turned and said to the person beside her,

"They know me."

If you think hard enough, you'll maybe remember someone in the edges of your world who needs to be seen and known again.

I hope you have the courage to find them.

Published: Mon, 10 Jun 2019

http://ruthwrites.online/2019/06/10/look-intently/

Look!

Mon, 24 Jan 2022

A new thing is coming!

As COVID throws its heavy blankets of fatigue over my already tired body, I have been close to giving up all hope. I forgot to laugh, to sing, to look out at the blue skies, to step into the garden and breathe in fresh air. The idea of making a change or trying something that may be scary but could be good didn't even enter my head. When we decide we are tired and everything is too much then it is very easy to give up.

Last week I was given a bunch of green stalks. On a second look I realised they were daffodils. Two days after that, the closed heads began to open. Then, full, bright, beautiful yellow flowers appeared. Just like that, I remembered that things can change. We can change.

As I write this I'm remembering that there are steps I can take to improve my situation. Like asking for help. That's a good place to start, isn't it? It can feel like we're beyond help, that we have left it too late. Not true. I'm working up the courage to get someone in to clean for me. But every time I look at the state of my usually pristine house, I don't want anyone to see it. I'll probably clean it myself then get a cleaner. Ridiculous I know.

If we wait until we are more presentable, if we put it off until 'a better time' it might never happen. When the flower heads are still closed, when the blankets are smothering us, that's the time for change to begin. And remember, there are people who are skilled in helping us. My husband would wander round a shop for ages, hoping to find things by himself. Don't be like that. Search for someone who can help and ask for it. It's much quicker and more thorough that way.

Do you see that things are overwhelming you right now? Even if you're giving up, there are still hands to reach out to, or ears to listen. If I had not realised the green stalks were the beginning of flowers, I would have missed their glorious change. If you can't see it yourself, ask someone else to point it out to you. Because you are on the cusp of something wonderful.

Watch for it.

Spring is coming.

Published: Mon, 24 Jan 2022

http://ruthwrites.online/2022/01/24/look/

Making do

Mon, 20 Apr 2020

During these sparse, empty cupboard times the phrase 'making do' keeps coming to mind. I've discovered that I am not gifted at this. Other people can make gourmet meals out of scraps, high fashion from rags and shop-worthy cards from things that were just 'lying around'.

There are some who are not realistically making do though. You know the types- 'all you need to make this simple meal is olives, fresh herbs from your garden and a small handful of things that have been languishing in your pantry.' You know, like strong white flour and a box of yeast. And a bottle of amazing prosecco to wash it down with. Friends, I do not have a pantry, and, unlike Nigella or Mary, I DO NOT have strong white flour.

A few days ago the Tesco man was unable to bring the naan I'd ordered, so I thought, fine, I'll make it myself. I didn't have the yeast or enough of the type of flour I needed but I thought I could wing it with the soda bread flour my husband had come sheepishly back with the other day. I optimistically left the dry, unkneadable ball to 'prove' for fifteen useless minutes, peered at it and then threw it out.

This morning I decided to make my best friend from school a birthday card. I was only sticking a photo onto card, what could possibly go wrong? Ha. The photo was bigger than the card so I thought I would just trim it. Even me and scissors don't mix well. The result, as you'll see in a few days Rebecca, looks like a five year old did it. I hate crafts and in these fuzzy, unmotivated times, nothing is suddenly, miraculously going to come together.

It's a little disappointing because I would say both my grannies would have done very well at this. One with her ability to make soup out of things she scavenged in the woods and the other with her 'waste not want not' mentality. That woman could make a tea bag last at least three times.

One thing I have learnt is to appreciate everything that arrives through my door from the weekly Tesco shop. Seeing the blue self-raising flour in the bag last week was a very happy moment. A month ago, I wouldn't have thought twice about it.

Beyond groceries and cards, I'm trying to appreciate the above and beyond parts of my life- the luxury (mostly) of having my family close by, the delight of knowing I will check in with my parents every day, the treat of stopping and sitting down with a good book. These things are so much better than flour or baking successes.

I probably won't come out of this desert time with a new skill, or the book I wish I had the focus to write, but I hope I will end it with more appreciation for the gift of the people around me.

Like my granny, I hope I won't waste it.

Published: Mon, 20 Apr 2020

http://ruthwrites.online/2020/04/20/making-do/

My candle

Mon, 04 May 2020

It started one day when I heard that someone had asked for people to light their candles to show solidarity with their self-isolating neighbours.

I can't remember quite how it became a thing I do every night. A few people seemed to appreciate it, and now the faithfulness they thanked me for has made me determined to keep it going.

There have been questions; is the photo an optical illusion, do you really light it every night, why is it still the same size? It is real, I do light it every night, and now it looks like this:

For years now I have been mainly sitting in my house, wishing I could do something, anything to help somebody else. There have been many times when I wanted to get up and give someone a hand but haven't been able to physically manage it. In another life, maybe I would have been the nurse holding the hand of someone struggling to breathe, or the social worker coming to the rescue of abused children, but right now, the one and best thing I have to offer is my candle and the prayers I say with it.

With my candle I say, I am standing with you, you are all my heroes. You are worth remembering and burning my finger tips for! One time I was walking towards the candle and I tripped spectacularly on the rug. It was the fastest fall-recovery I've ever done because I was on a mission to light my candle.

So, for the myriads of people I have named and those I haven't got to yet, this candle is for you.

Thank-you for giving me a tiny purpose in all of this.

Published: Mon, 04 May 2020

http://ruthwrites.online/2020/05/04/my-candle/

Neither up nor down

Mon, 16 Nov 2020

I feel like we are all living this wretched nursery rhyme at the moment. Levels, graphs, numbers are at the forefront of our minds morning, noon and night.

When the numbers go down, our hopes go up and vice versa. The problem is our grand old Duke keeps changing his mind about what direction we should be going and in Northern Ireland, well, our dukes are too busy fighting to lead us anywhere.

I'm not sure that anyone has been 'up' for months now. Most days we could probably describe ourselves as more down than up. Every time a small, good thing happens to me I try to grab onto it like a tiny balloon to help me get further up the mountain. But then, bad news comes along and bursts it.

When we're neither up nor down anxiety about going one way or the other dominates our thinking. We fear one and doubt that the other will ever happen again. But, you know what? The only way to get up the hill is to believe that we will.

Maybe you're sitting at the bottom, making your home there, forgetting that there's anything better for you. Maybe going up or going out is still too scary to attempt. Maybe you're resigned to living at ground level for the foreseeable.

That is why we need our ten thousand men right now. When you realise that there are others in the same position as you, you can share the journey with them, and they with you. For the first time in life, thousands, millions of people are going through the same thing, or similar, as you.

You are not alone. Look to your right, and to your left: we're all marching beside you. And if you have faith you will see that God, the grandest duke of them all, is paving the way for you to get through this.

Published: Mon, 16 Nov 2020

`http://ruthwrites.online/2020/11/16/neither-up-nor-down/`

#nofilter

Mon, 05 Apr 2021

Usually when people use the #nofilterneeded it's because the picture is perfect without any enhancement.

These days, when hairdressers, beauticians, fresh air and a good night's sleep are hard to come by, most of us are badly in need of a soft focus or even a no focus at all lens. It's funny (or not) how at a time when social distance is a mercy we then sit in front of a camera to see everyone else. As time goes on and hair gets greyer, fewer people are happy to be seen.

I have always gladly embraced ways of hiding the toughest sides of myself. Swimming used to be a great way to become like everyone else. Until I struggled out. Sitting on a bench is a fairly good way too, if my poles aren't visible. I used to try and hide them out of view for photographs. I've got over that now.

Is there anything about yourself you're afraid people will see? What do you think will happen if they do? Over this past year I've realised two things; first that people notice very little and second, they are more likely to be kind than not.

I'm a long way off from embracing my grey hair- I mean, if I already walk with a stick then that's enough old lady for me right now! But, beyond learning how to not care what people think is the wonder that people actually do care. A wee girl (she's Emily and she's six) approached me in the park recently, pointed to my poles and asked me what they were. I gave her the short explanation but she followed it up with many questions. She wanted the real story. I hope that when she's sixty she'll still be like that- not afraid of the unfiltered person in front of her, wanting to know the truth.

Is there someone hiding themselves from you right now? Are you strong enough to pursue their real story? Do you care enough? Can you be like Emily (with a touch more sensitivity perhaps)? The visual filters have been unexpectedly lifted away. Are you ready to look beyond the human ones too?

Published: Mon, 05 Apr 2021

http://ruthwrites.online/2021/04/05/nofilter/

Running on empty

Mon, 08 Feb 2021

During these hard pandemic times, everyone has run out of steam.

When I hear the health experts talk on the news these days, I see people who are fed up saying the same things with little result. When the garage door slowly opens to reveal my weary dad, when my mum stands at the door with a carton of freshly baked scones in her hand because she's unable to have us in, when my daughter comes to me with yet another hateful sheet of maths questions, when I realise I've heard more sighs than laughter from my children, when I look at the red ppe marks on our nurses' and doctors' faces, when case numbers are still relentlessly rising, when we realise it has been a year since we hugged our parents, we know we have had enough.

I wonder how ICU staff keep on getting up and going back into long days caring for patients with a sickness they've never encountered before. If one of those nurses was sitting in front of me I would ask them, what do you do when you've done all you can, when there's nothing left to give?

What do you do when you're running on empty? When you're all out of patience with the people you found easy to like when you didn't have to look at them every hour of every day? When you just want it all to go back to the way it was before?

When I feel like that, when I am wrung out, I stop working for a while. But then, if I can, I look about me for people who are not at the end of themselves yet, and use their strength instead. I hate doing that, but they don't hate helping me. In fact, I'm learning that giving away some of yourself can actually increase your strength. When I put down a dinner that everyone likes I get a rush of satisfaction. When I make myself ask the family to help out, there's a joy in watching them figure out how to do that.

When I'm running on empty I often find other things rise up. (Don't apply that thinking to an empty petrol tank though!) Interestingly, it's when I'm at my weakest that my best blog ideas appear, I remember others are struggling as well, I'm overwhelmed by the kindness of people around me and I fill myself up with their goodness to me.

All of us have enough, when we give it away.

What can you give to someone else today? Or how can you ask them to help you?

Published: Mon, 08 Feb 2021

http://ruthwrites.online/2021/02/08/running-on-empty/

The dawn will come

Mon, 23 Aug 2021

There's so much dark around us isn't there? Cases and deaths are rising, people are giving up, our world is battling with violence, injustice, poverty and disease. Our climate is facing catastrophe.

Personally I am going through one of the worst spells with my health. It is so hard to sit in the mud and see any light anywhere. But, I'm telling you and myself this true thing: even after the blackest of nights, the sun will rise.

Aye right I hear you say. Let me tell you, it's hard work to see good when we're swamped with bad. But it's possible, I promise. Two days ago, moments after me feeling sad, my husband made me laugh. Every day my children and my dog bring energy to me. The weather outside reminds me that change is possible. My mum used to always point out blue sky coming, even when the rest of us were moaning about rain. This week she didn't see any break in the bad weather but still she said she was very glad to be in Donegal for it.

I have realised that we have to hold on to hope, whatever hell we're in. Good things are on their way. Change is afoot. If you can believe that, it will transform the way you move through the hardest of times. The Bible tells us that joy comes in the morning and I pin my hope on that.

As my cousin Eilidh Patterson sings, 'this is just the darkest part of night before dawn'.

Watch for it, light is on its way.

Published: Mon, 23 Aug 2021

http://ruthwrites.online/2021/08/23/the-dawn-will-come/

The grey

Mon, 20 Dec 2021

It has been a very colourless time here. Weather-wise I would say for the past week or so but in general, for a lot longer.

The pandemic has kept us from the colour of meeting others, dining out and enjoying concerts. It has muffled our singing, stopped our touching and kept us hidden away in general.

Maybe your life is cloaked in other versions of darkness right now- weighed down by grief, childlessness, poverty, abuse, pain or poor health in mind or in body. The usual rescuers in red and blue are worn out, stifled by restrictions or overwhelmed with the sheer, relentless amount of need.

Where has the colour gone?

I've been thinking about the wise men recently. They were guided by readings and learning but was the star always bright as they traveled? Were they sometimes moving in the dark, just like us now? Did they ever wonder if they'd made a mistake? Even when they looked at an unremarkable baby in a darkened manger? Even if there were some uncertainties, they still gave him the best they had and were always, often silently, led by Someone higher than the heavens.

We're all moving in the darkness now and yet, there is still light to guide us, two thousand years later. The wise men stumbled towards it and now, living in the hope of what they found, we set one foot in front of the other and follow after.

It is so hard to walk in the dark, but others before us have left lights to guide us. I have a drawer stuffed with letters and cards of comfort and hope that give me the colour I need in my grey times.

Above them sits the Book that promises me that

The One True Eternal Light is still there to show us the way.

Published: Mon, 20 Dec 2021

`http://ruthwrites.online/2021/12/20/the-grey/`

The older the fiddle

Mon, 23 Nov 2020

The sweeter the tune.

In this time where our older people are hidden away, living alone, surviving on 'window visits' and masked encounters, I wanted to spend time honouring them.

Rightfully we show our appreciation for our NHS heroes, but what about the many facing the winter of their lives alone? What about the ones who do not understand why they can't be surrounded by their family? Those who don't remember from one day to the next why their children don't come visit any more? The dead who are only mourned publicly by a legally restricted few?

I don't know why we think that age brings this sudden tolerance of neglect. When does that happen? At 70? 80?

It doesn't. We just stop looking and listening to the seated members of our community. Maybe we stop because it's breaking our heart and we have no idea how to help.

Close your eyes for a moment and imagine you're sitting in a magnolia room, in a chair that was not chosen by you. The air is choking with disinfectant. The windows are shut. You know someone will come in and out but you will never see their smile, just their worn out eyes. You see the sun is shining but you won't be out to feel it. Once a day, if you're lucky, someone you love will stand at a distance from you and shout through the open window at you. You won't see their smile either, just tear-filled eyes. You'll reach out your hands but they won't be allowed to hold them.

These people once fought wars, taught, healed, mothered, farmed, campaigned and did so much for us. They are still here. Needing our acknowledgment and care. Never, never shrugged shoulders when they become another number.

Usually I like to end my blog with suggestions about what we can do now. Sadly, I've got very little this time. Write down your memories of your old people, if they're alive and you're able. Be their window person and crinkle up your eyes so they know you're smiling. Pray for them always.

And don't forget they are the sweetest tune you'll ever hear.

Published: Mon, 23 Nov 2020

http://ruthwrites.online/2020/11/23/the-older-the-fiddle/

The storm

Sun, 16 Jan 2022

Lying awake last night, listening to the coughs of family members, the story of Jesus calming the storm came to mind.

As I thought about the panic, fear and frustration the disciples must have felt, I saw the same in myself. When things are going badly, sometimes unexpectedly, we have a human tendency to shriek at Jesus for His intervention. It often feels that He is unresponsive and we panic on. But in the storm that day there were two true things: Jesus was there and He was doing something: resting, safe in the knowledge He was on His Father's path.

It comforts me that Jesus was there. And when He was pestered by human fear, He immediately dealt with it. Then. But what about now? When the waves in our lives are breaking into our boats? The fear is as real as it was for the disciples but the answer is, for our human time scale, slow. I heard someone say that that God is never early, but He's never late either.

The only way to keep going is to live in the knowledge that Jesus is still here with us, and our story is completely known by Him. He's patiently waiting for the perfect time to calm our storms. I'll not lie, I desperately wish there was a sudden, immediate answer. But that is held within the hands of our Eternal Father.

One day, I'll see Him stand up and calm every storm, in me and in you. After that, we will finally be able to stop fretting and start worshipping as we were designed to do.

Published: Sun, 16 Jan 2022

http://ruthwrites.online/2022/01/16/the-storm/

The void

Mon, 29 Mar 2021

This past year has been a time of learning new skills, getting used to staring at a screen or looking down a camera lens. It has felt like launching our talks, prayers, thoughts, even ourselves, into an empty void.

Being a writer I'm well used to publishing my work without much acknowledgement or thanks. When someone appreciates it, it makes my day and gives me the push to keep going.

Being heard is the most precious thing.

Do you know anyone who is giving their everything but not getting anything back? Is there something you can do for them? To say 'I hear you', 'I see you'. Right now I'm imagining you all bent over your phones or iPads reading this. I'm looking into the emptiness and hoping someone is there, benefitting from this.

I came across the line this morning, 'I don't need to be heard, I need to learn to hear.' Maybe it's time to pause our talking or writing or striving for recognition. Maybe it's time to hear; to look for people who are crying for help in the darkness, who feel like no-one is listening.

Of course I would love recognition for what I do, but I know that it's so much more important to acknowledge the people who need to be heard right now.

So, say a loud amen to the ministers preaching to a faceless congregation, wildly applaud the authors launching their work into the silent unknown, listen out for the whispered cries, search for the forgotten ones.

Everyone deserves that.

Published: Mon, 29 Mar 2021

http://ruthwrites.online/2021/03/29/the-void/

When life won't go clockwise

Mon, 01 Feb 2021

As it was during the first lockdown, something has been brought back now:

It's the clockwise one-way system round the parks.

That would be fine for most, but definitely not for me. For a long time now, the idea of doing a lap of anything is beyond me. The last time, when I had done enough, I had to step out of the circuit and take an alternative route across the uneven ground, not meeting the eyes of the other walkers following the correct direction. This time round, seeing the sign up again stopped me dead. I don't have the energy to follow zig zags or trip over lumps of grass. So I don't go in to the park any more.

When we can't be the people the world assumes we can be, when we can't do the things it asks of us, it's lonely, frustrating and often humiliating. Some days it's easy to hold our heads high and see other people's respect. Other days...

Years ago I made a T-shirt that said, 'Go against the flow'. Little did I know then that thirty years later I would be doing that in a literal sense. I still like the times when I'm doing the same things as everyone else- like sitting in a group, or driving. I still have to swallow strange shyness, (or is it pride?) when I have to do something that makes me different, like using trekking poles to walk in a residential area, or taking advantage of my blue badge to mount a kerb instead of using the car park that's further away. There's something that needs to happen in those times: either stop caring or, if that's too hard, stop thinking.

The mad thing is, I'm quite certain that nobody would ever challenge me on my contrary choices. My neighbour does ask me if it's snowing when he sees me with my poles and I laugh it off but one of these days... I hate walking away from a standing group to find somewhere to sit down. I wish I could be like 'most people'. But then the question rises up:

Who else is like me? There must be other people who have been stopped by the one-way signs, or mothers who are struggling to keep up with all the assumptions that life with a new baby is a pure joy, or homeschooling parents who post work that took tears and tantrums to achieve, or pastors who are quietly crumbling behind that smile, or people glad of face masks because they can't even look happy these days.

Life can't always go clockwise. Everyone falls off the treadmill at some point. We can't always keep going in the right direction. Brave faces can't hold up indefinitely.

So what can we do?

Don't be ashamed to step off the path, don't be afraid of the rough ground and don't forget that you are not alone.

Next time I venture into the park I will think about all of you, step off the path and go against the flow. I really hope to see you there too.

Published: Mon, 01 Feb 2021

http://ruthwrites.online/2021/02/01/when-life-wont-go-clockwise/

Parenting

429

A ribbon of grace

Mon, 01 Jul 2019

I had a disastrous cake day on Saturday. The day was already busy, but I found myself baking two cakes and encountering failure both times.

It was my son's birthday last Tuesday and I made him a perfect cake. But this weekend, all the relatives were coming expecting to sing around another one (or so I told myself). When the first came out overcooked I ignored instructions to just buy another and started a sponge cake. But I was tired, forgot to grease the tins properly and then failed to empty them out at the right time. As I was shaking them upside down later on and watching some bits fall out, some stay in, I realised I should never have started.

I cried a lot, always more than the situation merits, and just gave up. Thankfully, my husband skilfully stuck it all together with jam while I stood with my hands over my face.

The next day was singing around the cake day. I had feelings similar to standing there with no clothes on thinking about everyone seeing the state of that darned cake. But then I remembered the ribbon. It wrapped round the faulty cake, completely covering its messiness. If I hadn't said anything (naturally I told everyone the whole sorry tale), no-one would have noticed.

I found myself thinking about grace that day and hiding brokenness. It might be seeing the shadow of your neighbour, bowed with grief, through the narrow slits of the garden fence, or a friend hiding her sadness behind sunglasses, a lonely person laughing too loudly, a child backing onto a corner when everyone else has found a playmate, curtains never pulled back, doors permanently locked shut.

Sometimes, hiding away is the only way to cope, but other times we need someone to stand beside us and help us face the world again. I still much prefer it when my children walk beside me because somehow I feel like they cover me a little and give me courage too.

Is there anyone behind a door or a fence who needs your help with their lives? Maybe they just need somebody to hide with for a while. Maybe they need a ribbon of grace. Let's go softly and seek them out.

Published: Mon, 01 Jul 2019

http://ruthwrites.online/2019/07/01/a-ribbon-of-grace/

All those mattresses

Mon, 17 Jun 2019

Would squash the toughest of peas.

Let's be clear: I'm not rooting for the princess here. Show a little heart for the poor legume!

I'm discovering that June, albeit my birthday month, is a month where more and more stuff gets piled on-school events, teacher-presents to sort out, forms to fill in, books to sign, medical appointments to attend, school uniform to buy (because the shop has decided to have their sale on now. Unhelpfully). By the time the school holidays arrive, I'm ready to climb into bed and lie on top of the mattress, not beneath it.

It's the unexpected stuff that's the worst; an official letter lands on your doormat, someone you know gets sick, children break bones...

Do you ever think, how much more???

But somehow, we mostly get through to the other side. I wish I could have the energy to 'go to the mattresses' and deal with everything Marlon Brando style, but I'm done. Flattened. Weighed down. If only there was a way to get out. Writing this, making lists and taking one mattress at a time is my only solution. When they all pile up, it's impossible to see a way out. But, one at a time, they're easier to shift.

I wish life was about swooning onto a soft heap and complaining about the little things, but it's not as easy pea-sy (sorry!) as that. It's weight-lifting, prioritising, exhausting chaos.

Still, there's always a bed waiting at the end of it.

Published: Mon, 17 Jun 2019

http://ruthwrites.online/2019/06/17/all-those-mattresses/

Apron strings

Tue, 04 Sep 2018

I only really remember one harsh time when I noticed being set adrift by my parents and I was already eighteen! My dad dropped me off at the student halls of residence in Glasgow, shut the door behind himself and. just. left. My heart dropped. Now I see his probably did too.

The first time I left my firstborn at primary school, the afternoon I walked away from my wee girl at Brownie camp, today when my son headed off to get the bus to grammar school to begin his secondary education: they all felt like my being had been ripped apart. I kept having flash-backs to hugging them to my chest when they were babies, lying on my hospital bed staring over at them lying in their cots.

Tough love is not easy. Obviously. Sometimes I tell myself, 'you're making them stronger' but mostly, I just want to hold my children tight, keep them close, never let them go. But here's the rub: they want to leave. Not forever, but for a time. My job is to encourage them to go bravely, and be there when they come back.

I've always been a home bird, finding every time I was away more painful than rewarding. When I look back now, I'm very glad I faced the things I did. Ask me to do them again and I'd refuse. But I don't want that for my children. I want them to be adventurous, take risks, live. I must not cover them with the security blanket I always craved.

I have to let them fly.

Published: Tue, 04 Sep 2018

http://ruthwrites.online/2018/09/04/apron-strings/

Are you a worrier,

Mon, 14 Dec 2020

Or a warrior?

Last night I was trying to encourage my daughter as she faces yet another week of AQE tests in school. Any other year she would be finished, but because of lockdown they have been postponed until after Christmas. It's horrible. She's exhausted and more stressed than an eleven year old should ever be. At bed time last night I told her she was a warrior. 'Not a worrier?!' she quipped.

I wonder which one you are? I am definitely more a worrier than a warrior. Especially during this pandemic time, watching the numbers rise, seeing people disregard the rules, hearing 'sure it's Christmas' as if the virus will stay away then. What I hope for, for both my children, is that they don't become like anxious me, but find a fighting spirit within themselves to help them face every challenge life throws at them.

Thinking about it, I would argue you can be both. If you look at the child's face beneath that heavy chainmail you can see he or she is not particularly happy or brave. Sometimes we can show a fighting spirit even when we're trembling inside. That's why I persist in lighting a candle every night- I'm trying to put up a fight for everyone who is struggling at the minute. It's why I keep my head down and walk along the street even when I don't know whether I'm up to it or not.

Even through the storms of worry, you can put up a fight. In fact, that's one of the best ways to deal with anxiety: tell yourself you are stronger than you think and courage will come. Who are you fighting for today? Your friend? Family? Or yourself?

We are all warriors, fighting different battles, whether they're on the outside, or inside. Being a worrier doesn't mean we can't be brave as well.

I hope you can see that in yourself today.

I really hope my wee girl can too.

Published: Mon, 14 Dec 2020

http://ruthwrites.online/2020/12/14/are-you-a-worrier/

Everyone deserves

Mon, 23 May 2022

Something more. So fill up your bird feeders, put plans in your diary and get ready to really live.

Almost every day I phone my mum and we tell each other what we did since we last spoke. There are hard times when she has been too sick to speak let alone do anything. This past week, I haven't been much different. I've been thinking about my dear granny, who did so much with her life and then passed the end of it holding onto her diary and the tiny list of visitors she had each day. She was not an exception. Many are like her, sitting hoping for a new face to smile at them, or a small bit of news to talk about, surviving on the memories of a previous, busier life.

Some of you are run off your feet busy with packed schedules, but others may need to remind ourselves that life may be thinner now, but it is still there to enjoy. Having to do something, however small, to tell another person we have done it is not a bad way to live.

This way of living probably depresses most. Facebook is packed full of photos showing people #makingmemories. Maybe at one time that would have made me sad, but now I find I just love seeing them. There is something to be said for vicarious living.

On the other hand, what might be insignificant to most can be a big victory for you. Everything is relative. If one small thing fills you with a sense of achievement then that is more than enough. It might be a fear faced, a new change begun or a friend made. For one person it might seem easy but if it was hard for you, then that is worth celebrating. When I was finishing up my treatment today, another patient was away to get a Burger King. That was his reward to himself for sitting for five hours hooked up on a drip. You see? It might seem like nothing to you but it was the ultimate reward for him.

One person's molehill might be another person's mountain.

What's yours?

Published: Mon, 23 May 2022

http://ruthwrites.online/2022/05/23/everyone-deserves/

Fighting

Mon, 05 Jun 2023

to grow.

My daughter had to write a haiku last week and she picked the daisies she saw that were struggling against the nettles pushing against them. Her words contained the title of my post for today.

I was thinking about how many of us are struggling one way or another right now. Life is not easy and there are times when the nettles of despair, darkness and defeat seem to be taking over. If we give those negative feelings more time and space then they will fill it, no doubt.

This spell of hot weather is beautiful to look at but not easy to survive in, for plants, animals or humans. I stay out of the sun because heat saps all my energy and strength. I had to turn back on my cycle yesterday as my hip was hurting. My dad had to get the wheelchair out because my foot would not lift for me to walk inside. These are my nettles. What are yours?

I do hope that you can find a way of not letting them win; a way that pools your resources and overcomes that badness. I wonder how many fifteen/sixteen/eighteen year olds feel beaten by exams this term, or how many patients have been told the cancer has got worse. I have heard people saying 'they're going to beat this thing' but sadly no amount of will-power can stand against the unforgiving ravages of terminal disease. There are some nettles that will always win. But you can still search for the valiant daisies in the midst of them.

Last night I read 'The light shines in the darkness, and the darkness can never extinguish it.'John 1:5 (NLT) and it gave me hope. No matter how dark or painful your life is, nothing, no-one, can ever take away your light. Hold tightly to it and remember to look for it, even when you feel entirely swallowed up. My question for you is: where can you see it today?

Matt Redman gives a few clues.

'It's there in the newborn cryThere in the light of every sunriseThere in the shadows of this lifeYour great graceIt's there on the mountain topThere in the everyday and the mundaneThere in the sorrow and the dancingYour great graceOh such grace. '

Published: Mon, 05 Jun 2023

http://ruthwrites.online/2023/06/05/fighting/

Forget 'that'll do'

Mon, 28 Oct 2019

And start really living.When you look at that pumpkin you might think, 'oh what fun that must have been!' WRONG. It was potentially enjoyable for the first few scoops, but then I remembered how much I hated doing this every year-the mess, those dratted seeds, that slimy pulp. The worst thing about it is the staggeringly good pictures of everyone else's. Anyway, my daughter was happy so I'm happy.Two people, when I asked round, got close to what the pumpkin was supposed to be, and I promised to write this for them. It only took me a few minutes to know what to say because, as I see it, neither of them are 'that'll do' people. They are kitchen disco, night swimming go-getters.I met someone a few months ago who was diagnosed with MS around the same time as me. She asked me if I let it keep me back, and then told me she always did too much before she stopped. She fell doing the gardening and landed with her head on the bag of compost. Her husband came over and said "now was that a deliberate choice or...?!" She is not a 'that'll do' person either.Recently I discovered that I am a 'spoonie', that is, a chronically ill person who has to be very wise about conserving their energy, always remembering how much they've still got to do in a day. But, as I was spooning out that pumpkin I realised something- I need to be extravagant with the times and people that matter the most. The other insignificant spoonfuls can wait.

Published: Mon, 28 Oct 2019

http://ruthwrites.online/2019/10/28/forget-thatll-do/

Giants trapped in a small world

Mon, 18 Jun 2018

I was at one of the best weddings last weekend - it was a joyful start to a new chapter for the bride, after so much pain. We were on the edge of the beach, close to the sea. There was delicious food, good music and lots of happy reunions. I noticed something though, perhaps because I was sitting watching more than participating.

There were people there who couldn't hear. The racket of excited chatter and loud speakers built an impossible wall around them. They could not join in any conversation other than with the person sitting beside them, shouting in their ear. And if they were able, they would have been some of the best people to talk with. They had lived life to the full, and had so many stories to tell. When I noticed this kind of struggle, I just wanted to take them by the hand, find a quiet space and hear them talk.

It is so easy to forget, or just not feel bothered to try, but there are giants around us, shut in to a broom cupboard. If we can squeeze in there, or even better, get them out, they will have so much to teach us. Hard as it is to believe, we will be in their shoes one day too.

My own shrinking experience was of not being able to dance. All I could manage was swaying side to side, gripping on to the table behind me, watching everyone else. But. If I had been dancing, I would have missed the chance to watch my beautiful daughter, moving with joyful abandon.

I would have forgotten to sit with the giants.

Published: Mon, 18 Jun 2018

http://ruthwrites.online/2018/06/18/giants-trapped-in-a-small-world/

Goldilocks, smiley biscuits and a little red bicycle

Wed, 15 Jun 2011

My granny died this week, and as I was trying to grab hold of my best memories of her, these were three of the many things that came to mind.

Granny never did anything by halves, and before old age caught up with her, she moved through life like an unstoppable five-foot hurricane. She never walked; she always jogged or skipped everywhere, whistling under her breath. Or, if she was on her bike, she took no notice of the highway code, but zoomed back and forth in the middle of the road - so much so that the police had to ask her to start using the footpath. Granny did not observe protocol, in any setting, causing huge embarrassment to everyone but herself. Maybe she was still moving too fast to notice the carnage she left in her wake. And also the many many blessings...

Even though Granny always rushed, one of my most precious memories of her is when she sat on my bed and told me the story of Goldilocks and the 3 bears - every time she babysat in fact. She made me feel safe, and happy then. Another comfort was the frequent supply of 'smiley biscuits' - ginger nuts pressed with a cutter to mark smiles, clearly made by someone in a rush, but definitely the happiest biscuits I've ever eaten. Granny's 'no half measures' approach unfortunately made its way into the amount of salt she put into her cooking, and the Vesuvius-sized fires she built. How apt that she once taught me how to play syncopated piano music with the song 'Smoke gets in your eyes'.

What a larger-than-life person my wee granny was. Of course this meant that she sometimes rubbed people up the wrong way, but she often prompted them to change too. Granny always left her mark, and always will.

I can just imagine her skipping and whistling her way into heaven - no-one will miss that grand entrance!

Published: Wed, 15 Jun 2011

http://ruthwrites.online/2011/06/15/goldilocks-smiley-biscuits-and-a-little-red-bicycle/

Have a go hero

Mon, 02 Mar 2020

My daughter is scared of heights. It took her at least seven months to jump off the edge into a swimming pool. Up until that point she stood, knees bent, ready to go. But she always changed her mind at the last minute. It took the swimming instructor putting his hand out for her to grab to persuade her in. The days he tried to let her do it by herself, she always put out her hand, needing him to give her his. Then one day, when no-one was looking, she did it. I heard the splash and there she was. The instructor had been at the other end of the pool, and with no hand to grab, she did it all by herself.

I feel a lot like that these days. Everything seems like I'm jumping off safe ground into the scary unknown. Every day I'm faced with a choice: try with the risk of failing (or in my case, falling) or don't take any risk at all. It's the silly little things I'm making myself do, like picking up a basket instead of taking a trolley or hoovering downstairs by putting the other hand on every available surface. The challenges used to be going out on my bike, or walking the dog, but right now, the bar has had to be lowered considerably. Hopefully this will change, but when the tiny things turn into mountains, I have to set myself achievable goals.

Here's a question for you: what is it that you're hesitating in front of? Is there a hand you can grab before you face it? Is there a way of shrinking it down a little so it becomes more manageable for you? Facing our fears is a huge step, but maybe we can take smaller ones to get there, maybe there's someone else's hand right there beside you, ready for you to hold.

I have found that when I'm alone, I become stronger. I don't lean on the people beside me. Most days, I much prefer to rely on someone else, but there are times when I manage something independently and that puts a huge grin on my face.

What are you going to do today that frightens you? Use the hands around you, or maybe, take the jump all by yourself.

As Baz Luhrman advises, 'Every day, do one thing that scares you.' Go on, be a have a go hero!

Published: Mon, 02 Mar 2020

http://ruthwrites.online/2020/03/02/have-a-go-hero/

I'm still standing

Mon, 11 Jul 2022

My son is learning that Elton John song on the piano at the moment and with it pounding behind me every day, I couldn't not write a blog post about it!

Combine that with the fifteen minutes it took me to coax my daughter off the sofa and her phone to go get dressed this morning. The opposite dilemma I suppose!

Most days I have a battle with myself to get up, set my feet on the ground and see how well I can stay upright. It's amazing how fear can stop us from even giving things a go. But what's the worst that can happen?

I tried using my trekking poles for the first time in months a few days ago. It was too unsteady. But yesterday I tried again under watchful supervision and I was able to do it.

It has always been my deflecting response when people ask me about having MS: 'I'm still on my feet'. But what happens when we are beaten to the ground with hard times? Sometimes it's ok to tell the ugly truth. Sometimes it is impossible to put a bright spin on how we are. My question for you is, are you strong enough to say it, or, on the other side, are you strong enough to stand by someone and hear them telling it to you? Are you prepared to listen beyond the 'fine' to hear the full story?

When I was close to falling it was beyond reassuring to know there was another person there to keep me upright. Who is that for you? I remember when my son was a lot smaller he told me he wasn't going to let go of my hand until we were home. There's a Don Francisco song that my mum loves where Jesus promises the same thing; 'no matter what may happen child, I'll never let go of your hand.' I can't be the one who keeps you still standing, but I know Someone who can.

Life is a battle. Everyone knows that. But what matters most is how good we are at getting up again after we fall.

Or how well we stand by the ones who are falling beside us.

Published: Mon, 11 Jul 2022

http://ruthwrites.online/2022/07/11/im-still-standing/

In your head

Mon, 15 Apr 2019

Or, heaven forbid, on your head.

Last week the Letter came home. The one that strikes fear into my heart. The one that says cheerfully, 'someone in your child's class has discovered a louse.' The very minute, no, the second, I read those words my head starts to itch. Even after I peer at every dratted section of my daughter's hair, even when I make my husband check mine, little phantom tickles bury themselves into my scalp.

The sad thing is, this happens every time one of those cursed missives lands on my lap. I shouldn't be surprised really. When he was a lot younger, my dad read a book about horse diseases and diagnosed himself with every single one. Runs in the family.

Wait, what does?!

Of course, sometimes you can't rationalise yourself out of things because bad stuff happens. I told myself I was just imagining things until the consultant spelt it out. I looked away when I saw something moving in my daughter's hair two years ago.

But then, I wised up and faced the problems. Hiding doesn't make anything go away. That's what the wee pests want.

Sometimes, it's impossible to stand up and face things alone. That's when it's so important to ask for help.

I remember coming across a children's book about a little girl who lugged round a massive bag everywhere she went. Then one day a very kind lady sat beside her and between them they took out all her packages, which turned out to be her worries, and emptied that bag.

What's in yours? Have you ever tried getting someone to help you empty it? Most times, I carry my troubles round so much that I can't remember what a good night's sleep looks like. I even get dangerously attached to it. Like a head louse you might even say.

As I sign off, head still itching, I'll leave you to scratch yours.

I bet you do!

Published: Mon, 15 Apr 2019

http://ruthwrites.online/2019/04/15/in-your-head/

It all begins with middle C

Fri, 12 Jan 2018

It's been bothering me for a good while now- the hypocrisy of telling my son to practise his piano and clarinet every day when my own viola lies neglected below the stairs. 'My practising days are done' I tell myself as I stress the importance of starting with scales to him. I hated having to set up everything and tackle new music that was close to impossible to master. The exams were torturous. No matter what anybody says, you never get over the nerves, regardless of how many you've done before. Now, with my son, I'm revisiting those hideous feelings.

This week I looked at my viola and took it out. The experience was hugely frustrating and embarrassing. That's it, I told myself, I'm never going to play this wretched thing again.

Two days later I watched myself taking it out and this time all I did was a two octave scale of C. I played that about ten times and put my viola away. Satisfied because I realised that I could start again, that I was winning, that determination pays off.

Tomorrow I'll do it again, and the next day and the next. Maybe I'll let my children see I'm doing what I'm forever asking them to do. Maybe by Easter I'll play something new.

It's not just with music that I'm learning this. Since October I've been doing Pilates - one class a week but also myself for twenty minutes every other night. It was only when I took a break for a week over Christmas and then came back to it that I realised how much stronger the exercises had made me and how weak I was when I let it go. One position comically named Superman is the best measure of progress I have. Before Christmas I could only balance for the count of five. This week I'm holding myself up for forty.

The banality of repetitive practice is deceptively unrewarding, but think of the goal, whether it's the rich tones of Bach echoing through the house, a beautifully kept garden, a child who sees the point of scales or the body of superman, you choose.

Published: Fri, 12 Jan 2018

http://ruthwrites.online/2018/01/12/it-all-begins-with-middle-c/

Let's pretend

Mon, 08 Apr 2019

I was thinking of writing a blog about being yourself, but as I trawled through Winnie the Pooh quotes (because where else would you start?) I saw one that made me laugh. Pooh asks, 'is that you rabbit?' Rabbit replies, 'let's pretend it isn't and see what happens.'

Thinking about that, there have been many times when I've tried to be someone I'm not. When I was wee, my sister dressed me up as a made-up, bangle-covered lady of mystery called 'Esmerelda'. At twelve I bought beads and a mood ring, trying to look exactly like my friend in school. As a grown-up I make up my eyes and put on blusher to try and hide how tired or sad I get sometimes. I used to love swimming because I could be like everyone else- no wonky legs on show.

Last week my son cycled eleven miles to school because he wanted to show people he was 'more than a nerd who plays the clarinet'. When my daughter dressed up as Ginny from Harry Potter, her wig turned her into a super-confident wee girl.

The thing is, I love my clarinet-playing nerd and my timid little girl just the way they are. Being more aware of my family's support, I walk with my head held high. Most times I can't pretend because the truth of what I'm dealing with every day is out there, impossible to conceal.

What I'm discovering is, when you show the truth of what you're feeling, other people start to show you theirs. It takes courage but also a knowledge that you are loved 'just as you are'.

The best thing I've read recently was two words in an evaluation of an Alpha course I facilitated. Instead of circling a number on the scale they'd simply written in capital letters

'OUR RUTH.'

So long Esmerelda, I'm done with you.

You are the best version of you. No-one else can do it. So why don't you try climbing out of your rabbit hole, flinging off your mask and just revel in the person you really are?

As Piglet says, 'the things that make me different are the things that make me me.'

What are those things for you?

Published: Mon, 08 Apr 2019

http://ruthwrites.online/2019/04/08/lets-pretend/

Living in the now

Thu, 08 May 2014

Last year, I could…

My daughter said to me recently, 'Mummy remember when you carried me across the channel to the forest?"

That was then. Before my legs got so weak, I managed many things, and did many things. Before is a difficult place to think about, when you can't recreate it in the present. I know I'm not alone in that particular struggle. People who have lost somebody very dear to them, or an ability that defined their identity, struggle with the then/now conundrum much more than I do.

What I know I need to learn is how to face the now and turn it into something great. My family has not gone anywhere, my house with its enclosed garden and a kitchen you can fit a table in (the two stipulations I had when we moved) are still there. I can still sing, cook, laugh and write. There is a need to focus on the things I can still do, and not fixate upon the ones I've lost. There is also a need to create things that I never thought of doing before.

Come on strong character, stand up (or more likely - sit down) and fight for this! Don't just lie in a heap of self-pity. Cast your eyes around to see what you can turn your hand to, or who you can help.

This is the place I'm at right now, and I've got to find a way to dance in it. I'm writing this in Donegal, looking out as my 2 children and their daddy disappear round a corner on the beach, headed for new exploits on a further shore. My further shore is here, in this stationary moment. A harder challenge to face, but it's there if I push on, and don't look back. 'Further up and further in!" as Narnians would say.

Published: Thu, 08 May 2014

http://ruthwrites.online/2014/05/08/living-in-the-now/

More than a card

Sun, 10 Mar 2024

It's Mother's Day today. I didn't get a card from either of my two children but that didn't matter, because they both do more to show their love for me every day than most other children have to. For example, I came into the kitchen for breakfast earlier and my daughter told me to sit down as she brought everything to me. She hugged me then and said 'happy mother's day'. Better than a card, don't you think?

It wasn't always like this. I carried, fed and did everything that any mother would do until my health made it all difficult for me. But I am beginning to understand that mothering means more than doing the obvious, physical things. Sometimes the most crucial thing is about being there.

Being 'mother' can also mean more than being a 'mother'. There are many women (and men) who have a notable capacity to care for others. They don't need a label to prove it. A card, in those circumstances, might be welcome. So if you feel pushed out by the bunches of flowers, the official acknowledgement of mothers, remember that the caring you do is worth so much more.

Looking up to the mothers that brought us into this world: in precious memory or in the present, we are so grateful. My own mother does more for me during this more dependent time than she has done for more than twenty years. She and my dad make me coffee and lunch when I'm on my own. If my feet aren't lifting, they help with that too. It is not a situation I enjoy but, if I put my pride to one side, I am being cared for in a wonderful way. It is not a usual sight to see an eighty-seven year old father pushing his young daughter in a wheelchair but as he says 'it helps me to hold on to something when it's helping you'. So this, right now, is a gift I would not have been given if MS had not put me in an unwelcome situation. Every cloud...

If you are a mother, then treasure every second when you get to hold your child and watch thm grow. If you 'mother' people in your life, then know you are appreciated and noticed. If you are missing your own mother, let comfort come to you, perhaps in unexpected ways. And remember, every day can be a happy one if you look for glimpses of silver linings.

Published: Sun, 10 Mar 2024

http://ruthwrites.online/2024/03/10/more-than-a-card/

"Not I" said the goose

Tue, 12 Jul 2011

Reading The Little Red Hen to Samuel two nights ago, I was reminded of a truly valuable life lesson.

Ignoring the fact that I am furthering my education solely through children's books now, it was surprisingly effective. All of the little red hen's farm-yard companions repeatedly refuse her appeals for assistance with planting, threshing, grinding and baking, claiming that they are "too busy". Until she asks them if they can help her eat the end-product that is, but of course she doesn't let them.

How many times am I "too busy", too locked into my rigid daily routines and chores. to help out anybody else. And how many times does that mean I am missing out on sharing with them in their positive outcomes? Worse still, how often do they themselves miss out because they couldn't do it alone?

In the version of The Little Red Hen that we have, her friends are depicted performing circus acts - busy with trivialities, not anything useful. I wonder whether, for example, my 'need' to hoover the house twice a week - strictly on Tuesday and Friday mornings- is the tight-rope walking equivalent.

Writing this, and having it read, gives me an uncomfortable accountability though. But the next time I see somebody that needs me to abandon my own acrobatics to help them, I've got to do it.

And maybe, or maybe not, enjoy the fresh baking at the end.

Published: Tue, 12 Jul 2011

http://ruthwrites.online/2011/07/12/not-i-said-the-goose/

Why do we save things 'for good'?<$p>

Unsung heroes <$p>

Two companions <$p>

True colours <$p>

Tiny teachers. <$p>

Time to stop <$p>

The terrible and wonderful power of time. <$p>

The taco's getting cold. <$p>

The steps <$p>

The long-lost joy of giving <$p>

The importance of hugs <$p>

The heart of the matter <$p>

The 'heart of infancy'*. <$p>

That backbone <$p>

Take a nothing <$p>

Super mummy <$p>

Purposeful solitude <$p>

Pointless, valuable words. <$p>

More than a card <$p>

Let's pretend. <$p>

It all begins with middle C. <$p>

In your head <$p>

I'm still standing <$p>

Have a go hero. <$p>

Goldilocks, smiley biscuits and a little red bicycle <$p>

Giants trapped in a small world <$p>

Forget 'that'll do' <$p>

Everyone deserves <$p>

Are you a worrier, <$p>

Apron strings <$p>

All those mattresses <$p>

"Not I" said the goose <$p>

A ribbon of grace. <$p>

Living in the now <$p>

The heart of it. <$p>

Fighting <$p>

Super mummy

Sun, 06 Jun 2021

My eleven year old made this for my birthday last week.

All week I've been mostly staggering round the house/mostly lying on the sofa with heat fatigue. I've looked at it and wondered where is the super in all of that?

But when my two look at me, they see 'mummy' over everything else. They don't like it that I can't go up mountains with them but they still come home to me at the end of the day.

Maybe you feel that you have lost the person that you thought was you. Maybe you can't see a way to re-create someone different that you can be proud of.

Whatever you have lost, whoever you are, people still see you as YOU. Forget the physical changes or the painful things you have gone through. Those that watch you and know you still see you. Still love you.

Everyone has a bit of super in them and the best people will always see it.

Published: Sun, 06 Jun 2021

http://ruthwrites.online/2021/06/06/super-mummy/

Take a nothing

Mon, 19 Aug 2024

And turn it into a good something. Our little niece reminded me that sometimes, when there are no toys, games can still happen. She was running round the house laughing at nothing (that I could see) and was having a grand time when there were no amusements about.

How are you when your hands are empty and your phone is away? It is very easy to hide behind social media or 'busyness' when reality gets too great to bear.

When I lie down every night it doesn't take long before the worries flood in. The news headlines may change, but sadly they are never finished. Flower beds may be weeded but they will come back as soon as we leave them be. To-do lists are the same. Someone once told me to never fear the silence because it will be filled as soon as you leave it.

I am beginning to learn that silence and stillness can only be held for a very short time. Those things are to be treasured, never feared. When I think of my granny, she lived for visitors but needed a record to remind her that no, she wasn't alone all day; visitors were there.

So many people think that 'doing' is what defines us. But who are you when you step away from that? I'm sure retired people have that question on their minds. I have it too, but I remember my dad patting his chest recently saying 'I am still me'. You are still you, no matter how many professions, qualifications or achievements you can claim. Even when all that falls away or your memory fades, the essence of you still remains.

So next time you are faced with a feeling of nothingness, remember who you are has not canged. God is the Expert at creating something out of nothing. Have a look round you and you'll see 😊

Published: Mon, 19 Aug 2024

http://ruthwrites.online/2024/08/19/take-a-nothing/

That backbone

Mon, 25 Apr 2022

It's hard to lose it, no matter what life throws at you.

That's a photo of my twelve year old daughter, doing something she was nervous about. The only girl there. She has shown courage many times already. Just this week she walked in to the doctor's surgery by herself because I couldn't.

I started to think about where she got that determination from. Then I remembered that my dad, in his mid-eighties, cut the grass yesterday (front and back) and my mum, battling with dizziness and nausea, goes out for a walk 'even when she just wants to lie in bed'.

I'm very thankful for that legacy, although it is very hard to emulate. It makes me stand up and do the little I can do. It keeps me pressing on.

I read today about Ukrainians lighting candles and praying for peace as the Russians kept dropping bombs. I saw a picture of a soldier collecting food for Easter in his helmet. Even in terrible times, people try to keep going.

Can you recognise that in yourself or in people around you? Think back and see what you have got through, and remember that strength is still in you.

Make a list in your head of all the things you have done and remember it's not finished yet. There's more you can do still. The goals might have changed, but your backbone hasn't.

Published: Mon, 25 Apr 2022

http://ruthwrites.online/2022/04/25/that-backbone/

The 'heart of infancy'*

Mon, 25 Jan 2021

'have a childhood of the mind no less than a childhood of the body'.*

Over these past months of homeschooling, missed exams, changing criteria and restricting lockdowns my thoughts have gone back to a book by Dickens that I studied at university called Hard Times.

I know a lot of people have a 'hard time' (no pun intended) reading Dickens, but in fact there are a lot of ideas in his work that still resonate today. Hard Times deals with the heavy reality of industrialisation overcoming lighter tendencies towards imagination and childhood.

It didn't take long before I saw the care-free spirit in my children being choked by the new rules grim-faced adults on the TV set for the entire population, the ban on hugs with your friends and tea with your grannies. These days, nothing seems to surprise them and there are definitely more sighs than smiles.

Joy, for all our children, is seeping away. I keep on casting around to find ways to bring it back, but when you're feeling pretty weighed down yourself, it's hard to do.

It snowed today. All of a sudden child-like delight took over, not just in children but in put-upon dads and Facebook posting mums. Finally, unexpected joy has taken hold of us all. When I looked out this morning I kept saying 'oh!' over and over like I was a wee girl again. The children's dad said he'd start the snowman and then just kept going. My father-in-law built not one but three snowmen by himself for himself in his back garden.

You see, there is a child in all of us, and if we find it, we're more able to help our children re-discover it too. Even without the snow.

*Charles Dickens, Hard Times

Published: Mon, 25 Jan 2021

`http://ruthwrites.online/2021/01/25/the-heart-of-infancy/`

The heart of it

Mon, 25 Jul 2022

I was sitting on a deck chair while the rest of the family headed on to explore the beach when my daughter ran back to give me a beautiful heart-shaped stone she'd found in the sand.

I looked round at the magnificent views on every side - Hornhead, Tory Island, Muckish mountain and of course the ocean, but I kept glancing down at that heart. It reminded me, yet again, that if I stopped counting the things I have lost and focus on the most vital gift I have within my reach, life can feel a whole lot better.

Of course, the Beatles weren't quite right when they sang 'all you need is love', but it's a good place to start. That stone heart did not keep me warm as the wind blew around me, and it wasn't much company. I had to start my own conversations with strangers (don't tell the family) and zip up my coat to meet those needs. Sometimes waiting for a rescue starts with us helping ourselves.

I looked beneath the heart in the picture today and was reminded of a wooden cross. You see, the warm notion of love fades. The sentiment is not enough. My daughter found that heart and gave it to me. God sent His only Son to die so that we might know He loves us in a real, gritty, indisputable way.

How do you guarantee that the people around you know you love them? Do you tell them? Do you show them?

I came across the question a while ago which asked 'have you hugged your father today?' Or in other words, have you shown someone that you love them today?

Will you do it again tomorrow?

Published: Mon, 25 Jul 2022

http://ruthwrites.online/2022/07/25/the-heart-of-it/

The heart of the matter

Mon, 10 Dec 2018

When you can't do the things you always did, when circumstances have robbed you of any luxury, when you have to drop everything for someone else, what are you left with?

I was taught a simple lesson about that today. My daughter was too unwell to go to school. All my plans of writing, Christmas present wrapping, ham purchasing flew out the window. I could feel the frustration building from the moment I called the school.

But then, I just. let. go. I remembered the words I'd said out loud when I faced up to my diagnosis all those years ago: 'all I want is to marry (my now husband) and have his children.'.

When did that 'all I want' change to include time to write and buy a ham? I sat with my wee girl and we watched Elf. I had many chances to focus on one of the things I had wished for back then. This day has been a gift, not a hassle. Shame on me for losing sight of that.

When a loved one gets sick we get that same priority shift. Everything that truly counts comes into sharp focus. The things we normally do are thrown out and changed into 'what can I do for you right this moment?'

It's true we miss the daily grind and the drudgery then.

Isn't it a pity that we can't hold the things that matter at the top of our To Do Lists all the time? I know, that's not realistic. Here's what I'm going to do though- I'm stopping and I'm going to look after my daughter again.

Some things are worth more than this.

Published: Mon, 10 Dec 2018

http://ruthwrites.online/2018/12/10/the-heart-of-the-matter/

The importance of hugs

Fri, 02 Sep 2016

This morning, as I was speaking to another mum, my wee girl went in through the school door without me noticing, or saying goodbye. For the rest of the time since then, I have found myself feeling a bit out of kilter. It took a few minutes to diagnose, but then I got it: we didn't hug goodbye. It seems that even though it's been nearly seven years, and for my son, nine, I still need to take my leave of them properly, every day. I still need to hug them at least twice, every day. I still need to make sure they know I love them, every day. I have that feeling with my husband too, and I have been told that husbands who kiss their wives before they leave for work are less likely to have an accident getting there and back. Hmm, not sure that is anything more than a far-flung theory, but I'll run with it.

Yesterday, when my daughter was anxiously waiting for the first day back at school since the summer holidays, one of her friends spotted her, ran over and gave her a long hug. They're the best kind because you are saying, you matter to me, have you noticed that yet, don't forget it. There isn't a day that goes by without me recognising the need within myself for one of those hugs. Not from a random stranger (let's not push it), but from someone I care about. So, if that's how I feel, I'm pretty sure everyone else feels that too, well, apart from the really prickly people, I don't know what they want. My aunt had an obsession years ago with the 'inner child' that is in all of us - the part that has been carrying around hurts for a long time, the part that creates that need to be hugged. Perhaps that is the way we have to look at people - even the 'prickly' ones. Perhaps it all starts with empathy, and maybe it ends with a hug. But watch out for the spikes.

Published: Fri, 02 Sep 2016

`http://ruthwrites.online/2016/09/02/the-importance-of-hugs/`

The long-lost joy of giving

Fri, 18 Nov 2016

I have had a headache for days now, and I seem to have developed this terrible habit of waking at least an hour before the alarm goes. My stress levels are through the roof. Why? It's only a month til Christmas. Apparently the most wonderful time of the year. Is it really?

With every year that passes, I find myself feeling sicker and sicker around this time. Once Hallowe'en is done, shops bring out their Santas, trees, elves and bells. You cannot rest, breathe or recover from one season before you are dragged, kicking and screaming, into the next. The question now is not, 'how are you?'. It is the asking for a kicking query, 'have you started your Christmas shopping?', or the more baffling one, 'have you got everything in?' In where? In my overpacked head, yes, no thanks to you. Not anywhere else.

At five this morning it struck me -in the weeks leading up to what should be a celebration of God Incarnate, of Christ coming to earth, we have become banks. We ask for exactly what we want (or need, which in someways is worse), and if we don't get it, we take it back and exchange it, or get the money equivalent. We make lists with our children, guiding them carefully to what is possible, and allocating each item on their list to the appropriate aunt, uncle or grandparent. If we're stuck for small things, we just encourage a contribution system. That word makes my fresh crawl. Little Jonny, here's your single massive present that you'll probably use once and then forget about, and it's from everybody, because no-one could bring themselves to actually think of something to give you that would show you they love you.

Therein lies the crux of the matter. We give presents now because we feel we have to, that it is expected of us, that our relatives would stop liking us if we didn't. We don't give because we saw something and it immediately made us think of someone who would love to have it. We don't give because we are so full of deep gratitude for the ultimate gift offered to us all in Jesus. We just do it because we're stuck in the cold business of financial transactions.

If you stopped and asked yourself, what do I really want in my life, what do I really want to give, I don't think it could be found in a shop. I would put hugs from my children at the top of my list, closely followed by a chance to have dinner at home with my husband, just talking, putting the world to rights. Those precious things are non-refundable, unforgettable gifts that last a life-time. You say perfume or socks, I say love. And yes, in answer to your question, I do have everything in. It's right here, see. In my heart.

Published: Fri, 18 Nov 2016

http://ruthwrites.online/2016/11/18/the-long-lost-joy-of-giving/

The taco's getting cold

Thu, 10 Mar 2011

Which means: stand up, turn the oven on again and put the taco back in, because I don't have the energy to do it myself, but really don't want to be accused of nagging. Under some self-scrutiny, it seems that, most of the time, there is an unspoken current of discourse running through my life. A current that is presenting my husband with continual dilemmas, my family with ignorance, my friends with alienation and myself with frustrated loneliness.

It is an inherited trait - which is funny, because you would think if I have been on the other side of it, I would realise how completely futile and irritating it is. But no. The problem is that the times I have abandoned the sub-text it has been a terrifying, guilt-ridden experience and hasn't generated the outcomes I had hoped for. The only occasion that I can recall feeling satisfied with my honest communication was when I wrote it down and read it out without any spontaneous qualifications or apologies. But that was to a neutral observer, and not actually the real perpetrator.

So is unassertiveness a form of cowardice dressed up as consideration? I've always prided myself on my sensitivity towards others, but I'm beginning to think that perhaps I am actually under-estimating them, and cheating them out of ways to know me and love me. Maybe, my sensitivity needs to go one level deeper, and I need to begin tuning in to the goodness of those around me, and the things they long to offer to me. Maybe, that way, the relationships in my life will never be cold again.

Published: Thu, 10 Mar 2011

http://ruthwrites.online/2011/03/10/the-tacos-getting-cold/

The terrible and wonderful power of time

Mon, 08 Oct 2018

We still delude ourselves we can control it. But, here's the truth: we can't. Children screw their eyes shut and wish it was Christmas three months early. Their parents watch the days flying past and wildly hope it will be cancelled this year. Holidays end too soon. Work days crawl towards home-time. Appointments written up on the calendar seem to jump pages. Time spent on the dentist's chair feels like it's frozen as much as your mouth is. School trousers become shorts too quickly, but they'll never grow into that blazer. Time is relentless, but can somehow stand still when you wish it wouldn't.

I have a terrible habit of dreading bad things or anticipating good, as if I could stop one, or make the other happen quicker. The dreading eats away at me, and steals my sleep. The anticipating is a positive feeling, but doesn't change anything.

Looking back, I see that my dreading, wishing, anticipating younger self was blind to what was happening in the present moment. I have dreaded and wished myself through all the events of life, even when I was in the middle of them. When asked now about my children's early years I find that I've forgotten most of it. Why? Mainly because I was wishing they could cut their first tooth, walk, feed themselves, read, swim, kick a football, spell, put their own hair up (that's my daughter obviously) and walk home from school without me. Long before any of those things had happened. If I met that former self, I'd grab her by the arms and make her notice what was going on right in front of her. I'd tell her that she's going to forget if she doesn't pay attention. I'd tell her that all those things she's dreading or looking forward to will begin and finish in the twinkle of an eye. That she needs to hold the present carefully.

She has to treasure it before it disappears and becomes the past.

Counting down the days, for better or for worse, rubbishes the time in between. So, hold the people you love by the shoulders for a minute every day and just look at them. Forget about wishing and dreading;

Savour and cherish instead.

Published: Mon, 08 Oct 2018

`http://ruthwrites.online/2018/10/08/the-terrible-and-wonderful-power-of-time/`

Time to stop

Sat, 05 Apr 2014

A poor life this is if, full of care,

We have no time to stand and stare.

W. H. Davies

A few weeks ago, I was hunting for stones and shells on the beach with my wee girl. Knowing these would have to be brought home, and probably displayed, I was encouraging her to really look for 'special ones'. She got a fair amount, and then lost interest, but I didn't. Feeling weak, I sat down on a rock while she ran about. From that sitting place, I spotted a beautiful, tiny white shell. I stood up to go and get it, but from up there, I couldn't see it. I had to get down again, and then, I found it. It's now placed on top of a glass vase of beach finds, and every day, I see it and am reminded that sometimes stopping gives you gifts that you'd pass over otherwise. Like having to get down on your knees to help your child get dressed, feeling her throw her arms around you and meet your eyes as she tells you something important. Or sitting in between my two on a tough, post-injection Wednesday, watching a film. Would I have heard them laugh like that if I'd been rushing around, doing something 'busy'? I don't think so.

It takes discipline to stop too. If I looked at the wrong things, like the dust on the shelves, or the dirt on the windows, I wouldn't let myself be. Just being is a scary thing - facing your deepest anxieties, confronting who you are at that moment. But if we keep on running past ourselves, or the things that are beautiful in our worlds, I think that is, perhaps, a life half-lived.

So okay, my greatest achievement is never going to be running a marathon, or building up a company from scratch, but I definitely can say, I took time to stand and stare. This life is full of care, but it's also full of precious shells, waiting to be treasured.

Published: Sat, 05 Apr 2014

http://ruthwrites.online/2014/04/05/time-to-stop/

Tiny teachers

Mon, 04 Feb 2019

The other week I learnt a life lesson. From my nine year old daughter. We'd had a disagreement over something, and, very quickly, she put her arms round me and said 'I'm sorry'. No reasons, no excuses, no anger at all. Any time I, or possibly any adult, apologises there'd always be qualifications.

When was the last time you put your arms round someone and said sorry, no addendums?

There are many moments in my life every day where my children, or even my dog, teach me. There are lessons in humility, forgiveness, patience (lots of those) and joy. Watching my dog dig furiously on the beach, my daughter laugh, my son beam with pride about an achievement, show me so much about living. Even when they're far from perfect, I learn forbearance.

It's a sad day when we forget to learn the lessons set out for us. When we think we can get on just the way we are thank-you very much.

Honestly, there are days when I don't want to go to that life school, but I find myself in it anyway. I can't write myself an absence letter. The second the alarm goes, I'm there, with so much still to learn.

What school do you go to?

Published: Mon, 04 Feb 2019

http://ruthwrites.online/2019/02/04/tiny-teachers/

True colours

Mon, 04 Sep 2023

Yesterday my daughter was looking for wrapping paper to back some of her school books in. She found an old sheet of Peppa Pig. But she did a funny thing; she turned the paper round so the white back of it was on the outside. I held my tongue and realised yet again it's better not to question.

Thinking about that, I thought of how many times we hide who we are or how we really feel. I used to be pretty good at that until my disability took over and it was impossible to conceal. The days of appearing normal at the swimming pool or walking without a stick are long gone. But what does it matter? Showing your life to others is never as bad as you think. Because, you know what? Most people are kind and some even love you.

If someone else sees the real you, don't forget that the difficult bits are just a small part of who you are. Think about a person you really care about: can you sum them up in a couple of words or are they much more complicated than that? See the people around you not in monochrome but in multicolour! Because that is what they are!

One of my favourite parts of the day is when I can pull the curtains over and no-one can see me. Maybe it's time to open them wide, turn over the plain paper and show your true colours! I have discovered that being myself is so much less effort than pretending. You should try it sometime. 😊

Published: Mon, 04 Sep 2023

Two companions

Wed, 21 Aug 2013

Since they were born, I have devoted most of my life to them. At the beginning, it was definitely a one-sided thing, and I foolishly wished it over. But after the first while of simply giving, feeding, getting up repeatedly through the night, kneeling down time after time to change nappies, it started to change. I got payment in smiles, then hugs, then jumbled words. Those were times i hope I never forget, even when 20 years have passed.

But right now, they are becoming my friends. I can have a conversation with them, and know they understand. We laugh a lot, they hug me a lot, and we are happy. (Of course, the picture I'm painting has blemishes of irritation, rage and disappointment, but let me talk about the good side.) Yesterday they went with me to pick up my medicine at the hospital, and nearly every afternoon they play quietly together while I have a rest. They don't question my need for any of these things, but know more than I give them credit for, I'm certain. When my legs are weak, one of them will notice and take my hand. When there are tears in my eyes, they will hold onto my legs, and say nothing.

This summer has been a real blessing. I have shared a lot of beautiful moments with my two, and most of the time, that has made me very happy. When school starts, I will not breath a sigh of relief as I walk away. I will miss them both, and be so thankful for their company, so thankful for their childhood, When that passes, all in a flash, they will be independent, and mostly not need me anymore. But, funnily enough, I will always need them. My two companions.

Published: Wed, 21 Aug 2013

http://ruthwrites.online/2013/08/21/two-companions/

Unsung heroes

Mon, 06 Jan 2014

Today was my granny's birthday, and feeling sad she's not here anymore, I got to thinking about how much I missed of her when she was still around. When she was younger, fitter and more lucid, she was too busy asking me about me, (or, more importantly to her, what my husband did and what exactly was a computer anyway!) than telling me much about her own past life. Admittedly, she was quick to boast (quite justifiably) about being one of the first female doctors in Ireland, and married to a man who came from a small farm in Donegal to become the moderator of the Presbyterian church. I remember her telling me about the Belfast blitz, and many funny tales about her work, like when she asked a lady how long her father had been ill when the patient lying in bed was actually her mother, or the time she taught herself to drive a car in a day so she could do the job as a locum GP (she had to ask a man at her patient's house to reverse it for her though!) There were so many laudable things about this little lady, and yet, painfully, she passed her last years sitting, mostly alone, in an old people's home. The visitors steadily tailed off, and my granny, previously sociable, ever admirable, was frequently forgotten.

I wonder how many wonderful, praiseworthy older people sit by themselves, their many achievements overlooked, as they're called 'love' and 'pet' a thousand times more than 'hero'. Because that is what they are: they lived through turbulent times, they broke down previously unassailable boundaries, and now, they're belittled, and unheard. How many inspiring stories do they have, now silenced by neglect and loneliness? How many lessons are we missing by not taking the time to listen? As the third age extends in years and numbers, these questions need to be taken seriously. And not just because this will be us as well one day.

The one thing I am sure about is, any time I have sat down with an elderly person, I have walked away feeling blessed, and humbled. There is frailty of body, but rising above that, there is often unparalleled strength.

Published: Mon, 06 Jan 2014

http://ruthwrites.online/2014/01/06/unsung-heroes/

"Why do we save things 'for good'?"

Mon, 27 Jul 2020

Monday 27th July 2020

Yesterday, my daughter and I snipped off the masking tape on a box with a label saying it contained her great granny's china coffee set destined for her when she's old enough.

Last week I thought, 'why do we always save things up until they end up being forgotten?' Also last week I turned my back on my old dripping teapot and got out my 'good' Denby one to use instead. The tea, I tell you, was infinitely superior.

I think I'm going to leave behind the 'saving for the right occasion' mentality and start using everything right now. So maybe there'll be unwelcome breakages, but there will also be joy in the using before that.

What do you have packed carefully away for a suitable occasion in your house? How long has it been there? What event are you waiting for?

Sometimes it is good to be careful with precious things, but today, I'm asking why? My mum cut up her wedding dress to use for my sister's dolls' dresses. The rest lived in the rag bag. I hear you gasp, but really, I severely doubt that either my sister or myself would have relished walking down the aisle in a mini-skirt bridal gown! Even though I loved mine, I'm not going to pass it down because all dresses change with time and fashion.

I'm not going to haul out the china because it belongs to my wee girl, and she doesn't have any reason to use it just yet. However, I will keep the box in an accessible place so we don't ever forget about it.

Sometimes, when life is just plain hard, there is valid reason to pull out the cherished things and enjoy them.

I would encourage you to hoak around in the back of your cupboards, heck, climb into your roof-space, and bring your forgotten treasure out into the light.

The pleasure of discovering and holding it will make it worth your while, I promise!

Published: Mon, 27 Jul 2020

http://ruthwrites.online/2020/07/27/why-do-we-save-things-for-good/

Our kintsugi story

Mon, 27 Oct 2025

If you think back over the last few encounters you have had, you will have come across people who have had their fair share of hardship. Actually, everyone has.

Rather than thinking life is tough for us all, see that it is always interesting. There is a Japanese art of mending broken pottery with gold called kintsugi. A broken vase is not a useless bit of pottery; it can be restored, pouring golden seals into the cracks, joining all the shattered pieces together.

So, when you meet someone, listen to their story and believe there is a gentle way to redeem it. Never see anyone as hopeless. See them as broken, in need of repair. Not fixing. Not hiding their pain, but seeing who they are, cracks and all.

Being able to see myself as a whole person, not someone who is lacking, is a saving truth. If God was a potter, He is well practiced in the art of kintsugi, in fact I'm pretty sure He was the first to do it.

So don't look at yourself and only see your pain. Look and see there is a way to make something beautiful out of your broken pieces.

Published: Mon, 27 Oct 2025

http://ruthwrites.online/2025/10/27/our-kintsugi-story/

www.ingramcontent.com/pod-product-compliance
Ingram Content Group UK Ltd.
Pitfield, Milton Keynes, MK11 3LW, UK
UKHW052058141225
465963UK00006B/55

9 781068 344022